DRY

ALSO BY AUGUSTEN BURROUGHS

SELLEVISION

RUNNING WITH SCISSORS

DRY

AUGUSTEN

BURROUGHS

ST. MARTIN'S PRESS ≋ NEW YORK

AUTHOR'S NOTE

This memoir is based on my experiences over a ten-year period. Names have been changed, characters combined, and events compressed. Certain episodes are imaginative re-creation, and those episodes are not intended to portray actual events.

www.stmartins.com

Design by Phil Mazzone

ISBN 0-312-27205-7

10   9   8   7   6   5

In memory of George Stathakis

For my brother

And for Dennis

ACKNOWLEDGMENTS

I am so fortunate to have St. Martin's Press as my publisher, specifically: John Sargent, Sally Richardson, Matthew Shear, John Murphy, Gregg Sullivan, Tiffany Alvarado, Kim Cardascia, Jeff Capshew, Ken Holland, the entire Broadway sales force, Lynn Kovach, Darin Keesler, Tom Siino, George Witte, Lauren Stein, Matt Baldacci, John Cunningham. With love to Frances Coady. I would also like to thank my literary agent, the brilliant and generous Christopher Schelling at Ralph M. Vicinanza, Ltd. (Hi, Ralph.) With love for Lona Walburn, Jonathan Pepoon, Lawrence David, Suzanne Finnamore, Lynda Pearson, Jay DePretis, Lori Greenberg, the beautiful Sheila Cobb and her handsome and goofy husband, Steve. Also, when I needed blurbs for my memoir *Running with Scissors,* I wrote to a bunch of my favorite authors, and they wrote back. Thank you so, so, so much: Kurt Andersen, Phillip Lopate, Jay Neugeboren, Gary Krist, Tom Perrotta, A. L. Kennedy, Maxine Kumin, Jerry Stahl, Neil Pollack, and a special thanks to David Rakoff and Haven Kimmel. Thank you, Amy Sedaris, for your astonishing support and cupcakes. More gratitude must now drip on the booksellers who invited me to read *Running with Scissors*. Thank you also to Booksense for your support. And to the many hundreds of people who wrote me e-mails about *Running*—thank you. Most of all, I would like to thank Jennifer Enderlin for believing in me from the very first word.

PART I

JUST DO IT

Sometimes when you work in advertising you'll get a product that's really garbage and you have to make it seem fantastic, something that is essential to the continued quality of life. Like once, I had to do an ad for hair conditioner. The strategy was: *Adds softness you can feel, body you can see.* But the thing is, this was a lousy product. It made your hair sticky and in focus groups, women hated it. Also, it reeked. It made your hair smell like a combination of bubble gum and Lysol. But somehow, I had to make people feel that it was the best hair conditioner ever created. I had to give it an image that was both beautiful and sexy. Approachable and yet aspirational.

Advertising makes everything seem better than it actually is. And that's why it's such a perfect career for me. It's an industry based on giving people false expectations. Few people know how to do that as well as I do, because I've been applying those basic advertising principles to my life for years.

When I was thirteen, my crazy mother gave me away to her lunatic psychiatrist, who adopted me. I then lived a life of squalor, pedophiles, no school and free pills. When I finally escaped, I presented myself to advertising agencies as a self-educated, slightly eccentric youth, filled with passion, bursting with ideas. I left out the fact that I didn't know how to spell or that I had been giving blowjobs since I was thirteen.

Not many people get into advertising when they're nineteen, with no education beyond elementary school and no connections. Not just anybody can walk in off the street and become a copywriter and get to sit around the glossy black table saying things like, "Maybe we can get Molly Ringwald to do the voice-over," and "It'll be really hip and MTV-ish." But when I was nineteen, that's exactly what I wanted. And exactly what I got, which made me feel that I could control the world with my mind.

I could not believe that I had landed a job as a junior copywriter on the National Potato Board account at the age of nineteen. For seventeen thousand dollars a year, which was an astonishing fortune compared to the nine thousand I had made two years before as a waiter at a Ground Round.

That's the great thing about advertising. Ad people don't care where you came from, who your parents were. It doesn't matter. You could have a crawl space under your kitchen floor filled with little girls' bones and as long as you can dream up a better Chuck Wagon commercial, you're in.

And now I'm twenty-four years old, and I try not to think about my past. It seems important to think only of my job and my future. Especially since advertising dictates that you're only as good as your last ad. This theme of forward momentum runs through many ad campaigns.

A body in motion tends to stay in motion. (Reebok, Chiat/Day.)

Just do it. (Nike, Wieden and Kennedy.)

Damn it, something isn't right. (Me, to my bathroom mirror at four-thirty in the morning, when I'm really, really plastered.)

. . .

It's Tuesday evening and I'm home. I've been home for twenty minutes and am going through the mail. When I open a bill, it freaks me out. For some reason, I have trouble writing checks. I postpone this act until the last possible moment, usually once my account has gone into collection. It's not that I can't afford the bills—I can—it's that I panic when faced with responsibility. I am not used to rules and structure and so I have a hard time keeping the phone connected and the electricity turned on. I place all my bills in a box, which I keep next to the stove. Personal letters and cards get slipped into the space between the computer on my desk and the printer.

My phone rings. I let the machine pick up.

"Hey, it's Jim . . . just wanted to know if you wanna go out for a quick drink. Gimme a call, but try and get back—"

As I pick up the machine screeches like a strangled cat. "Yes, definitely," I tell him. "My blood alcohol level is dangerously low."

"Cedar Tavern at nine," he says.

Cedar Tavern is on University and Twelfth and I'm on Tenth and Third, just a few blocks away. Jim's over on Twelfth and Second. So it's a fulcrum between us. That's one reason I like it. The other reason is because their martinis are enormous; great bowls of vodka soup. "See you there," I say and hang up.

Jim is great. He's an undertaker. Actually, I suppose he's technically not an undertaker anymore. He's graduated to coffin salesman, or as he puts it, "pre-arrangements." The funeral business is rife with euphemisms. In the funeral business, nobody actually "dies." They simply "move on," as if traveling to a different time zone.

He wears vintage Hawaiian shirts, even in winter. Looking at him, you'd think he was just a normal, blue-collar Italian guy. Like maybe he's a cop or owns a pizza place. But he's an undertaker, through and through. Last year for my birthday, he gave me two bottles. One was filled with pretty pink lotion, the other with an amber fluid. Permaglow and Restorative: embalming fluids. This is the sort of conversation piece you simply can't find at Pottery Barn. I'm not so shallow as to pick my friends based on what they do for a living, but in this case I have to say it was a major selling point.

A few hours later, I walk into Cedar Tavern and feel immediately at ease. There's a huge old bar to my right, carved by hand a century ago from several ancient oak trees. It's like this great big middle finger aimed at nature conservationists. Behind the bar, the wall is paneled in this same wood, inlaid with tall etched mirrors. Next to the mirrors are dull brass light fixtures with stained-glass shades. No bulb in the place is above twenty-five watts. In the rear, there are nice tall wooden booths and oil paintings of English bird dogs and anonymous grandfathers posed in burgundy leather wing chairs. They serve a kind of food here: chicken-fried steak, fish and chips, cheeseburgers and a very lame salad that features iceberg lettuce and croutons from a box. I could live here. As if I didn't already.

Even though I'm five minutes early, Jim's sitting at the bar and already halfway through a martini.

"What a fucking lush," I say. "How long have you been here?"

"I was thirsty. About a minute."

He appears to be eyeing a woman who is sitting alone at a table near the jukebox. She wears khaki slacks, a pink-and-white striped oxford cloth shirt and white Reeboks. I instantly peg her as an off-duty nurse. "She's not your type," I say.

He gives me this *how-the-hell-do-you-know* look. "And why not?"

"Look at what she's drinking. Coffee."

He grimaces, looks away from her and takes another sip of his drink.

"Look, I can't stay out late tonight because I have to be at the Met tomorrow morning at nine."

"The Met?" he asks incredulously. "Why the Met?"

I roll my eyes, wag my finger in the air to get the bartender's attention. "My client Fabergé is creating a new perfume and they want the ad agency to join them tomorrow morning and see the Fabergé egg exhibit as inspiration." I order a Ketel One martini, straight up with an olive. They use the tiny green olives here; I like that. I despise the big fat olives. They take up too much space in the glass.

"So I have to be there in a suit and look at those fucking eggs all morning. Then we're all going to get together the day after tomorrow at the agency and have a horrific meeting with their senior management. Some global vision thing. One of those awful meetings you dread for weeks in advance." I take the first sip of my martini. It feels exactly right, like part of my own physiology. "God, I hate my job."

"You should get a real job," Jim tells me. "This advertising stuff is putrid. You spend your days waltzing around the Met looking at Fabergé eggs. You make wads of cash and all you do is complain. Jesus, and you're not even twenty-five yet." He sticks his thumb and index finger in the glass and pinches the olive, which he then pops in his mouth.

I watch him do this and can't help but think, *The places those fingers have been.*

"Why don't you try selling a seventy-eight-year-old widow in the Bronx her own coffin?"

We've had this conversation before, many times. The undertaker feels superior to me, and actually is. He is society's Janitor in a Drum. He provides a service. I, on the other hand, try to trick and manipulate people into parting with their money, a disservice.

"Yeah, yeah, order us another round. I gotta take a leak." I walk off to the men's room, leaving him at the bar.

We have four more drinks at Cedar Tavern. Maybe five. Just enough so that I feel loose and comfortable in my own skin, like a gymnast. Jim suggests we hit another bar. I check my watch:

almost ten-thirty. I *should* head home now and go to sleep so I'm fresh in the morning. But then I think, *Okay, what's the* latest *I can get to sleep and still be okay? If I have to be there at nine, I should be up by seven-thirty, so that means I should get to bed no later than*—I begin to count on my fingers because I cannot do math, let alone in my head—*twelve-thirty.* "Where you wanna go?" I ask him.

"I don't know, let's just walk."

I say, "Okay," and we head outside. As soon as I step into the fresh air, something in my brain oxidizes and I feel just the slightest bit tipsy. Not drunk, not even close. Though I certainly wouldn't attempt to operate a cotton gin.

We end up walking down the street for two blocks and heading into this place on the corner that sometimes plays live jazz. Jim's telling me that the absolute worst thing you can encounter as an undertaker is "a jumper."

"Two Ketel One martinis, straight up with olives," I tell the bartender and then turn to Jim. "What's so bad about jumpers? What?" I love this man.

"Because when you move their limbs, the bones are all broken and they slide around loose inside the skin and they make this sort of . . ." Our drinks arrive. He takes a sip and continues, ". . . this sort of rumbling sound."

"That's so fucking horrifying," I say, delighted. "What else?"

He takes another sip, creases his forehead in thought. "Okay, I know—you'll love this. If it's a guy, we tie a string around the end of his dick so that it won't leak piss."

"Jesus," I say. We both take a sip from our drinks. I notice that my sip is more of a gulp and I will need another drink soon. The martinis here are shamefully meager. "Okay, give me more horrible," I tell him.

He tells me how once he had a female body with a decapitated head and the family insisted on an open casket service. "Can you imagine?" So he broke a broomstick in half and jammed it down through the neck and into the meat of the torso. Then he stuck the head on the other end of the stick and kind of pushed.

"Wow," I say. He's done things that only people on death row have done.

He smiles with what I think might be pride. "I put her in a white cashmere turtleneck and she actually ended up looking pretty good." He winks at me and plucks the olive from my drink. I do not take another sip from this particular glass.

We have maybe five more drinks before I check my watch again. Now it's a quarter of one. And I really need to go, I'll already be a mess as it is. But that's not what happens. What happens is, Jim orders us a nightcap.

"Just one shot of Cuervo . . . for luck."

The very last thing I remember is standing on a stage at a karaoke bar somewhere in the West Village. The spotlights are shining in my face and I'm trying to read the video monitor in front of me, which is scrolling the words to the theme from *The Brady Bunch*. I see double unless I close one eye, but when I do this I lose my balance and stagger. Jim's laughing like a madman in the front row, pounding the table with his hands.

The floor trips me and I fall. The bartender walks from behind the bar and escorts me offstage. His arm feels good around my shoulders and I want to give him a friendly nuzzle or perhaps a kiss on the mouth. Fortunately, I don't do this.

Outside the bar, I look at my watch and slur, "This can't be right." I lean against Jim's shoulder so I don't fall over on the tricky sidewalk.

"What?" he says, grinning. He has a thin plastic drink straw behind each ear. The straws are red, the ends chewed.

I raise my arm up so my watch is almost pressed against his nose. "Look," I say.

He pushes my arm back so he can read the dial. "Yikes! How'd that happen? You sure it's right?"

The watch reads 4:15 A.M. Impossible. I wonder aloud why it is displaying the time in Europe instead of Manhattan.

THOSE FUCKING EGGS

I arrive at the Metropolitan Museum of Art at a quarter before nine. Fifteen minutes early. I'm wearing a charcoal gray Armani suit and oxblood red Gucci loafers. My head throbs dully behind my eyes, but this has actually become normal. It usually wears off by the end of the day and is completely gone after the first drink of the evening.

I didn't technically sleep last night, I napped. Even in my drunken stupor of last night, I realized I couldn't show up here this morning looking like a total disaster, so I managed to call 1-800-4-WAKE-UP (*You snooze, you lose!*) before I laid down on my bed, fully dressed.

I was awake by six A.M. and still felt drunk. I was making wisecracks to myself in the bathroom, pulling faces. This is when I knew I was still drunk. I just had way too much energy for six A.M. Too much motivation. It was like the drunk side of my brain was trying to act distracting and entertaining, so the business side wouldn't realize it was being held hostage by a drunk.

I showered, shaved and slicked my hair back with Bumble and bumble Hair Grooming Creme. Then I ran the blowdryer over my head. Afterward, I arranged my hair in such a way that it appeared casual and carefree. A wisp of hair falling across my forehead, which I froze in place with AquaNet. After having gone on more fashion shoots than I care to count, I've learned that terminally unhip AquaNet is the best. The result was hair that looked windblown and casual—unless you happened to touch it. If you touched it, it would probably make a solid knocking sound, like wood.

I sprayed Donna Karan for Men around my neck and on my tongue to oppose any alcohol breath I might have. Then I walked to the twenty-four-hour restaurant on the corner of Seventeenth and Third for a breakfast of scrambled eggs, bacon and coffee. The fat, I figured, would absorb any toxins.

As a backup safety measure, I swallowed a handful of Breath Assure capsules and wore a distracting, loud tie.

Everyone somehow arrives precisely at once, even though they all came from different places. I make a mental note: read Carl Jung. I need to understand synchronicity. Maybe I can use it in an ad someday.

I shake hands and greet people with an unusual amount of energy and enthusiasm for nine o'clock in the morning. I hold my breath when I face people and exhale when I turn away. I make sure that I stay at least ten paces ahead of everybody else. The group is small: my Fabergé client—a petite young woman who wears handcrafted needlepoint vests, the account executive and my art director, Greer.

Greer and I have been a "creative team" for five years. She's been getting a bit bitchy lately about my drinking. "You're late for work . . . you look disheveled . . . you're bloated . . . you're always impatient. . . ." The fact that I've missed a few important presentations hasn't helped matters. So I told her recently that I'd cut my drinking way back. Almost to nothing. To this day, Greer has never forgiven me for calling one of our clients at home at two in the morning and initiating phone sex. I was in a blackout at the time, so I am spared the actual memory.

As we walk into the first room of the exhibit, I cruise to the display case in the center of the room. I pretend to be interested in the egg that's illuminated by four spotlights. It's hideous; a cobalt blue egg smothered with gaudy ropes of gold and speckled with diamonds. I walk around the case, looking at it from all sides, as though I am intrigued and inspired. What I'm really thinking is, how could I have forgotten the words to *The Brady Bunch*?

Greer approaches me with a quizzical look on her face, quizzical not as in curious, but quizzical as in disbelief. "Augusten, I think you should know," she begins, "the entire room reeks of alcohol." She waits a beat, glaring at me. "And it's all coming from you." She crosses her arms over her chest, angrily. "You smell like a fucking distillery."

I steal a glance at the two other members of our group. They're huddled in a far corner of the room, looking at the same egg. They appear to be whispering.

"I even brushed my tongue. I took half a box of Breath Assure," I tell her defensively.

"It's not your breath. It's coming out your pores," she says.

"Oh." I feel betrayed by my body chemistry. Not to mention my deodorant, cologne and toothpaste.

"Don't worry," she says, rolling her eyes. "I'll cover for you. As usual." Then she walks away. Her heels sound like ice picks on the marble floor.

As we continue through the museum, I feel two things. On the one hand I'm depressed and feel like a loser, having been caught in the act of being a lush. But on the other hand, it's a huge relief. Now that she knows, I don't have to make such an effort to cover up. This is the dominating emotion and at times, I almost feel giddy. Greer manages to keep the group away from me for the rest of the morning, so I am able to pretty much ignore the eggs and instead focus on the Met's amazing use of recessed lighting, their beautiful hardwood floors. I feel inspired to make renovations to my apartment and am cataloguing ideas. At lunch we go to Arizona 206, a funky Southwestern place that elevates corn into cuisine.

Greer orders a glass of Chardonnay, something she never does. She leans over and whispers in my ear. "You should order a drink too. In case nobody else noticed at the museum that you reek. So this way, if somebody gets too close to you and smells the liquor, they'll think it's from lunch."

Greer. Forty-five-minutes-per-day-on-the-treadmill, no-saturated-fat, alcohol-is-bad-for-you Greer is so rational. I, on the other hand, am living proof of the chaos theory. To oblige her, I order a double martini.

Somebody says, "Oh, well, since you two are being wild . . ." and the client and the account guy each order a light beer.

The rest of the day passes smoothly, groceries on a conveyer belt. Soon, I am home.

I'm so relieved when I walk in my door, so grateful to be home where I don't have to hold my breath or explain myself that I have an immediate tumbler of Dewar's. *One drink*, I tell myself. Just to calm my nerves from today.

After I finish the bottle, I decide it's time for bed. It's after midnight and I need to be at tomorrow's global brand meeting at ten. I set two alarm clocks for eight-thirty and crawl into bed.

I wake up the next day seized by panic. I bolt out of bed and stumble into the kitchen where I look at the clock on the microwave: 12:04 P.M.

The answering machine is blinking ominously. Very reluctantly, I hit PLAY.

"Augusten, it's Greer. It's a quarter of ten, I was just calling to see if you'd left the house yet. Okay, you must be gone."

Beeeeeeeeeeep.

"Augusten, it's ten o'clock and you're not here. I hope you're on your way."

Beeeeeeeeeeep.

"It's ten-fifteen. I'm going into the meeting now." In this last message her voice had a hard, knowing edge to it. An I'm-through-with-you-motherfucker edge.

I shower and throw on my suit from yesterday as fast as I can. I don't shave but that's okay I figure since I have light facial hair anyway and besides, looking a little scruffy seems sort of Hollywood-ish. I walk outside and hail a cab. Naturally, it's red lights all the way uptown. And as I step into the lobby of my office building, my forehead is soaking wet, despite the mild May temperature. I swipe my sleeve across it and then get into the elevator and stab the button for my floor: thirty-five. The button doesn't light up. I stab it again. Nothing. A woman steps into the elevator, pushes thirty-eight and her button lights up. The doors slide shut and she turns to me. "Whew," she says, "you just get back from a five-martini lunch?"

"No, I overslept," I say, instantly realizing how bad that sounds. Her smile fades and she looks at the floor.

The elevator stops on my floor and I step out and walk down the hallway to my office. I toss my attaché case on the desk and take a tin of Altoids out of the front pocket. I crunch a handful of them while I try to think of an excuse. I stare out my window at the East River. I would give anything to be the guy on the tugboat who is pushing a garbage bin upriver. I bet he doesn't have to deal with this kind of stress. He just sits at the helm, the wind rushing through his hair, the sun on his face. Perhaps he reminisces about his days sailing the North Atlantic, yellowed snapshots of his grandkids scotch-taped to the sun visor. Either that or he listens to Howard Stern, a warm can of Coors between his legs. Either way, his life is certainly better than mine. He certainly isn't late for a global perfume meeting.

I decide to give no excuse, to just be as friendly as possible and become as involved with the meeting as I can. I will sneak in and take my place and say things that will make people believe I have been there all along.

I try the conference room door but it's locked. "Shit," I say under my breath. This means I'll have to knock. And somebody will have to get up and let me in, thus foiling my plan to be invisible. So what I do is I knock very softly. This way, only the person closest to the door will hear me.

I knock and the door is opened. It is opened by Elenor, my boss, the executive creative director of the agency. "Augusten?" she says with surprise when she sees me. "You're a little late."

I see that the conference room is filled with suits. Twenty, thirty of them. And everybody is standing up, stacking papers in their briefcases, throwing their empty Diet Coke cans in the trash.

The meeting is just now ending.

I spot Greer over in the corner of the room talking with our Fabergé client. Not only my Fabergé client, but my Fabergé client's boss, the product manager, the brand manager and the global head of marketing. Greer catches my eye and her eyes narrow into small and hateful slits.

I say to Elenor, "I know, I'm sorry to be late. I had a personal emergency at home."

She scrunches up her face like she has just smelled a fart. She takes one step closer to me and leans in, sniffing. "Augusten, are you . . . *drunk?*"

"What?" I say, shocked.

"I smell alcohol. Have you been drinking?"

My face flushes. "No, of course I haven't been drinking. I had a couple drinks last night. But—"

"We'll talk about this later. Right now, I think you should go over to the client and apologize." She slips past me out of the room and her panty hose make an important *hush, hush* sound as she walks away.

I make my way over to Greer and the clients. They stop speaking the moment I appear. I manage a smile and say, "Hi, guys. I'm really sorry I missed the meeting. I had a personal matter that I had to attend to. I'm terribly sorry."

For a moment, nobody says anything, they just look at me.

Greer comments, "Nice suit."

I start to say thanks, but then it dawns on me that she's being sarcastic because it's the same suit I had on yesterday and looks like maybe it should have been taken to the cleaners a few weeks ago.

One of the clients clears his throat and checks his watch. "Well, we need to be going. We have to get to the airport." They move past me as a group, all pinstripes, briefcases and itineraries. Greer pats each on the shoulder as they go. "Bye," she says after them. "Have a great flight. Say hi to the baby, Walter. And Sue?" She beams. "I want the name of that acupuncturist next time I see you."

A few moments later, Greer and I are in my office, "having a talk."

"It's not just about *you*. It's about *me*, too. It reflects on *me*. We're a team. And because you're not holding up your half of the team, I'm suffering. My career is suffering."

"I know. I'm really sorry. I'm just really stressed out lately. I honestly have cut way back on the drinking. But sometimes, well, I fuck up."

Suddenly, Greer takes an Addy Award off my bookcase and hurls it across the room against the wall. "Don't you *fucking* understand what I am *fucking* telling you?" she screams. "I'm telling you that you are bringing us down. You are destroying not only your career, but mine."

Her rage is like a force in the room that flattens me into complete silence. I stare at the floor.

"Look at me!" she demands.

I look at her. Angry blue veins have erupted on her temples.

"Greer, look. I told you I was sorry. But you're being ridiculous. This is not ruining anybody's career. Sometimes people are late to meetings; sometimes they miss them. This shit happens."

"It doesn't happen *constantly*," she spits. Her blond, icy bob is so perfect it irritates me. There is, literally, not a hair out of place and somehow this strikes me as insanely wrong.

Now I want to throw an Addy. At Greer. "Calm down, will you? Christ, you crazy bitch, this is insane. If I'm such a mess, explain why we're so fucking successful," I say, making a motion with my hand around the office as if to say, *Look at all of this!*

Greer glances at the shelf, then to the floor. She inhales deeply and then lets it out. "I'm not saying you're not good," she states more calmly. "I'm saying that you have a problem. And it's affecting both of us. And I'm worried about you."

I fold my arms across my chest and stare at the wall behind her, needing a break. It's weird how my mind goes blank. I hate confrontation, despite the fact that I was raised with so much of it. My parents' shrink was big on confrontation. He encouraged shouting and screaming, so you'd think I'd be better at it. But I just freeze up. So I stare at the wall and I'm not really thinking so much as feeling guilty, I guess. Like I've been caught. The thing is, I know I drink too much, or what other people consider too much. But it's so much a part of me, it's like saying my arms are too long. Like I can change that? The other thing that is starting to annoy me as I stare at the wall is that this is Manhattan and everybody drinks, and most people are not like Greer. Most people have more fun.

"So I drink a little too much sometimes. I'm in advertising. Ad people sometimes drink too much. Jesus, look at Ogilvy. They've got a fucking bar in their cafeteria." And then I actually *point* at her. "You make it sound like I'm some bum in the Bowery."

Bums, I want to remind her, do not make six-figure salaries. They do not have Addy Awards.

She looks at me without any trace of uncertainty. She is unmoved by my comments. "Augusten," she says, "you're going down. And I'm *not* going with you." She turns and walks out of my office, slamming the door hard behind her.

Alone in my office. It's over. She's gone. She's probably right. Am I worse than I think? I get so angry all of a sudden, like I'm a kid and am being forced to stop playing and go to bed. My parents used to have parties when I was a kid, and I hated being sent to bed just when they began. I hated the feeling that I was missing everything. That's why I ended up living in New York City, so I wouldn't miss anything. That fucking bitch has ruined my day. I will be unable to concentrate on work at all today. Part of the reason Greer and I are such a good team is because we are fast. We cannot stand for something to be unresolved—so we work at a frenzied, concentrated pace to solve problems fast and come up with the right campaign. There are some creatives who will piss away days or weeks. But after a briefing, we get to work immediately and we always try to have four ideas within a day; then we can coast.

But her little scene means I don't get my resolution. I get to stew. And this makes me hate her. And I can't live with that, so I want to drink.

That night at home, I watch a video of my commercials. Even my old American Express stuff is cool after all these years, though I do regret the wardrobe decisions. Still, whatever our little problems, Greer and I have done some great work together. I can't be *that* bad, I think as I check the level on my bottle of Dewar's. There's a third of a bottle left. Which means I've already had two-thirds of a bottle. Which doesn't seem like "a problem" to me. People often drink a bottle of wine with dinner. It's just not so unusual. And anyway, I'm a big guy: six-foot-two. Besides, I'm almost twenty-five. What else are you supposed to do in your twenties but party? No, the problem is that rigid Greer obviously has control issues. And she's judgmental.

Another problem is that I am thinking these things while perched on the edge of my dining room table, which I never use for dining, but as a large desk. And when I reach for the bottle of Dewar's to refill my glass, I lose my balance and fall over on the floor, smashing my forehead against the base of my stereo speaker.

There is a gash and there is blood. More blood, really, than the gash calls for. Head wounds are so dramatic.

I finish the bottle and still do not have that sense of relief that I need. It's like my brain is stubborn tonight. So I have some bottles of hard cider and these gradually do the trick and I get my soft feeling. I lose myself on the computer, at porn sites. It's weird that no matter how drunk I get, I can always remember my Adult Check password.

The next day, I am summoned to Elenor's office. It is on the forty-first floor and has floor-to-ceiling glass, polished blond hardwood floors, a glass-topped table with beveled edges and chrome legs. It would be austere except for the leopard-print chair behind the desk which lets you know the person in this office is "creative." I have a beautiful view of the Chrysler Building's spire. Because Elenor is sitting behind her desk and talking on the phone, the spire appears to be coming out from the top of her head like a horn. Which is apt. She motions me in.

Once I am inside her office I see that we are not alone. Standing against the far left wall of the office, as if they had been hiding from my view until I was inside, are Greer, Elenor's asshole partner, Rick, and the head of human resources.

Elenor hangs up the phone. "Have a seat please," she tells me, pointing to the chair in front of her desk.

I look at her, then the chair, then the others in the room. All is eerily quiet. I feel as if I have walked into the room during the Nuremburg proceedings. "What's going on in here?" I say warily.

"Close the door," Elenor says, but not to me. She says it to *them*. Rick steps away from the wall and closes the door.

I have a feeling I know what this is about, but at the same time I think it can't possibly be what I'm thinking. What I'm thinking is too unthinkable. This can't be about my drinking.

Again, Elenor tells me to sit. Finally, I do. And Greer, Rick and the human resources woman all move in unison to the large sofa.

"Greer?" I say. I want to hear the magic words: "Nightmare of a pitch, get ready," or something worse, "Guess which account we just lost." Except I know she will not say these things. And she doesn't. She looks down at her shoes: polished Chanel flats with interlocked gold Cs. She says nothing.

Elenor rises from her chair and walks around her desk. She stands before me and then sits back on the edge of her desk, clasping her hands in front of her. "Augusten, we have a problem," she begins. Then in a rather light and playful tone she adds, "That sounds almost like an insurance commercial, doesn't it? 'Nan, we have a problem. These sky-high premiums and all this confusing paperwork . . . if only there was an easier way.'" Her smile dies and she continues. "But seriously, Augusten. We *do* have a problem."

So if she's joking, maybe I am crazy and this is nothing. I feel like I'm in a department store and I've just pocketed a keychain flashlight and the security guard comes over to me and asks the time. Am I going to get off?

"It's your drinking."

Fuck. Greer, you cunt. I don't look at her. I continue looking right at Elenor, and I don't blink. A person with a drinking problem would deny it, would shout or create a scene right at this moment. But I smile, very slightly, like I am listening to some client's stupid comments on a commercial.

"You have a drinking problem and it's affecting your work. And you're going to need to do something about it immediately."

Okay, I need to slow things down a little. "Elenor, is this about being late to that meeting yesterday?"

"*Missing* the global brand meeting yesterday," she corrects. "And it's not just that. It's many, many instances where your drinking has had an effect on your performance here at the office. I've had clients speak to me about it." She waits a beat to let this sink in. "And your coworkers are concerned about you." She motions with her head to the sofa, in the direction of Greer. "I myself have smelled alcohol on you numerous times."

I feel tricked by these people. They have nothing better to do than obsess over how many cocktails I have? And Greer, she just has to control everything, has to get her way. Greer doesn't like that I drink, so all of a sudden my drinking is a big agency affair. Greer wants me to drink diet soda, I will be forced to drink diet soda.

"Right now, as one example," she says. "I can smell alcohol on you right now. But there have been other things. That shoot we had last year in London where you took the train to Paris for three days and nobody heard a word from you."

Oh, that. My Lost Weekend in Paris. I'd done my best to forget what little I remembered. Still, I dimly recall a young sociology professor with a soul patch, which is that little tuft of hair under the bottom lip, which I had never heard of before him. That much I remember. But really, so what? The commercial got shot.

"This isn't about just one thing here and there. It's about a progression of behaviors. And it's about our clients. Because more than one has spoken to me. See, Augusten, advertising is about image. And it just doesn't look good to have a creative on the account who misses meetings, shows up late, shows up drunk or smelling like alcohol. It's just not acceptable." Framed behind her head is the *Wall Street Journal* ad profiling her. The headline reads, MADISON AVENUE, ACCORDING TO ELENOR.

It's horrible, but I immediately think I can't wait to tell Jim about what's happening right now, when we have drinks later. Thinking this makes me accidentally smirk.

Greer gets off the sofa and stands next to Elenor. "It's not a joke, Augusten. It's serious. You're a mess. Everybody knows it. I knew the only way to get through to you would be to have an intervention." She is trembling, I see. Her bob is quivering ever so slightly.

The human resources woman speaks up. "We feel that it would be in your best interest for you to admit yourself into a treatment center."

I look at her, and realize I hardly recognize her without a stack of paychecks in her hand. Next to her, Rick is doing his best imitation of somebody who is not a psychopath. He looks at me with such sincere concern and compassion that I want to harm him with a stick. Rick is the most insincere, backstabbing person I have ever met. But he fools everyone. They are all tricked by his kindness. It's amazing how shallow advertising people truly are. Rick is a Mormon and although this is not a reason to hate him, I hate all Mormons as a result of knowing Rick. I want to say, what's *he* doing here? But I don't because he's Elenor's partner and they are a team, like me and Greer, only they are also my bosses.

The human resources woman drones on. "There are many treatment options, but we feel a residence program would be the best course of action under the circumstances."

Oh, now, this is just way over the top. "Are you saying I need to go to rehab?"

Silence, but nods all around.

"Rehab?" I say again, just to make sure. "I mean, I can cut back on my drinking. I do not need to leave work and go to some fucking rehab."

More solemn nods. There's a thick tension in the room. As if everyone is ready to pounce and restrain me should I break out in a rash of denial.

"It would only be for thirty days," the human resources woman says, as if this fact is supposed to somehow comfort me.

I feel this incredible panic and at the same time, I am certain there is nothing I can do. The thing is, I recognize what's happening here, have seen it before in meetings when I am trying to sell a campaign to a client that they will never, never, never buy.

I will either have to quit right now and find another job or I will have to go to their ridiculous rehab. If I quit, I'm sure I can get another job. Pretty sure. Except advertising is sort of a small world. And I just know that Rick would be on the phone in five minutes calling everybody and telling everybody in the city that I'm a drunk who refused to go to rehab, so I quit. And really, what could happen? It's actually possible I could be without a job. Even though I make way too much money, I still live paycheck to paycheck, so I would actually be broke. Like the bum that Greer already thinks I am.

It's simple: I lose. "Okay," I say.

Every shoulder in the room relaxes. It's as if a valve has been released.

Elenor speaks up. "Are you saying you'll agree to a thirty-day stay in a treatment center?"

I glance over at Greer, who is looking at me expectantly. "It doesn't really seem like you're giving me a choice."

Elenor smiles at me and clasps her hands together. "Excellent," she says. "I'm very glad to hear this."

The human resources woman rises from the couch. "There's the Betty Ford Center in Los Angeles. But Hazelden is also excellent. We've had many people check into Hazelden."

Roaches check in but they don't check out is what I want to say. And then I remember the priest. It was about three years ago and he was giving me a blowjob in the back of his Crown Victoria. I was drunk out of my mind and couldn't get it up. He told me, "You really should check yourself into the Proud Institute. It's the gay rehab center in Minnesota."

So maybe I should do this instead. The guys will definitely have better bodies at a gay rehab hospital. "What about Proud Institute?" I say.

The human resources woman nods her head politely. "You could go there. It's, for, you know, gay people."

I look at Rick and he has turned away because he hates the word *gay*. It's the only word that can crack his veneer.

"That might be better," I say. A rehab hospital run by fags will be hip. Plus there's the possibility of good music and sex.

And the confrontation suddenly becomes no different from any other advertising meeting. An agreement has been reached. It's decided. I'll take the rest of the week off to make the necessary arrangements and I'll coordinate the details with human resources. I'll be expected back in just over a month, clean and sober. Perhaps somebody will even write a conference report highlighting the main points of the meeting.

On my way out, Greer kisses the air on each side of my cheek. "Good luck," she says. She grips my shoulders. "Someday you'll thank me for this."

What movie did she get that from? I wonder.

As I leave the building, I begin to feel somewhat elated. The bright side of the situation steps forward in my mind: I managed to escape from that awful intervention unscathed, I have over a month off from work, and it's only two in the afternoon.

I do not have to go to work tomorrow or the next day or the day after this. As I walk away from the building, I have a sense of flight. The sun is strong, with heavy clouds in the sky. I can get seriously drunk tonight without that awful, annoying concern about how much I will stink in the morning.

I feel high, as though I have been handed some incredibly good news.

What I really like to do is get drunk at home so I don't feel so nervous and inhibited, then go out to some dive bar and talk to guys. You never know who you'll meet or where you'll end up.

It's like this fucking incredible vortex of possibility. Anything can happen at a bar. Unlike Greer, I like options, I like to not really know what's going to happen next. Resolutions can be very dull.

Then it hits me. An awful glitch. Something so unfathomable that it dawns on me with a slow blackness that makes me feel hollow.

In order to get away with this, I may actually have to do something so horrifying that I can barely admit it to myself.

I may actually have to *go* to rehab.

That evening, I call my best friend, Pighead, and tell him that I am checking into rehab. Pighead isn't a drinking buddy like Jim, the undertaker. Pighead is more like, I don't know, my *normal* friend. Plus he's older than I am, he's thirty-two. So maybe I think of him as being wiser in some ways.

"Good," he says. "I'm glad you're going into rehab. You're a disaster."

I take offense. "I'm not that bad. I'm just a little excessive, eccentric." I make it seem like I am somebody who mixes stripes with plaids, somebody who laughs too loudly in restaurants. "All I'm going to do there is learn how to be a little more normal."

"Augusten, do you know how you get when you drink? You get nasty. You don't get silly and put a lampshade on your head or say witty, philosophical things. You get foul, dark and ugly. I don't like you when you drink, not at all."

I think of the karaoke bar. That's not foul or dark. Just publicly humiliating.

"If I'm so foul and awful, why be my friend?" I hate people who don't drink. They understand so little.

"Because," he explains, "you, the person, are good. And I love you the person. But unfortunately, in order to get you the person, I also have to put up with you the drunk. I think this could be a real transformation, if you take it seriously."

Somehow I feel a little stung by his response, like he's taking *their* side instead of mine. I don't know what I expected him to say. Maybe I expected him to say, "But why? Why you of all people?"

I have known Pighead since the first week I lived in New York. This makes him my official rock. The thing that grounds me.

I'm his rock, too, although he would never admit this. He would say, "I'm my own damn rock." But he's an investment banker, so for him, admitting the truth is something to be done only in the event of a plea bargain.

The reason I know what we are to each other is because we fight freely and almost constantly, about even the smallest thing. In fact, once we didn't speak for an entire week because he didn't like the way I loaded his dishwasher.

"Augusten, it's just common sense. You don't put a heavy frying pan on the top rack next to the drinking glasses, they'll break."

I thought it was uncommonly considerate of me to load the fucking thing in the first place. "Well how the hell am I supposed to know these things? I don't have a dishwasher, I use plastic." I can't decide if we're exact opposites, or somehow exactly the same except for minor cosmetic differences. I do know that all of his friends hate me and all of my friends hate him. We drive each other crazy in ways that nobody else can even touch. We never bore each other. And we both realize what a rare thing this is. What amazes me is that I never drink around him and still we get along, or rather *don't* get along, so perfectly.

Pighead is HIV-positive. Or, as he simply says, "I'm an AIDS baby." He got this phrase from watching *20/20*. Diane Sawyer was profiling babies in Africa who were born with the disease, born to infected mothers. We were both sitting on his white sofa drinking Ocean Spray cranberry juice as the parade of bony children flashed across the screen. It was grim and depressing. "That's me," Pighead said in his mock, pity-me tone of voice. "I'm an AIDS baby. Hold me?"

But because he's been healthy and virtually symptom-free for six years, baffling his entourage of physicians, neither of us ever really thinks about it. Or talks about it. He's completely normal and healthy in every way. In fact, I'm so accustomed to the dozens of bottles of prescription medicines on his kitchen counter that I don't even notice them anymore. There must be fifty of them, all in a group. But all I ever see is counter space and Post-it notes. I don't even see the hypodermic needles he uses to inject himself with white blood cell boosters.

"When are you leaving?" he asks.

"In three days."

"For how long?"

"A month."

"Did you tell the office yet?"

"Well, they're sort of the ones making me go. Elenor said I have to get cleaned up or I'm outta there."

"Lucky for you they didn't just fire you. It's nice of them to give you a chance. So what are you going to do to prepare?"

I see a book of matches on the table in front of me, matches that read CEDAR TAVERN, NEW YORK CITY.

"Drink," I say.

"Guess what?"

"What?" Jim says, taking a sip of his drink.

"The office did an intervention thing on me. They're making me go to rehab for thirty days."

Jim explodes into a fit of laughter, coughing over his gin and tonic. A little spray lands on me.

I wipe my forehead with a napkin, grinning at his reaction. We're in a dive bar on Avenue A in the East Village.

"You're kidding!" he cries, choking. His face is red.

"I'm serious. I don't have to go to work for thirty days. Plus the whole rest of this week." I bum a cigarette from his pack on the table, light up.

"That's fucking awesome, man," he says. "Congratulations."

I take a long sip from my martini. "I know. The more I think about it, the cooler it seems. At first, I was sort of horrified. But now, well." Now I'm thinking rehab could turn out to be great. I'll dry out for thirty days and it'll be like going to a spa. When I come home, I'll be able to drink more like a normal person drinks. Why was I so freaked out before? There is a certain glamour to rehab. I almost feel like, what's wrong with me that I resisted in the first place?

And Jim is totally on the same page. "No, it's great. Think of all the celebrities you'll see. Plus, it's just great material." He polishes off the last of his drink and crunches some ice in his mouth. "I mean, we'll be able to laugh about this for years."

"Right," I agree.

"So what'd your buddy Pighead say? You tell him yet?"

I signal the bartender to get us another round. "Yeah, I told him. He thinks it's a good idea, actually. And I mean good idea in the wrong sense. In the hospital sense, as opposed to the rehab sense." When I say "rehab" I raise my chin, as though talking about the Oscars.

"That wuss," Jim says.

"Yeah, he is." But I feel a little bad saying this. And also, I can't explain Pighead to Jim. But I also can't ever have any of my friends meet each other. I have to keep them all separate. And they all think this is a little strange, but for some reason it's normal to me.

"Pighead is a stick in the mud if you ask me," Jim says, sliding his empty glass forward toward the bartender to make room for the fresh drink. "So un-fun."

I can't really tell Jim that I like that about Pighead, I like his un-fun-ness. I can't say it's comforting. "Yeah, I guess," I say flatly.

"Anyway, you'll have a blast," he says. He raises his glass in a toast. "To rehab," he says.

"To rehab," I say and we clink. "Hey, why don't you come with me?" I ask.

"Can't," Jim says as he swallows. "Gotta work. I don't have some cushy-ass job like you."

I leave the bar feeling confident and excited by the prospect of checking into rehab. Back in my apartment, I strip off my clothes, change into some sweats, crack open an ale and drink it quickly. I play early Blondie on the stereo. The more I think about it, the more I like the idea of this rehab thing. There's no telling who I might see there. And Jim's right, it is the sort of story you can laugh about for years.

I call 411 for Minnesota and ask for Proud Institute. I scribble the number on my hand then go to the refrigerator for another ale. I spend the next forty minutes on the phone with someone from the rehab hospital and my enthusiasm withers. I answer a litany of questions: How much do you drink, how often, have you ever tried to stop before? Blah, blah, blah. I tell them I drink all the time, it's only recently become a problem and I could probably stop on my own but my office sort of pushed me into this, so that's why I'm going to rehab instead of those alcoholic meetings.

In the middle of the conversation, I open a third ale. I cup my hand over the mouthpiece so they don't hear the tab of the ale being popped. It dawns on me that this is a slightly contrary action. Like stopping into Baby Gap before having an abortion.

After I hang up I walk into the bathroom and look in the mirror. "What have you done? Man, are you fucking *crazy?*" I watch myself take a sip of ale. "You don't even like ale," I tell my reflection. My reflection takes another gulp and goes back to the refrigerator.

I'm expected at Proud Institute in three days. I have a reservation, as if I am simply going to Shutters on the Beach in Santa Monica.

I go into the living room and sit on the sofa. I stare at the blank wall across from me. Suddenly, rehab doesn't seem so fun after all. The dour woman on the phone depressed me completely. If ever there were a person you would not want to invite to a keg party, it was she.

Suddenly I feel very uncomfortable on my sofa, so I get up. I pace around my apartment and no matter where I go, I still feel cagey. Like I ought to go out, but I just got back. I look at the ale in my hand and the other empty bottles that are sitting in the sink.

The fact is, I have accepted Pulitzer Prizes, Academy Awards, met wonderful people, and had healthy, loving relationships, all in my mind, all while drinking. How did this happen to me? I need to figure it out before I get to rehab so I don't make a fool of myself there.

Is it because when I was eleven I saved up my allowance for three weeks in a row and bought a faux crystal decanter and glass set from J. C. Penney for nine dollars, then filled it with cream soda, pretending it was scotch? I remember thinking about that decanter set constantly until I was finally able to buy it one Saturday, allowance day, and take it home. I set it up on my desk. But it didn't look right, so I went into the cellar and found one of the old silver serving trays my grandmother had given my parents when they were married. My mother hated all that silver, thought it was garish, and relegated it to a box next to the hamburger-filled freezer. My mother was much more down-to-earth and preferred wood to silver; she liked jazz and poetry. I brought one of the trays upstairs and polished it in the kitchen while I watched cartoons.

Then I brought the shiny tray into my bedroom and set the decanter plus the four glasses on top of it. It looked exactly right. I shined my desk lamp through the decanter filled with cream soda. I believed it to be the most beautiful thing, like something on *The Price is Right*. But within a few weeks, the cream soda grew a top layer of furry green mold.

So maybe that's what did it. Or maybe it's my father's fault.

I can remember my father telling me to "never, under any circumstances" touch his bottles. He had all sorts of bottles, and they never gathered dust. They were beautiful and colorful, like jewels, especially in the late afternoon when sunlight entered the room from a low angle and made the bottles glow. I remember one of them was square-ish and had frosted glass on the outside. This would be gin.

When he was at work or downstairs in the basement drinking and sitting in the dark, I would uncap one of his untouchable bottles, place the palm of my hand over its mouth and turn it upside down. Then I'd quickly recap it and lick my hand. I couldn't have been any older than eight.

Actually, it's surprising that I drink at all, considering my father. He drank so much that I didn't even see it. It was like some fathers had mustaches and some fathers had baseball caps and my father had a glass attached to his hand. It wasn't strange. I didn't think, *Oh, my dad's an alcoholic*. I just thought he was always thirsty.

Then again, this could all be the result of *Bewitched*.

I was addicted to *Bewitched* as a kid. I worshipped Darren Stevens the First. When he'd come home from work, Samantha would say, "Darren, would you like me to fix you a drink?" He'd always rest his briefcase on the table below the mirror in the foyer, wipe his forehead with a monogrammed handkerchief and say, "Better make it a double."

I go to the bed and sit on the edge, sinking into the plush down comforter and the featherbed below. I feel a prick of good fortune, an awareness that I am lucky to have such a nice bed to sit on during my anxiety attack. Why am I so anxious? And then it hits me. I'm not anxious, I'm lonely. And I'm lonely in some horribly deep way and for a flash of an instant, I can see just how lonely, and how deep this feeling runs. And it scares the shit out of me to be so lonely because it seems catastrophic—seeing the car just as it hits you. But then all of a sudden, that feeling is gone and I'm blank. So it's like a door quickly opened, just a crack, to show me what a mess I was inside. But not enough to really stare for long and absorb all the details. Just enough to know the room needed a major spring cleaning.

I get drunk and call my father. "I'm checking into a rehab hospital, I'll be gone for thirty days."

Silence. Then, "Well, what about your work, son?"

"I'm in *advertising*, Dad," as if this explains everything. I don't tell him that work is the reason I have to go in the first place. Then I say, "It's your fault I'm going. I caught this from you."

He exhales loudly into the phone, and I can feel him move further along up the family tree, instantly branching out to become a distant relative. "I don't want to talk about this with you. You do what you have to do. I'm just damned worried about that job of yours. You take that job for granted like you do, and you're just not going to have it. It'll be taken right away from you. And for Christ's sake, you have to get over your past. You are a grown man now, not a little wounded boy."

The animal portion of my brain seizes control and my blood is filled with hatred molecules. "Do you remember the time we were in the car together and you said you were gonna kill the thing that meant the most to my mother and you glared at me and sped up? Heading for a rock? And I had to jump out of the fucking car? When I was like nine, you motherfucker," I spat.

More silence. Then he growls, "I did no such thing and you know it. You just make crap up, and I'm very tired of it, very tired."

I know he remembers. "What about the cigarette burn on the bridge of my nose, between my eyes?"

Silence, except I swear I hear the thin pulse of the artery in his neck beating against the phone. "I do not know what you are talking about." But the tone of his voice does not match his words. His tone says *yes*.

When I was much younger, maybe six, I was sitting on his lap in the La-Z-Boy and he very slowly brought his Marlboro toward my face, aimed the tip between my eyes and landed.

I had forgotten about this until I was twenty and had eczema.

I went to a dermatologist for the rash. She said, "What's this?" as she touched my scar.

My mind went absolutely blank. The kind of blank where it's not that you're forgetting something, but your mind is not allowing you to remember. It's a thicker, dumber blank. Like trying to run underwater in a dream. "I don't know, just a mole or a glitch or something," I said dismissively.

She leaned so close to my face that I could see the individual pores of her skin. "No, this is a burn, this is definitely an old burn."

I told her it couldn't be a burn. I used the same tone of voice I would have if she'd told me that I was pregnant. But that night, I went home and got very drunk. And that's when I saw the burning tip of the cigarette. And I knew it wasn't because I was drunk that I was imagining it, it was because I was drunk and my own head was out of the way and I could remember. This is maybe one of the best things to ever come of my drinking. Or maybe it's one of the worst.

I tell my father, "I know you remember. Maybe you were drunk yourself when you did it. But I know how it is to be drunk. There are some things you just can't forget."

I think I hear him sniffle. But before I can decide if it's a sniffle of recognition or a sniffle of allergy season, his wife takes the phone away from him and says to me, "That's enough," and hangs up. Two words and I'm gone.

I hit REDIAL but the line is busy. I sit and think, *She just doesn't know. She married him after he stopped drinking, she never saw any of it.*

I walk into the bathroom to piss and as I'm pissing, I think, *Did I make it all up? Is it all some Oprah/repressed memory thing?* This seems likely.

Now I feel vacant. I guess it's sad. Crushed?

I wake up the next morning curled against the bathtub, my head resting on a balled-up towel. When I stand up, I bring my hand around to touch my back where it had been in contact with the tub and my back is cold, like a dead person.

NOTHING TO BE PROUD OF

I am to be picked up at the airport in Minnesota when my flight arrives. As the plane circles in its holding pattern, I try to imagine what the person who is going to meet me might look like since the administrator on the phone couldn't give me a description. "It'll be one of the staff assistants, I'm just not sure who yet. They'll find you, don't worry."

I wonder how they'll find me. Do alcoholics emit some sort of daiquiri-scented pheromone that only other alcoholics can detect? I visualize an older man, a father figure with a Freudian beard and knowing, recovered-alcoholic eyes made kinder through years of inner growth and abstinence. Perhaps in the car he will quote from the *I Ching*.

As the plane is coming in for its landing, it seems to be rocking hard from side to side. I believe they call this a cross-wind landing. First one wing will hit the tarmac, and the engine on that

side of the plane will explode. Then the other side will hit and
that side will explode. The fireball will then scream down the
runway, scattering debris and body parts until it comes to a stop in
the field past the airport, smoldering and unrecognizable.

The plane hits hard, bounces back up into the air and hits
again. At first I feel relief. This is immediately replaced with
dread.

Inside the airport I make an effort to look like I am from New
York so that the alcoholic driver has an easier time spotting me. I
am wearing dark sunglasses to hide my bloodshot, swollen eyes
even though it's overcast. I try not to look at anyone. I pretend I
am at Gotham Bar and Grill, bored by the same old bunch of
models and actors. I stand by baggage claim, my two overstuffed
bags at my feet. The same bags I've taken with me on commercial shoots around the world and now to rehab. I have failed my
luggage.

I wait ten minutes. Everybody I see seems to look like a recovering alcoholic looking for somebody.

I decide to ditch the New York thing, try to look more like
someone on the brink of hospitalization. I tap my foot nervously.
I look from side to side, quickly. I bite my lip. I think, *Should I just
sit down, right here at carousel seven, and shake until somebody's arms
are around me and they're saying, "It's okay, I'm here, I'm here, come
with me to the institute."*

I wait four more minutes. It's time to get out of here before
the drug-sniffing dogs catch on to me. It's inconceivable that a
piece of luggage could sit in my closet for a year and not have at
least a gram of coke dust on it.

I hoist both bags onto my shoulders and make my own way
out the automatic door to the taxicab waiting area. The cab driver
asks where I'm going. I give him the street address instead of the
actual name. I don't say "Proud . . . you know it? It's the gay
rehab center in Duluth, and by the way my name is Augusten and

I'm an alcoholic . . ." I just give him the address, anonymous and factual: 3131 North Drive, Duluth.

I am only slightly mortified that he gives no pause before accelerating toward the exit gate and onto the interstate. He appears to know exactly where he is going. I am glad he says nothing.

"Had another drunk fag today," he will tell his wife over a dinner of honey-glazed ham and Betty Crocker scalloped potatoes. He'll shake his head. "And boy, was this one puffy."

As seemingly endless miles of brown, drab Minnesota landscape pass by the window, I try to imagine what the institute will be like.

I have replayed my internal Rehab Hospital Tourism tapes over and over. My favorite goes like this: A discrete, Frank Lloyd Wright–ish compound shrouded mysteriously from public view by a tasteful wall of trimmed boxwood trees. Ian Schrager, of course, created the interior. Spare rooms, sun-drenched, with firm mattresses and white, 300-count Egyptian cotton sheets. There is a nightstand (probably made of birch with a galvanized steel top) and on it: *Chicken Soup for the Alcoholic Soul* and a carafe of ice water with lemon wedges. I imagine polished linoleum floors. (By allowing this one clinical detail into my fantasy, I believe I will be allowed all the other details I envision.) Nurses will be far too holistic and nurturing to wear white polyester; they will wear, perhaps, tailored hemp smocks and when they are backlit by one of the many floor-to-ceiling windows overlooking the lily pond, I will see the outline of their lean, athletic legs.

There will be a large pool. I will forgive its heavy chlorination. I will understand. This is a hospital, after all.

Lap swimming will be supplemented with personal training in the modernly equipped gym. Here is where I will lose the twenty pounds of cocktail-belly that has accumulated around my middle.

I will eat only small, restrained portions of their steamed local trout and seasonal field greens. I will politely refuse the dessert of fresh berries in a marzipan nest.

But as the landscape transforms from flatlands to industrial parks, I begin to worry. Nowhere in my vision have I encountered so many parking lots filled with minivans. My internal Rehab Hospital Tourism tape has been snagged inside my internal VCR.

Where is the lush scenery? The pond with the rare Japanese goldfish? Where are the meandering hiking trails?

The driver turns left onto Maiden Lane. The hospital is supposed to be on the corner, but all I see is the Pillsbury factory outlet store among other industrial park buildings. And across from Pillsbury (complete with a giant inflatable Dough-Boy on the lawn) is a brown, 1970s professional office building with missing shingles on its overhanging roof. The lawn has been worn away to bare dirt from heavy foot traffic. And the sign out front is missing a few letters. It reads: P   OU   INS   T   E.

Signs with missing letters can only mean bad things. When I was a kid, the "e" went out in the local Price Chopper grocery store and stayed out for many years. Because the "Pric Chopper" logo happened to be a man wielding an axe, the sign sent out an eerie and powerful castration message, which, at the age of twelve, affected me deeply.

Oh, fuck.

Inside the building is the busy, clinical atmosphere of a suburban doctor's office. A receptionist answers one call while placing another on hold. Two people sit reading out-of-date magazines, a chair between. A large artificial ficus tree looms in the corner near the window, its leaves layered with dust. "May I help you?" says the receptionist, a twenty-something woman with short mousy hair and no chin. She is all bubble eyes, nose and teeth, flowing into neck. I tell her I'm here to check in. She looks at me pleasantly, as though I am here for a teeth whitening. "Just have a seat and somebody will be right with you."

I can feel my ears throb with blood, my face go hot. Suddenly, unexpectedly, this whole scene is becoming dangerously close to being real.

I could leave now. I could say, "I forgot something in the cab . . ." and then walk back out to the parking lot, give myself fifteen good feet of distance, and then run like hell. Back in New York, I could tell everyone, "I had an epiphany on the plane . . . it was almost *spiritual* . . . You won't see *me* drinking anymore."

Then I see her.

"Hiiiiiiiiiiiiii," she sings as she comes towards me. "You must be Augusten. I'm Peggy. Come with me." She is a short woman, but extremely wide. And she's dressed entirely in white polyester. Her hair is blond, frizzy and past her shoulders, but dark at the "roots" which comprise half the length of her hair. She is saying things to me but I am too stunned to comprehend a word. All I know for sure is that I have accidentally fallen through a wormhole in the universe and stumbled into someone else's grim life.

She leads me down a flight of stairs, we turn right, walk through a doorway and suddenly we're in a long hallway. Doors on either side, all of them open. As we walk, I peer into the rooms. This is not hard to do since each one is lit brightly with overhead fluorescents. I notice that each room has three beds. The air smells vaguely of disinfectant and baby powder and magic markers. There are people sitting on some of the beds, doing nothing but looking blankly out into the hallway. My first impression is that combs are banished here. A man looks at me fearfully while he chews his fingernail. His hair is an unruly mass of silver and black threads.

An emaciated great-grandfather crosses in front of us wearing

a blue hospital gown. The back is wide open, drawstrings hanging. I see his concave butt cheeks and wince.

This is not good. This is very, very bad.

I take deep, Lamaze breaths, but then remember that smells are
molecules and take smaller ones. In order to control what is
quickly becoming real panic, I focus ahead of me, on Peggy. She
wobbles slightly from side to side. The heels of her shoes are
worn thin, unevenly—she seems to lean to the left. Does this
mean she's on her feet a lot, making many unexpected moves?
Lunges? Quick bolts?

She leads me into an office with four gray steel desks and lots
of matching gray steel filing cabinets. One entire wall of the
room is a window that overlooks the public inpatient "community area." The window is the kind with chicken wire inside of it.
The kind that can withstand a direct blow from, say, a loveseat.

Peggy hands me over to a woman who's sitting behind one of
the desks. "Sue, this is Augusten from New York City, he's here
for an intake."

Sue looks up from her paperwork, smiles. Her face immediately strikes me as both friendly and intelligent. She looks like
somebody who might understand why I will not be able to check
in after all.

"Just give me one sec here, *Augustine,*" she says, mispronounc-
ing my name and stacking one mound of papers on top of
another. She takes a sip of coffee from a permanently stained mug
that reads in swashy, cheerful type, GO AHEAD, MAKE MY DAY!
"Okay then, you're Augustine," and suddenly I have her complete
and undivided attention. Her face is molded into an expression
of, *What can I do for you today?* yet her eyes say, *Just you wait.*

I can think of nothing to say, so I say, "Yes, Augus*ten*," correcting her without actually correcting her. My first display of
passive-aggressive behavior, something sure to be noted in my
chart.

She asks if I met my ride okay at the airport. I tell her I took a cab. She looks troubled.

"But Doris was supposed to pick you up!" She frowns and looks at the phone. "How long did you wait?" she wants to know.

Afraid I'll get this Doris person into trouble, I do what comes most naturally to me when put on the spot: I lie. "Oh, I didn't wait. I thought I was supposed to get here myself, so I took a cab." Then for authenticity, "Cabs are so much less expensive here than they are in New York, I was really amazed." I'm smiling like somebody who has just pocketed a pair of ruby cuff links at Fortunoff.

She looks at me for what seems like a very long time. For some reason, it occurs to me that I forgot to pack deodorant.

"Well, anyway. Let's get you checked in and settled." And before I'm able to say "I have changed my mind," she has me filling out paperwork, takes a Polaroid (for curious "legal" reasons), and tells me my bags will have to be searched. "For cologne, mouthwash, anything containing alcohol."

"Cologne?" I ask, incredulously.

"Oh, you'd be surprised," she says, "by the things alcoholics will try and sneak in here to drink."

In my mind this settles the issue. I would never drink cologne and therefore am not an "alcoholic" and am, in fact, in the wrong place. This is clearly the place for the die-hard, cologne-drinking alcoholics. Not the global-brand-meeting-misser alcoholics, like me. I begin to say something, and make it as far as actually opening my mouth but she stands abruptly and picks up my bags. "I'll just take these into your room and have them inspected while you finish up your paperwork, okay."

It's not a question. And again, I have this feeling of powerlessness, of forward propulsion against my will. I am strangely impotent.

I look at the papers in front of me: insurance forms, releases, next-of-kin, places for me to sign my name and initial over and over again. My handwriting is messy, confused. My signature, different every time I sign it. I feel like an imposter. As if some deranged spirit has overtaken the body of Augusten and is right this very moment willfully committing him into a rehab center.

The real Augusten would never stand for this. The real Augusten would say, "Could I get a Bloody Mary, extra Tabasco . . . and the check."

I finish signing the forms and stare ahead. My eyes fall on the filing cabinet beneath the window. On top of it is a disposable aluminum cake pan containing the ravages of a supermarket birthday cake. A car-wreck of garish pink and blue frosting, green sprinkles, canary yellow sponge cake. It has been hastily, greedily devoured. As if frantic nurses have made mad dashes into this room between crisis interventions and scooped whole handfuls of the cake into their mouths, desperate for the sugar rush, before running back out to strap somebody onto the electroshock therapy gurney, which I am certain is just around the corner, out of view.

I make a mental note to check Peggy's uniform and chin for evidence of frosting.

Sue pops back into the room. "Your bags are clean. Got your paperwork finished?"

"I think so," I say meekly.

She glances over the forms. "Looks good. Let's get you all set up in your room, follow me."

I follow her for exactly twelve feet. My room is directly across from the nurses' station. It's a "detox room," and I'm told it will be mine for seventy-two hours, then I will be moved to one of the long-term rooms. The floor plan is basically a V with one corridor for men, the other for women. At the spot where the two corridors meet is the nurses' station with the chicken-wire window, overlooking the conversation pit, which is three sofas and various chairs, plus one huge coffee table. The furniture is a heavy wood-crate style, covered in industrial plaid fabric. It speaks not of good design, but indestructibility. Ian Schrager clearly had nothing to do with any of it. Ian Schrager would take one look and order the building doused with gasoline as he climbed back into his silver Aston-Martin Volante. This is the anti-Royalton.

My room, like the others, has three beds, each a single.

"Here you go, sweetie," Sue says as she hands me a folded white terry cloth towel. On top is a thick blue bible-ish looking book called, cleverly, *Alcoholics Anonymous*. She also hands me a pair of paper slippers. "I'll give you five minutes to freshen up and then we'll get started," she says as she leaves. "Oh, by the way, this door is never to be closed, *never*." There is threat in her voice. But then she adds happily, "See ya in a few."

I take off my leather jacket, hang it on the hook next to the mirror above the sink and sit on the bed. The sheets are paper-thin, smell of bleach. Not Rain Fresh bleach, or Lemon Summer bleach—these sheets smell like Acme Institution Supply bleach.

There is one flat foam pillow. A framed print of a single foot-step in the sand with a rainbow emanating from the sole hangs at the head of my bed, crooked. Printed below the footstep is the phrase, A JOURNEY OF A THOUSAND MILES BEGINS WITH A SINGLE STEP.

I stand up, look out the window. It's a ground-level view of the backyard of the institute; dirt with a picnic table, cigarette butts scattered all about. In the distance, I can see a small creek and beyond that, more industrial park.

Liz Taylor wouldn't be caught dead here.

I notice that one of the other two beds is unmade, luggage haphazardly stuffed beneath it. How perfect. One roommate, with the threat of a third.

"Knock, knock," Sue says at my door.

I spin around, alarmed.

"All set?"

I nod, since I am now a mute.

Sue leads me into the conversation pit, which is empty. She explains that the other patients are upstairs in "group" and that they should be down in about ten minutes and then there will be lunch in the cafeteria.

She points to a folding chair next to what appears to be a substandard airport bar, like what one might encounter at the Kitty Hawk Lounge in the Fresno airport. But it's actually a freestanding nurses' station.

Nurse Peggy appears from nowhere, her great whiteness causing me to squint. She is unnaturally happy as she tells me to roll up my sleeve so she can take my blood pressure. As I roll, she slides an electronic thermometer into my mouth and looks down at me. She smiles. The thermometer beeps and she withdraws it. Next, she wraps the blood pressure cuff around my arm and pumps. She releases the valve with a hiss. She frowns.

"Hmmm, that reading was a little high, so I'm going to take it again, okay? This time I'd like you to do a little something for me. Just sit back, close your eyes and relax. Try to think of something calming."

I think of an icy martini, single olive dead center at the bottom. There's a gentle quiver of the surface tension as the liquid threatens to—but doesn't—spill over the edges.

She takes my blood pressure again.

As she folds the blood pressure apparatus into the pocket of her uniform she explains that my pressure is very high. "I'd like to give you a Librium to calm you down. What we don't want is for you to go into physical shock from the alcohol withdrawal, as that would be a dangerous situation and we'd have to send you to the emergency room at St. Jude's by ambulance."

My blood pressure skyrockets as she leaves to retrieve the pill.

And then I think, *Wait a minute here: Librium? The pill commonly known as Mother's Little Helper?* I feel certain that had I chosen to go to a normal, *straight* rehab I would not be given Mother's Little Helper to lower my blood pressure. I would have just been expected to rough it out.

I hear commotion upstairs. Then all at once, a thunder of feet, laughter on the stairway behind me. I feel them see me.

Peggy hands me the pill along with a tiny paper cup of water. She looks up and throws out some hi's to the crowd.

I watch as people glide down one of the two corridors, gather in the conversation pit. One person comes over to us.

"Hi, Kavi," Peggy says.

Kavi smiles only at me, as if I am something new on the menu. He's wearing black jeans with a coin-studded belt and a tight white shirt. His eyebrows are thick and undivided, a chalkboard eraser arched across his forehead. He looks Indian, but highly gay-Americanized. This strikes me as a sort of a sacrilege. A lock of his thick, black hair falls precisely across his forehead in a glossy, deliberate curl. "I'm Kavi. What are you here for?"

"Thirty days."

He smirks, puts one hand on his hip. "No, I mean what's your drug of choice?"

I understand nothing he says. Suddenly I speak a different language, one that only chairs and light fixtures can understand.

He waits for my answer.

I wait for my answer.

He rolls his eyes. "You know . . . like alcohol . . . crack . . . crystal . . ."

I suddenly hear one word I can understand. "Oh, alcohol. Sorry."

Kavi seems bored by my answer. "I'm a sex addict, that's why I'm here, but also cocaine. I never really was much of a drinker. I'm from Corpus Christi. I'm a flight attendant."

I think, *From now on it's Amtrak.*

Peggy gets an idea, looks at Kavi. "How'd you like to be a buddy, Kavi? Show Augusten around?"

Kavi appears delighted. "I guess," he says, twirling his curl in a nonchalant fashion.

"Great," she says. Then to me, "You're free."

I wish.

Now I'm standing next to Kavi in the center of the conversation pit. Other patients look at me, come over. They stick their hands out and say things. I keep repeating my name and that I'm from New York. I believe that I am meeting people, shaking their hands, but I have left my body and am operating purely on muscle memory.

Kavi pulls me away, turns to the crowd, says something. He leads me down the length of the men's corridor; I am his.

"This is the gym. Ellen holds her drama therapy workshops in here. Ellen's unreal." He rolls his eyes and shivers.

The gym is filled with boxes and folding chairs, stacked in rows against the wall. I see, in the far corner, a small bench press without weights. The basketball hoops have no nets, boxes stacked high beneath them. I feel fairly certain I am the only person ever to have broken a sweat in this gym. And my sweat is from panic.

"On Fridays we have an AA meeting here that's open to the public."

It hits me that "the public" is a group to which I no longer belong. "Is there a pool here?" I ask idiotically.

"Ever go skinny dipping?" Kavi answers, his finger scratching his left nostril.

I need very badly to escape from Kavi. "Well, thanks for the tour," I say, turning toward the exit.

He shrugs and leads me back out into the common area with the indestructible furniture and fireproof ceiling.

A big, friendly-looking man approaches me. "Hey, I'm Bobby," he says with a thick Baltimore accent, ". . . and I'm an alcoholic."

Saturday Night Live, this is a skit. I'm actually home, drunk, watching TV. This is my worst blackout ever. Somebody must have put something in my drink.

Big Bobby looks at me like a dog waiting for a treat after performing a trick. He is a very happy man. He looks brainwashed. Or worse. I check his forehead for a large surgical scar.

He continues to smile expectantly.

I take a step back. I don't want to catch whatever he has. He's a disturbing, out-of-uniform Santa.

Kavi slinks over to us. "Lunch," he purrs.

All at once, people appear from various unseen places. It's as if their minds share one collective thought. *Time . . . for . . . lunch . . .* I'm surprised they don't move with their arms extended out in front of them, like in *Night of the Living Dead*.

I follow Bobby and Kavi up the back stairs, past the main room and down the hallway, which leads to the cafeteria. People are talking, joking with each other, taking red plastic trays and moving along the cafeteria assembly line. I follow. A fishcake sandwich is smacked onto a dishwasher/microwave-safe plate and shoved onto my tray by a bitter and underpaid cafeteria woman. As I move along the line, other food items are plunked onto my tray: a small salad of iceberg lettuce and Bacos, a slice of white bread with a pat of Hotel Holiday butter and a blob of red Jell-O with fruit cocktail trapped inside. Instantly, I feel compassion for the trapped fruit.

A welcome tumbler of Dewar's on the rocks is substituted with a sealed pint of whole milk.

Behind the assembly line, the room is filled with round tables, all of them on wheels. I follow Bobby and Kavi and sit with them because they are familiar, and therefore less of a threat than the other patients.

I look at my tray and think, *$13,000 a week for a deep-fried fish sandwich?*

Then I get it.

Before they can build you up, they've got to break you down. Crush you into small, manageable pieces and then reassemble you as a new, better and nonalcoholic member of society. The pulverizing begins here. I eat only the red Jell-O.

Big Bobby notices. "Hey, aren't ya hungry?" he says, real upbeat and hopeful.

"No," I say, "not really."

Then his large paw reaches over the McFishThing and hovers there. "You mind, then?"

I tell him to go for it.

He plucks the sandwich up and consumes it in three wide, experienced bites. "I love the food here," he says, still chewing. He is a polite Ignatius from *A Confederacy of Dunces.*

"You have a sesame seed on your lip," I tell him.

His wide, meaty tongue darts out and snatches it with expert skill.

While Big Bobby swallows, Kavi sucks on his pinkie. He watches me intently. He's a sex addict, I remember. And suddenly, he ceases being a person and takes on the appearance of an anonymous roadside restroom stall. The kind used by passing truckers for quick sex with people like Kavi. Yellow, I believe. Kavi would be a yellow stall with no lock.

I glance at my watch; it's just before two in the afternoon. I haven't even been here an hour and a half and already I'm thinking it's not going to work out. I could get sober in New York, on my own. Take the thirty days off from work. Do my own minirehab. Buy some self-help books and maybe go to AA meetings. I feel sure I could become sober on my own now, after seeing this place. I think it's quite possible I have been "scared straight" in only a matter of hours. The only person ever to be spontaneously cured of alcoholism. I decide to be fair, I will give it one day.

That seems more than fair. That seems outlandishly generous.

After lunch, I go to "Group." My particular group has about twenty patients in it, plus David, the chemical dependency counselor. David is almost handsome. But he also looks borderline homeless with his greasy hair and untucked shirt. I calculate that for me, he is two light beers away from being doable. And nine away from being a Baldwin brother.

We sit upstairs in a circle we have made by dragging chairs and sofas across the thick gray indoor/outdoor carpeting and forming a cozy little "safe" area. I look for Big Bobby, but he's not here. He must be in the other group, down the hall. Or he's crouched under one of the tables in the cafeteria licking the floor.

David says, "Okay, Augusten is new today, so let's go over the rules of Group. Would anyone like to begin?"

An enormous woman with very sad eyes raises her plump hand.

"Great, Marion, thank you," says David. He smiles at her with a potty-training grin.

I begin to feel a small, creepy feeling start up my legs.

Marion looks at the floor as she speaks. Each time she names something from the list, I see a finger extend from her fist, so she's counting off the fine points like a child learning math. "There is no eating in Group. You can bring a beverage. There's no crosstalk. When somebody's talking, you never interrupt them. You let them finish before you speak. Also, if somebody starts to cry, you don't hand them a tissue because that can interrupt the grieving process. Ummmm. Oh, also, put everything you say into 'I' statements. So, like, if somebody says something, and you want to share, you would say 'Well, I can relate to that because *I* . . . ' or whatever. And never give advice to people."

David nods, pleased.

She almost smiles, but then stops herself.

I don't belong here. I make over two hundred thousand dollars a year as an advertising professional. The CEO of Coca-Cola once complimented my tie.

David claps his hands together and says, "Okay then, let's begin."

Paul is the first person to start. "My name is Paul and I'm an alcoholic." Paul is the first pregnant man I have ever seen.

The room screams, "Hi, Paul!" back at him with such startling force that I flinch.

"And I just want to say that I am a little uncomfortable with the new person being here today because the group no longer feels safe. And I'm sorry but that's how I feel."

David cocks his head, studies Paul. Probes him. "You feel unsafe? How else do you feel, what other feelings do you have?"

Paul concentrates, hard. He looks as if he can't decide between a vodka tonic or a screwdriver. "I feel scared and excited and angry and curious and also tired because I didn't sleep very well last night. I think I need to have my meds upped."

David nods his head looking exactly like a compassionate therapist. "You can speak to the nurse after group about your meds, Paul."

Then David turns to me. "Augusten, how does it make you feel, what Paul's expressed? What do you feel about his feelings?"

I am overcome with a thickness of the mind. It's a sensation I've had before during extreme stress. A memory floats to the surface, like a dead fish:

I am thirteen years old, in bed with Neil Bookman, who is thirty-three. His bed, in his apartment that he invited me to so he could show me some photographs he'd taken, because I'm interested in photography.

He is forcing his penis down my throat, all the way to the back and I am gagging, it's hard to breathe. "You like this?" he says as he pounds. "Huh? You like my big fat dick?" Neil is a friend of my parents and he is the "adopted" son and patient of their psychiatrist, whom I now live with. I have known Bookman since I was five. I look past him at the ceiling and see the thin black cracks in the plaster. I go inside one of the cracks. I leave my body on the bed, let Bookman do anything he wants to with it.

"Augusten?" David asks. "Would you like to share your feelings?"

I look at all the faces looking at me. Except Pregnant Paul; he is looking away.

I can't be here, this can't be happening. I don't know what to say. I don't know what I feel. "I feel like I want to leave. Like this was a big mistake."

Paul turns, quickly looks at me. "That's exactly how I felt when I first came here," he says.

Then somebody else says, "Me too."

And then somebody else, "It took about a week before I finally accepted it."

"Good, good," David says in a soothing tone.

A WASPy looking man who is slumped down in his chair suddenly bursts into tears. The room falls silent. I could be wrong, but I believe I sense palpable excitement in the air as everyone suddenly turns to him. He buries his face in his hands and sobs so hard that his entire body rocks. A couple people whisper something back and forth.

David turns to them with his finger on his lip. *"Shhhhhhhhhh."*

The WASP chokes and then, much to my horror, looks directly at me and says, "I don't belong here, either. I don't belong in this room or in this goddamn world. I should be dead."

He continues to look at me and I look at him back, afraid that if I break eye contact he will hurl a chair at me.

David asks in a very soft voice, "Tom, why do you feel you should be dead?"

The WASP looks at him. *Phew.* Let this mess transfer onto a trained professional.

Then the WASP starts talking. He's talking about how he drank every single night and on the nights he didn't drink would get really sick. He's been in and out of rehab six times and he feels this is his last chance. And the reason he is here this time is because he was driving his parents to a party and they didn't realize he was drunk. They thought he was on the wagon. But he was in a blackout. He veered off the road and the car rolled over an embankment and landed against a tree. His mother's legs were crushed. Now she's paralyzed from the waist down. And every time he looks at her, he realizes that if he had killed himself earlier, his mother would be okay. Now he can't even look at her without reliving that night.

I notice he is wearing cuff links on his pinstriped shirt. Cuff links and loafers. But when you look at his eyes, all you see is destruction and emptiness. Something so sad it scares me. It scares me because I almost recognize it. He could be an ad guy.

"I had a car accident," says another man who is wearing a cowboy hat. "My face went right through the windshield, thirty-two stitches," he says, pointing to the scar that runs across his forehead, just below the brim of his hat. "Think that stopped me? Hell no. And you know why? 'Cause I didn't hit nobody else. It was only me that got hurt, and I don't count, see?"

Tom, the WASP, looks at the cowboy and nods his head. Yeah, he knows.

Car accidents, facial lacerations, paralyzed mothers . . . I am definitely in the wrong place. This is for hard-core alcoholics. Rock-bottom, ruined-their-lives alcoholics. I'm an Advertising Alcoholic. An eccentric mess. I fold my arms across my chest and look out the window at the lone tree in the distance. The tree looks homeless. It looks like—oh, I don't know—an advertising copywriter who refused to go to rehab and got fired. A general sense of doom swells inside of me.

A woman says, "But Dale, you are important. It's your disease that makes you feel you're not."

David looks at the woman who just spoke. He's wearing a naughty face. "You know the rules Helen. If you have something to say, *use an 'I' statement.*"

Helen blushes slightly and stammers. "Okay, okay, you're right. I'm sorry." She inhales very deeply, slides her eyes up to the ceiling. "What I mean is that *I* could relate to your story because I have felt that my drinking was okay as long as it didn't hurt anybody. But in the program, I'm starting to realize that I do matter, that I am somebody who is worth something and it's the booze and the crack that make me feel I'm not. If I don't use, I can't lose." Then she looks at the cowboy. "Dale, I'm very glad you shared that. And you too, Tom. I really got a lot out of what both of you said . . . so thanks." She shrugs and smiles.

I'm thinking, *In the program . . . thanks for sharing . . . if I don't use, I can't lose . . .* What language are these people speaking? I remember I was really freaked out on my first day in advertising, because I could barely understand a word people said. It was as if I had taken a job in Antwerp: Storyboards, VO, Tag, Farm-out, CA, Rep, Donut-middle. It was like, *Huh?* My favorite phrase was "Two-Cs-in-a-K." This referred to the standard packaged goods commercial. It stood for Two Cunts in a Kitchen.

I say, "There seems to be an alcoholic language and I don't speak it." I have never had an ear for languages, which is yet another reason why I should leave right now.

People chuckle knowingly.

David smiles.

I turn red and mentally scold myself for actually *involving* myself with these people. Better to sit quietly, avert the eyes. Do *not* ask the Iranian hijackers for an extra pillow.

David says, "Yup, there's a language all right. You'll pick it up really quickly. But if there's some particular thing you heard that you don't understand, just tell us and we can explain it to you."

Marion briefly departs her world of low self-esteem long enough to smile at me.

I wipe my hands on my pants. They leave dark wet marks behind. I am feeling so out of place and uncomfortable, not to mention threatened. Like it's the first day of high school and I showed up in a red Speedo. I swallow hard. "Well, this woman here . . ." I point to the woman who had just "shared." "Helen, is it?"

She nods.

"Yeah, so Helen, she said something about 'in the program' and I guess I was wondering what a 'program' is." Somehow, I do not think *a program* in any way resembles something Julie from *The Love Boat* would dream up.

"Would anybody like to answer Augusten's question?"

Pregnant Paul smiles at me, looks like he's about to open his mouth.

"Sure. Hi, Augusten, I'm Brian and I'm a drug addict," says a guy who has been silent the whole time. He has been not only silent, but borderline smirky.

"Hi, Brian!" says the room.

"A 'program' is basically AA terminology and it refers to the steps. You know the Twelve Steps?"

I shake my head vaguely and shrug. I only know the first step, which seems depressing enough: admitting I am powerless over alcohol, even bad sangria. That there are eleven additional steps is daunting.

"Okay, well, when you 'work your program' all that means is that you're doing everything you can do to stay sober, according to the steps. You'll see. You'll see a lot of AA when you get out of here."

That should be interesting. I've always wondered what an AA meeting is like. The reason I've never been to one—aside from the fact that you can't drink at them—is because I'm afraid what I see in my head might be close to the truth: Held downstairs in the dank, unused basements of churches, I envision a shamed group of people wearing long dark coats and old Foster Grant sunglasses, sitting in folding metal chairs. Everyone is clutching a white Styrofoam cup filled halfway with bad coffee. Filled only halfway so the coffee doesn't slosh out, due to the fact that everyone's hands are trembling from withdrawal. I see one person after another introducing themselves. . . . ". . . and I'm an alcoholic." And I hear the other alcoholics applauding. "Congratulations!! Welcome!! One day at a time!!" Maybe they talk about how much they want to drink. "And I would kill for a Manhattan right now." And somebody else says ". . . on the rocks, a Manhattan on the rocks . . ." And a few people moan and you hear all of these frantic sips of coffee all at once. Maybe there's even a secret handshake, like the Mormons who also don't drink. My feeling has always been that if AA means sitting around in the bottom of a church talking endlessly about how much I want to drink, I'd rather never talk about drinking. I'd rather talk about modern art or advertising or screenplay ideas, while tossing back shots. So yeah, it'll be interesting to see what the mystical force of AA really is. I can hardly wait. Check please.

Why does this have to be so complicated? I wish they could just cut your "drinker" out of you. Like having a kidney stone removed. You check into the hospital as an outpatient, get anesthetized from the waist down, they put headphones on you and you listen to Enya. Fifteen minutes later, the doctor lifts the headphones off and shows you the small, turd-colored organ he extracted from somewhere inside you. I see it looking like a snail.

"Would you like to save it . . . as a souvenir?"
"No, Dr. Zizmor, toss it. I don't want any reminder."
The doctor slaps you on the back on your way out. "Congratulations, you're now a sober man."

"Could I say something to the group?" Brian asks.

"Of course," says David.

"I would just like everyone to know that I am down to my last doses of Valium and by Monday, I should be off of it entirely."

The room applauds.

Why does he get Valium? All I get is a McFishThing sandwich, along with Mother's Little Helper so I don't go into some alcoholic withdrawal shock. I want Valium.

Yet there's something about this Brian person I like. I sense that he is extremely intelligent. There's a professionalism to the way he speaks, like he's a therapist, that I find comforting. That's just my gut instinct. I think tonight at dinner, maybe I will sit with him instead of Big Bobby and Kavi the Sex Addict.

Group lasts for an hour and a half. Having survived, I now have fifteen minutes before my next piece of structured therapy: chemical dependency history, or CDH.

At the bottom of the stairs, Tom the WASP catches up to me. "It really does get better," he says. "In a few days, you won't want to leave this place."

I smile, say, "Thanks," and walk to my room thinking, *you are so wrong.*

I'm standing in front of a white marker board, upstairs, writing down "to the best of your ability" a complete history of my drinking.

"I want you to go back as far as possible and list everything . . . alcohol, barbituates, tranquilizers, speed, everything . . . even prescription painkillers. And don't minimize. List your age, the substance, the quantity consumed and the regularity."

So far on the board, I have written:

Age 7: Given NyQuil for cold. Grandfather is NyQuil salesman so we have cases of it. Green is favorite color so
sometimes sneak sips.

Age 12: First real drunk. One bottle of red wine. Threw up
on friend's sheepdog.

Ages 13–17: Smoke pot once a week. Drink alcohol maybe
once a week.

18: Drink nightly, always to intoxication. Five drinks per
night, + or -

19–20: Drink maybe ten drinks per night, with occasional
binges. Coke once every six months.

21 to present: A liter of Dewar's a night, often chased with
cocktails. Cocaine once a month.

I stand back and look. A jumble of blue words, my messy writing, my magic marker confession up here for all to see. I've never
actually *quantified* before.

People look at the board, then back at me.

Tracy, the leader of the CDH group, looks at me with eyes
that seem to belong to someone three times her age. It's something beyond wisdom, all the way to insanity and back. It's
like her eyes are scarred from all the things she's seen. "When
you look at what you've just written, what do you feel?" she
asks.

I look at the board. Now that it's up there, it does seem like I
drink a lot. "I guess I drink a lot." I feel ashamed, like I wear the
same pair of underwear for days at a time.

Brian, from Group, says, "Given the quantity of alcohol you've consumed, it's a wonder you're alive at all."

And what makes Mr. Valium such an expert? I wonder.

A lesbian wearing a blue MALL OF AMERICA sweatshirt tells me, "I am so happy that you're here. You need to be here."

A couple of other people agree. *Glad you're here. You need to be here.* They may be right or they may be wrong. But the one thing that I know for sure is that this will make a great bar story.

"The amount of alcohol you consumed would be associated with late-stage alcoholism. You were very much in danger of alcoholic poisoning, an overdose. And I'm glad you're here, too." Tracy looks at me with genuine warmth and understanding. Something else, too. Something that makes me think we could have really partied together.

I figure I'll up the ante. "Does Benadryl count?" A couple of people look at me. I shrug innocently like, *Shucks, I don't know these things.*

"Benadryl? The antihistamine?" asks Tracy.

"Yes," I say. "Does that count?"

"It depends," she says, suspiciously.

"Oh. Well, the thing is, I can't drink alcohol, not *any* alcohol, without having an allergic reaction. My face swells, my chest gets red, I get a metallic taste in my mouth and it's hard to breathe. Even one drink will do it. But I found that if I take Benadryl before I drink, I'm okay."

"How much Benadryl?" she asks.

Other people look at me, then at her, then back at me. This could be Wimbledon.

I suddenly realize that the amount is so staggeringly large that I am ashamed to admit it. "Ten pills a day. Usually. Sometimes fifteen."

Her eyes widen in alarm. "And the recommended dosage? What is that?" But she's not really asking me the dosage, she's asking me if I recognize insane when I see it. I play along.

"Two."

She looks at me. Actually, right through me to the back of the chair. She can see its upholstery despite the fact that my body is blocking the view. She says nothing. Because she knows she doesn't need to say anything. She knows that I already know. All she does is close her eyes and give me a small smile. "Yep, I'm very glad you're here."

I sit quietly and a strange and unfamiliar feeling comes to me. It is almost a feeling of relief, ears popping, pressure released. But it's something else, too. I think for the first time I can see, right up there on the board, that I do drink much more than normal. And the pills I have to swallow to drink. Like my body is allergic to alcohol and is telling me I shouldn't be drinking, but I do anyway. And when I sit there looking at what I've written, I almost can't help but feel like it's possibly a good thing I am here. Or rather, that this has been drawn to my attention, made serious and not just a joke.

Maybe that's enough and I can go?

Dinner goes like this: on the way upstairs, I avoid Kavi, the sex addict from Corpus Christi, a city whose name now sounds obscene to me, like the technical term for a Blue Whale penis. *"The Corpus Christi of the Blue Whale is typically between nine and twelve and a half feet long, when fully erect."* Once inside the cafeteria I am greeted by some of the other patients, a few of whom I recognize from group or the chemical dependency history class, some of whom I have never seen before. "Thanks . . . yeah . . . culture shock . . . thirty days . . . alcohol . . . I'm sure . . . Thanks anyway . . ." I take a red plastic tray. Dinner is served by the exact same bitter, underpaid woman who served lunch. Her name tag reads MRS. RICE. So she has lived up to her name, fulfilled her destiny to work somehow with food. She's a tall woman, fleshy without being fat. Her hair is gray and because it is also long and straight, parted in the center, this for some reason makes me think she used to be a blonde. She is now a former blonde working a double shift in a rehab hospital. I smile at her because I feel guilty, like the fact that I wear Armani means I should somehow have my life more together, that I am ungrateful and spoiled and deserve no empathy or dinner. All of which is probably true.

I take the tray of gray shepherd's pie, canned cream of corn soup, tapioca pudding and milk and stand there looking at the tables, trying to see if Brian from Group is here. I spot him. I make a beeline.

He seems unsurprised that I chose him to sit next to. "Brian, right?" I ask.

"Shit, you're doing good. It took me two weeks before I learned even one person's name." There's corn on his chin.

I smile, genuinely for the first time in twenty-four hours. "You've got corn there," I say, pointing to my own chin.

We find an easy rapport. He hates the food here. I agree. The people are freaks. Exactly what *I* thought. The place is in shambles. Obviously. But it works.

"Really?" I ask, unsure as to how this is possible.

He tucks into his meal, placing his arms on the table in such a way that they surround his food, protectively. Between bites, he tells me that he is a psychiatrist and has been involved in treating chemically dependent people for six years and that these are some of the best, smartest and most dedicated counselors he's ever seen.

"You're a shrink?" I'm stunned by this news. *So then why . . . how?* I don't actually ask, but he seems to be able to read me.

"Yeah, at San Francisco General. Here for Valium. With shrinks, it's always the Valium that takes you down. Occupational hazard."

For some reason, I never considered that any of this could happen to a doctor. I buy the whole white jacket, stethoscope slung around the neck, double-parked Saab convertible thing.

"Then it was, ' . . . *one* Valium for you . . . *two* for me."

He's not some nut. He's a *doctor.*

"That became 'one Valium for you . . . *five* for me."

Oh my God, I think, *that's exactly the kind of bartender I would be.*

He looks down at his tray and continues. "At the end, which was a little over two weeks ago, I was swallowing all of my patients' Valiums, about twenty a day, and giving them aspirin instead. I got caught." He brings his eyes up to meet mine and I see sorrow in them. Sorrow edged with fear. "I might lose my license."

Sometimes there is nothing else to say except, "Oh."

We spend the next five minutes in silence, eating. He asks me to pass the pepper.

I drop my napkin on the floor and lean over to pick it up. I finish before he does because I only sip the starchy white broth around the corn in the soup. It'll be easy to play Karen Carpenter in this place—I bet I get down to ninety pounds by the time I leave.

I watch him stab an overcooked green bean with his fork and the gesture strikes me as tragic. Suddenly, there is a buzzing in my chest. As if wasps are trapped inside of me, stinging. That a *doctor* could sink so low. I mean, what does that say about me? Surely, an advertising guy would sink even lower. "I really don't like it here," I tell him.

He looks at me like he knows something, but won't tell.

I go on. "It's dilapidated, unprofessional—and the people. I don't know. It's not what I expected."

He stands up, bringing his tray with him. I do the same and we walk to the trash area, dump our plates.

"It'll take a few days, but you'll see. You'll *get* it."

A skinny woman with long, dark, straight hair grabs Dr. Valium by the arm and whispers something in his ear. He cracks up and they head off down the hallway together, her arm around his waist, laughing. "I'll see you downstairs," he calls back to me.

I think about what Dr. Valium just told me. "It'll take a few days, but you'll see. You'll *get* it."

This is probably exactly what the Reverend Jim Jones said to his followers as he stirred the Kool-Aid.

It's called simply "Affirmations." There's a nighttime Affirmations and a morning Affirmations. I was lucky enough to miss the morning show.

I'm sitting upstairs in the main room with all the other patients. Marion, the large woman who can only make eye contact with the carpeting, is obviously the "leader" of this group. She begins by asking out loud, "Who would like to volunteer to read tonight's affirmation?"

Kavi volunteers by leisurely raising his arm in the air and allowing his hand to flop back and forth at the wrist in a vague and affected fashion.

I notice that he has changed into eveningwear. Gone is the tight white T-shirt. Now he's wearing a black fishnet tank top and his long, springy chest hairs are sticking out through the wide weave. The hairs are strangely glossy, as though he has used conditioner on them. I think I even catch the perfumed scent of Finesse in the air. But it could just be a nasal hallucination.

He reads from a heavily fingered paperback with a sunburst on the cover. "April fifth, taking a single footstep toward change." As he reads the inspiring and motivational entry, I look at people's feet. I notice that almost everyone is wearing the pale blue hospital slippers that came in my hospital welcome pack. I morbidly wonder if it's possible that I will be so broken by this place that I, too, will wear the little booties. And then I'll cry when they rip, sharing my pain with the others.

Big Bobby keeps blinking his eyes really hard with what is

some sort of nervous tick. Pregnant Paul stares out the window, but because it's dark, I suspect he's really watching the group reflected in the glass. The WASP has changed from a pinstripe shirt into a white oxford, as though he is on a cruise.

After Kavi finishes reading the affirmation, Marion the Low-Esteem Leader says, "I guess I'll begin the Grateful Statements. I'm grateful to be here tonight. . . . I'm grateful that I'm alive and feel loved . . . and I'm grateful for you, Augusten, for being here."

Oh, I really wish she hadn't done that. I do not want more attention drawn to me. I mentally vanish from the room, Endora from *Bewitched*.

Somebody else says, "Steve, I'm grateful you watered the plants while I was at 'individual.' And I'm grateful that I didn't *use* today and I'm hopeful about tomorrow."

A few people sigh, heads nod in appreciation.

The man with the cowboy hat from my group says, "I'm grateful to have you here too, Augusten. And I'm grateful to be here myself. I'd like to thank God for another chance. And say, one day at a time."

Dr. Valium smiles to himself and stares at the floor. Is he biting the inside of his cheek to halt a smile?

And so it goes, that for fifteen minutes the patients express their gratitude to each other for such things as "saying hello to me in the hallway . . . sharing what you did in Group this afternoon . . . splitting your chocolate-chip cookie with me."

I can feel the artery on the left side of my head pulsing, moments away from bursting into an aneurysm. Whatever Librium was in my system has already been metabolized by my urban liver. My liver wastes no time. It's the New York City cabdriver of livers. I'm thinking it can't get any worse than this.

But of course, then it absolutely does.

"Okay, everybody, what time is it?" Marion asks playfully, leading everybody on.

Two of the patients reach behind their chairs and retrieve two large, well-worn stuffed animals; one is a monkey, one is a blue kitten. They hug the dirty plush toys to their laps and wear great big smiles.

At once, the entire room breaks into an alarming musical chant. "It's Monkey Wonkey time . . . Monkey Wonkey was a lonely monkey. Then Blue Blue kitten became his friend . . . now Monkey Wonkey and Blue Blue Kitten want to make friends with . . . YOU!!!"

And both patients suddenly lunge off their chairs and sprint over to me, giggling and dropping the stuffed animals onto my lap before returning to their seats like obedient children.

I sit motionless and confused, bathed in applause. *Why a song about codependent stuffed animals? And why am I now holding them on my lap? And more essentially, what time is the first flight in the morning?* At this point, I would even take a bus, gladly the rear seat next to the toilet.

I look at Dr. Valium. He lifts his eyebrows smugly, as if to say, *And there you have it.*

Marion explains, for once looking up from the carpeting, "Don't worry, Augusten, it's just a little tradition we have here. Each night, we hand out Monkey Wonkey and Blue Blue Kitten to somebody special who needs a little lift. And since you're new, that's why you got them." Then she adds, as if it were a perk, "So you get to curl up with both of these guys tonight—and tomorrow, you get to choose who pass them along to!"

Before I am able to say a word, the group rises to its feet and joins hands. My own hands are forcibly grabbed by the alcoholics on either side of me. The stuffed animals tumble from my lap.

Then, as if genetically programmed to do so, a young male alcoholic who had been previously slumped in a chair with his hair hanging over his eyes begins, "God . . ." and the group joins him in spooky unison, ". . . grant me the serenity to accept the things I cannot change, the courage to change the things I can, and the wisdom to know the difference. Amen."

I think, *How bizarre*. They're quoting the opening of Sinéad O'Connor's "I Feel So Different." I love that song. I associate it with vodka and Rose's lime juice, back when I first moved to New York City and lived downtown in a Battery Park City high-rise apartment. I'd blast that CD and lean out the window in my living room, watching the traffic blur up West Street, the unfathomably gigantic World Trade Center towers illuminated always, even at midnight.

The crowd breaks up, people laugh, somebody says, "Race you to the coffee machine." I find myself carried by the flow of the group, down the stairs, still clutching the stuffed animals.

"Look, I know this seems really corny, but you've got to trust me. Once you get past all the crap, the program here is truly amazing," Dr. Valium says. "Give it some time," he adds. "It needs time to sink in."

Big Bobby waddles over. I want to tell him, "I have no food, go away."

He says, "Don't worry, they're clean."

"Huh?" I say.

"Monkey Wonkey and Blue Blue Kitten. We throw them in the washer once a week." He smiles, clomps down the stairs.

I imagine the entire inpatient community standing in the laundry room wringing their hands while they wait anxiously for the plush toys to dry. I go to my room. My roommate is on his bed, curled up into the fetal position. I drop the animals on the floor at the foot of my bed and sit.

It's nine o'clock. Let's see. Right about now, I'd be at the Bowery Bar, working on my seventh martini of the night. I'd have napkins with ad campaign ideas scribbled on them strewn on the bar in front of me. I might even be flirting back and forth with the actor/bartender.

I look at my roommate, an older, withered black man who checked in only hours before me. He hasn't left the room all day. It was whispered to me that he has terminal liver cancer. Earlier he'd been taken to the other, normal hospital, for some additional tests, which is why I didn't see him when I first arrived.

I undress to my boxers and T-shirt and crawl under the thin sheet. The flat pillow under my head offers no support. I stare at the beige water stains on the suspended ceiling.

I sigh.

So far, mental health sucks.

ALCOHOLISM FOR BEGINNERS

M̲y name is Marion and I'm an alcoholic and drug addict," says Low-Esteem Marion as she looks at the two plump hands in her lap.

"Hi, Marion," chants the circle.

"I'm right where I need to be," says Marion to the hands.

"You're right where you need to be," echoes the circle.

"I feel my feelings and share them with others."

"You feel your feelings and share them with others."

Marion looks across the room at a member of the circle, briefly, before looking away. "I love myself."

"You love yourself," affirms the group.

"And I am somebody."

"And you *are* somebody," the room says in unison.

A brief, small smile passes across Marion's lips, her cheeks flush with color and she wipes the palms of her hands across the legs of her jeans, turning to the person sitting to her right.

"My name is Paul, Alcoholic," says Pregnant Paul.

"Hi, Paul Alcoholic," says everyone verbatim, including Marion who is now able to look directly at Paul, who himself looks at the floor and represses a nervous smile.

"I'm a good person."

"You're a good person," promises the room.

"I will get well," says Paul optimistically.

"You will get well," promise the addicts.

"I'll lose my spare tire and find a cute boyfriend," grins Paul.

"You will lose your spare tire and find a cute boyfriend," sing the patients.

"And I am somebody," he says, hands clasped across his belly.

"And you are somebody," says everyone, except me.

As was explained by a counselor this morning, Affirmations are a time when we affirm in ourselves something we would like to strengthen. For example, if I feel I am fat, I would say, "I am thin," and the group would affirm this in me. "You are thin." It's as simple as that. And you always end with the phrase, "I am somebody."

Funny, but similar affirmations haven't worked for me in the past. I do recall many times telling Greer, "I'm not drunk. I would never show up to work drunk." And her telling me, "Bullshit, you lying fuck."

When the circle finally comes to me, there's a brief moment of silence, because I have stopped paying attention to the affirmations, and am instead imagining how it would feel to walk into a jewelry store in downtown Minneapolis and buy an expensive watch to replace the one that I gave to the ex-cop after sex one night during a blackout in my apartment.

There is a clearing of a throat. All eyes slide my way.

"My name is Augusten and I'm an alcoholic," I grumble.

"Hi, Augusten," says the room.

"I'm glad to be here," I lie.

"You're glad to be here," they repeat.

"I won't check out after lunch," I say.

"You won't check out after lunch," they affirm.

There, I think. *Done.*

"And . . . ?" somebody says.

"And what?"

"And you ARE somebody," three or four people say with some hostility.

Jesus Fucking Christ. "And I *am* somebody," I say sarcastically.

"And you are somebody," they overemphasize.

When Affirmations are over, I go straight into Group. Today, nice David is not the counselor of the group, but instead there's Rae. Rae's a big woman. And to add an exclamation point to this fact, she wears a loud floral print; gigantic blossoms all over her body. There's something in her voice that makes me think I won't get away with anything, that I shouldn't even try. I feel pretty confident Rae's clubbed more than her fair share of baby seals in her life.

"Today we're going to talk about consequences. The consequences of our drinking. Does everybody know what consequences are?"

Nobody says a word.

She looks around the room, stares each and every person directly in the eyes, including me. This takes a while. I feel a shiver pass through me. Worse, I think, than making eye contact on the subway with someone you suspect belongs to a gang because they are wearing a Halloween mask in June.

Rae gives a bloodthirsty grin. "Oh, I see. None of you have experienced any consequences as a result of your drinking. My oh my, what a lucky group of alcoholics you are."

The only thing that I can think is, *Oh shit.*

Still nobody says anything. People just sort of shift around in their seats, we don't even look each other. I sense we are all looking at our shoelaces, concentrating hard on the knot.

"Okay then, let me tell you what a consequence is. A consequence is when you're a drunk and you meet another drunk at a bar. And you and this other drunk start a relationship. Every night you drink together. And every night this drunk that you hooked up with beats the shit out of you. And every morning, he apologizes. And you forgive him. So what if he breaks four bones in your face? You have plenty more."

She pauses. My hands are sweating. I have the sensation of ascending on a roller coaster.

"When your friends tell you that you are crazy to stay with this man, you tell them that it's none of their business. Eventually, you lose your friends. But you don't care, because you have your booze and you have your man. But that's just an example."

She pauses. "Of course, a consequence could also be losing a job because of your drinking, or losing a friendship, or even losing your self-respect. Maybe letting the dishes pile up in your sink until you can't see your sink anymore."

A bell rings. I think of my apartment. It's my deepest, darkest secret. The fact that I drink is not a secret. The fact that I'm usually already drunk when I meet Jim for drinks is not a secret.

My apartment is my secret. It's filled with empty liquor bottles. Not five or six. More like three hundred. Three hundred one-liter bottles of scotch, occupying all floor space not already occupied by a bed or a chair. Sometimes I myself am stunned by the visual presentation. And the truly odd part is that I really don't know how they got there. You'd think I'd have taken each bottle down to the trash room when it was empty. But I let two collect. And because two is nothing, I let three collect. And on it went. The ironic thing is that I'm not the kind of person who saves things. I don't have boxes filled with old postcards from friends, cherished mementos from childhood. My apartment is clean and modern in design, kind of what you'd think a New York City ad guy's apartment would look like. I even spent half my paycheck one month on a single end table.

Except there are bottles everywhere. And magazines all over the floor.

Every time I've removed the bottles from my apartment, promised myself it would never happen again, it always happens again. And when I used to drink beer instead of scotch, the beer bottles would collect. I counted the beer bottles once: one thousand, four hundred and fifty-two. You have not felt anxiety until you have carried a plastic trash bag stuffed with a few hundred beer bottles down the stairs in the middle of the night, trying not to make a sound.

Quickly, before I can change my mind, I speak up. "Something you just said, I can relate to that." Already, "I" statements.

She looks at me, folds her arms across her chest and nods. "Go on."

I tell her about the bottles. And how because of them, I never invite anybody over to my apartment. "Actually, whenever I hear somebody in the hallway, I freeze in case they knock on my door, so I can pretend I'm not home."

I feel a pang of sadness, and it's actually for myself. Why would somebody live that way? I also feel like I have broken a confidence. So this is what I say. "It's funny, but admitting this out loud, I feel really strange, like I'm saying something I shouldn't."

She claps her hands together. "Exactly! What you are doing is 'telling on your addict.' You need to visualize your own internal addict. Think of it as a separate 'being' that lives inside of you. And it wants nothing more than for you to drink. When you don't drink, it says, 'Oh come on, just one.' Your addict wants you all to itself. So when you talk about the bottles, or any other consequence of drinking, you are in effect, 'telling on your addict.'"

I play along. I try to imagine a nasty little man living inside my forehead, kicking the backs of my eyeballs for telling. Then I imagine myself wearing the hospital slippers.

"Of course, your addict is not really a separate entity within you, but I think it helps to visualize it as such." She smooths the front of her dress. "Now, how are *bottles* a consequence of drinking?"

"Um, I guess because they make the apartment messy," I say.

"And?" she questions, sounding like a prosecuting attorney.

I just look at her, puzzled. Someone forgot to give me my script.

"Anybody else?" she asks the room.

Big Bobby straightens in his chair. "Well, if he's got all those bottles in there, then, like he said, nobody ever visits him. So that must be lonely."

I feel instantly pathetic. More transparent than jellyfish sashimi.

"Yes," she says, "That's it exactly. The bottles allow you, Augusten, to place a wall—a wall of glass if you will—between you and other people. Effectively, you are a prisoner in your own home. And your internal addict loves this. Because the goal is to have you isolated. Your addict is very jealous and wants you all to itself."

I think of how I'm always in a rush to leave the office early, come home and drink. How lately, I don't even care if Jim's busy or if I don't see any friends. I don't mind at all staying home alone. And drinking. In fact, I think I'm starting to crave staying home alone instead of going out. And then I think of Pighead. How we never talk about his HIV because we never need to because he's fine. Except for sometimes.

"Augusten," he will say to me, "I'm not asking for any favors. I'm not asking you to take a vacation to Hawaii with me for a month. Just come over for dinner once in a while, come for roast beef. Call me up and say, 'Hey, how's it going?'"

I think of how demanding I consider him to be. Needy. "I can't," I always tell him these days. "Work." Even roast beef and *60 Minutes* is too much to ask of me. Even a phone call.

Dr. Valium goes next. He talks about how he might lose his medical license for his Valium addiction. How all those years of schooling could end up being for nothing.

"That's a *consequence* all right," Rae says.

The others bring out their greatest hits. The WASP talks about the car accident and his mother's paralysis. Low-Esteem Marion talks about her failed relationship with her girlfriend of six years. Big Bobby talks about not being able to hold a job and hating himself because he's thirty-two and still lives with his parents.

It's all very Ringling Brothers. And as freakish as these people may be, it's not exactly like I can't relate to what they're saying. It's more like I can sort of relate. Sort of completely.

"Ten years ago, I was a prostitute in Green Bay, Wisconsin. I would fuck or blow anybody for enough money to buy a bottle of booze. And hey, it didn't have to be good booze. Gut rot was perfectly fine, just as long as it was a liter. Then I met my 'Mr. Right,'" Rae says, spitting out *Mr. Right* like it's something toxic. Like she bit down on a thermometer and is now spitting out the mercury.

I look at her face while she talks, seeing if I can spot any signs of the leftover broken bones. I see no evidence, and, in fact, her skin is very smooth and she has an expression of calmness that seems, to me, almost like a vacation destination—a place I want to go.

"I hit rock bottom in my bathtub. I'd been unconscious in it for two days. When I woke up, my hair was glued to the side of the tub with my own blood. I was lying in my own excrement."

I look at her in her loud floral print and think, *No way*.

"But that was ten years ago. Five years before that, fifteen years ago, I was a doctor's wife. I drove a Cadillac and went to night school. I had plans. Except, my marriage was beginning to fall apart; my husband was having an affair and I refused to admit this to myself. So I picked up a new hobby: drinking. At first, it was just a cocktail at night, before dinner. Then two cocktails. Then six. By the end of the first year I was having a drink in the morning, instead of coffee. And after three years I had dropped out of school and was drinking full-time."

Wow, I think. *Does a Bloody Mary count? I love a Bloody Mary in the morning. Doesn't everybody?*

She continues. "I realize my case is a little different. It was a little faster. Five years, from nothing to rock bottom. I guess I learn quick."

She's an excellent presenter and would have succeeded in advertising, is what I think. She generates a sense of excitement in the room and I become aware that my hands are moist with sweat, but not from fear. From needing to know what happened next. I like the drama. I glance around the room and other people look rapt as well. And I feel like, *That's the reason to go to a gay rehab. People appreciate the drama.*

"When I got out of that tub and looked in the mirror, I did not recognize the creature looking back at me. And on that day, I went to my first AA meeting. That was ten years ago. Today, I'm sober, I have a Ph.D. and I'm sitting here with you, trying to help *you* become sober."

Sober. So *that's* what I'm here to become. And suddenly, this word fills me with a brand of sadness I haven't felt since childhood. The kind of sadness you feel at the end of summer. When the fireflies are gone, the ponds have dried up and the plants are wilted, weary from being so green. It's no longer really summer but the air is still too warm and heavy to be fall. It's the season between the seasons. It's the feeling of something dying.

"See, alcoholism is exactly like bubble gum. You know when you blow a bubble and it bursts, some of the gum sticks to your chin?"

Small, tentative laughter.

"What's the only thing that gets the bubble gum off your chin?" she asks.

Sometimes I will chew grape bubble gum because it stinks and hides the smell of alcohol. I answer, "Bubble gum. You have to take the gum out of your mouth and press it against the gum on your chin and it'll pick it up."

Rae beams. "You've got it."

Slam dunk. I am on the road to recovery.

"Only an alcoholic can treat another alcoholic. Only other alcoholics can get you sober." Then she slaps her hands down on her legs, exhales really fast and says, "Okay, that's it for Group. Time for lunch."

Still, I'd kill for a cosmopolitan.

I am released from the detox room and the rainbow footprint poster and placed in a regular room, directly across from the men's showers. My roommates are Dr. Valium and Big Bobby. Without trying, I've kind of fallen into a routine here. Much like a worker at a labor camp. The morning and evening Affirmations (and I AM somebody!!) are cheesy bookends to each intense day of what amounts to Alcoholic Academy.

The days here tend to blur together. Because once you've gone through four days, you've experienced every "class" there is and then it's just a matter of doing the same day over and over again. Like the movie *Groundhog Day,* it's an endless loop.

Recently, a skinny girl named Sarah piped up in group. "I can only have an orgasm if my girlfriend cuts my legs with a razor blade. The thing is, I feel so inhuman, like I'm just a shell, a husk. But when she cuts me and I bleed and see the blood and taste it off my fingers, well, then I realize I'm human, real."

So she's one of those girls on *Lifetime, Television for Women,* who stabs her knees with a fork until her parents catch her and take her to an expensive shrink, played by Jaclyn Smith. And while that's moderately entertaining, I still don't understand how any of this directly relates to me. On the plus side, they're feeding me Librium like candy. It gives me the sensation of floating just a few inches above the floor. It's a nice feeling, one I'd like to carry with me when I leave this place. It's great that rehab has turned me on to a new drug.

David gave the group a writing assignment the other day that we had to go over in Group today.

"I want you to write a letter to somebody very close to you. And I want you to tell this person exactly what you honestly feel about them and your relationship with them."

Dr. Valium wrote a general letter to his patients, apologizing for taking their Valiums and giving them aspirins. The WASP wrote to his mother, apologizing for being drunk, driving her to the party and going off the side of the road in the car, paralyzing her. He apologized for being born.

I wrote to Pighead.

Dear Pighead,

The reason I am so distant is because, well, there are two reasons actually. The first reason is my drinking. I require alcohol, nightly. And nothing can get in the way.

The second reason is your disease. I can't stand the idea of getting close to you, or closer, only to have you up and die on me, pulling the carpet out from under my life. You're my best friend. The best friend I ever had. I have to protect that.

I don't call you or see you much because I'm killing you off now, while it's easier. Because I can still talk to you. It makes sense to me to separate now, while you're still healthy, as opposed to having it just happen to me one night out of the blue.

I'm trying to evenly distribute the pain of loss. As opposed to taking it in one lump sum.

I read my letter out loud in David's group and something completely unexpected occurs. I mortify myself and get choked up. Tears fill my eyes. Marion reaches for the box of tissues.

"No, Marion, don't," says David.

"Oh yeah, I forgot . . . how stupid of me," she says in a hard, punishing voice.

I mouth the words *thank you* to her and she gives me a small, private smile. I make her know that she handed me a tissue even though she didn't and that it was just what I needed. Then I clear my throat. "I don't know what *that's* all about," I say. It scares me that I can have emotions so close to the surface and yet not even be aware of them. And really, I thought I had all my Pighead stuff worked out.

"I, uh," I begin. I'm surprised when my voice comes out thin and shaky, like I'm sitting on top of a washing machine during the spin cycle. And then I'm crying. And it's humiliating to sob in front of these people, but I can't help it. Something in me has snapped. After what feels like ten minutes, I'm able to pull it together.

"You okay?" David asks.

I nod, wiping my eyes on my sleeve.

He leans forward, elbows on knees. "What's going on inside you?"

I bite the inside of my mouth. "It's Pighead stuff, I guess. Reading that letter, you know. It makes me think back, I don't know, to when it started."

Pighead and I met on a phone sex line. I'd just moved to Manhattan and didn't have any furniture except for a yellow inflatable raft to sleep on that I bought at Wal-Mart. But I had a phone, and a *Village Voice*. A number advertised in the back of the *Voice* promised, "Hook up with other guys." So I called the number and drank beer while I chatted with guys. I adopted a British accent.

The way it worked was, you called the number and were connected to another caller. If you didn't like him, you pushed the pound sign on your phone and you got somebody else.

Usually I would wait for the other guy to talk first. "How big is your cock?" was the standard question.

I adopted a British accent and started asking the question, "So what brand of toothpaste do you use?"

Mostly, I got pound-signed. Except one guy answered, "Crest."

And I said, "Really? And why not Colgate or Gleem?"

And he said, "Because I like the taste of Crest better. And doesn't Colgate have MFP? I don't know what MFP is, you see. So I'm really mistrustful of that. It's like Retsin in Certs."

This caused me to laugh.

"You know," he said, "You have an excellent British accent. Except it falls away when you laugh. You need to work on that."

I said in my normal voice, "Shit. But you bought it up until the laugh?"

He said he did, indeed.

"Good, because I almost never laugh," I said.

He said, "That really is something you need to change about yourself. Do you believe in changing yourself? Or are you one of those tiresome people who prefer to stagnate?"

I said, "I grew up near a pond, so I understand the dangers of stagnation."

He said this was very good news. Then he asked, "So why haven't you asked me how big my dick is? Everybody else wants to know. Aren't you curious?"

I said, "Okay. How big is your dick?"

And he said, "I thought so. So you really are just looking for sex. You're not looking for anything more than sex. What was I thinking? Calling this line looking for a deep, personal connection."

"That was a trick," I told him.

"Or treat," he said.

We went on like this for an hour. Back and forth. Until finally he suggested that we meet. "Just for a drink," he said.

We met the next day, at the Winter Garden, downtown in the

World Financial Center. I wore jeans and a yellow oxford and he was in a crisp Armani suit. He wore a gold pinkie ring, which I commented on immediately. "That," I said, "is something Donald Trump would wear."

He said, "Take that back."

I smiled at him and said I wouldn't because it was the truth.

He said, "I think I may need alcohol in my system in order to spend any more time with you."

There was a Chinese restaurant in the courtyard on the first floor, so we sat at the bar in front of a long aquarium filled with orange fish. He ordered an Absolut and tonic, with a splash of Rose's lime juice. I ordered the same thing, in a tone of voice suggesting my surprise that we both drank the same drink. *What a coincidence*, my eyes said. It seemed essential that I appear to know exactly what I was doing.

Pighead was extremely—and there is no other word for it— slick. Even his thick, black hair was so glossy, it looked nylon. He was charming and witty and he smelled of Calvin Klein Obsession.

I told him about my life in advertising, impressing on him my lack of formal education beyond elementary school and my suc- cess at an early age. These were the two things about myself that I could display for others to admire. I could not talk about my parents or my childhood or my adolescence because these things would seem insane to other people and I would appear an iffy risk, especially to a mortgage banker.

Pighead checked his gold watch and told me he had to leave.

I did sort of feel that the rest was mere formality and we should just move in together. I was too new to New York City to understand that many people must have felt this way about him. That I was not unique. A handsome banker is not hard up for a date in Manhattan, ever.

• • •

On my bookcase at home, there's a photo of Pighead trying on a
leather jacket I bought for him one Christmas. I can be seen
behind him in the mirror taking the picture. I'm wearing a
ridiculous red Santa hat and my wire-framed nerd glasses. In
another picture, I'm swimming in some motel pool in Maine. It
was the Lamp Lighter Motel, I remember. It was fall and the pool
was freezing cold and had orange leaves floating in it. Leaves and
beetles. This was one of our first road trips. We'd known each
other for about a year. I remember that after getting out of the
pool, we went back to the room and I took a hot shower. When I
came out, we ended up fooling around on the bed. We stayed in
bed for two full days, leaving only at night to get prime rib or
spaghetti at the only restaurant in town that served water in glass
instead of paper.

Back in Manhattan, I told him one night, "I think I'm in love
with you." We were leaning against the railing of the esplanade at
Battery Park City, watching the planes circle in their holding pat-
terns above us. For New Yorkers, planes circling above at night
replace stars, in terms of romance.

He turned to face me. "I love you too, Augusten." Then gently
he said, "But I'm not *in love* with you. I'm sorry about what's
happened between us. It shouldn't have happened. I should never
have let things get sexual, A. And B, I should have never made you
feel that we could be anything more than friends. It's my fault."

I was trapped because I did love him, but also now wanted to
cause the most massive harm possible. *You* will *love me*, I thought.
And then it will be too late.

It went on like this for a year. The sex, always intense, fast and
hungry. And the friendship. But no romance. I'd go over to his
apartment (mine was always too messy for his taste) and he'd
make roast chicken or beef stew. I'd watch his hands work: slic-
ing, stirring, grinding pepper. I would watch his hands and think,
I love those hands. And all the while, I knew I had to get over him.

It didn't matter *why* he wasn't interested in me romantically. Just that he wasn't.

I started dating. First there was Tim, which lasted three months. Then there was Ned, which lasted a couple of weeks. There was Julian, Carlos, Eric. All of them in some way resembled Pighead. Tim was a banker, like Pighead. Julian and Carlos resembled him. Ned didn't look like Pighead but he was Greek and I thought, *Maybe this will be enough.*

It was a year later when I finally thought I was over him. When not every song reminded me of him. And I was able to go for entire days without thinking about him on a constant basis. I was able to imagine the possibility of someone else.

One evening he called me from his car and told me to meet him downstairs. It was a Friday. Probably I had plans with Jim, maybe we would be going to the Odeon or Grange Hall. "You need to come downstairs. *Now.*"

I climbed into his car and foul mood. "Jesus, what the hell is the matter with you?" I remember asking him. Maybe not those exact words, but close enough. "You have to keep things in perspective. Nothing is this bad. Your fucking job is just a job. It's not like you're HIV-positive."

But it was. He'd tested positive.

That night, I slept over at his house, holding him, showing him that it didn't matter to me. I wanted him to know that even if there was no cure, there was hope. The kind of hope that is powerful, because it comes from such need. That was the night he told me that he loved me. That he was in love with me.

But hearing him say it made me feel like he was saying it only because he was afraid. Afraid he'd never get anything better. I made it my mission to fall completely out of love with him, yet be there for him as a friend. That virus was something I just didn't want anything to do with. And I was angry with him. Furious that I had spent so much energy falling out of love with

him, only to have him fall in love with me after he became diagnosed with a fatal disease. Part of me felt deep compassion. And
another part felt like, *You fucker.*

So now we're friends and I thought I was way past all that
crap. But obviously I am not over all that crap. Obviously I am a
sort of a mess.

For a while the room is silent. Then Kavi speaks up. "When my
lover was diagnosed with AIDS, I left him. Couldn't deal with it."
He is fiddling with the gelled curl on his forehead as he says this.
"And what I regret the most is that he died not knowing how
much I loved him. And how the only reason he didn't know was
because of my using, and my selfishness. I was already married, I
guess. To coke. I couldn't even deal with the two of us together,
let alone his virus, which made it three of us. I hate myself for
that."

He looks at me. "He died never knowing how much I really
loved him. He died believing that it was his virus I was afraid of.
But that's not it. I left him before he could leave me. Because I've
been left a lot in my life. Except by coke. Coke never leaves me.
Coke is always there. I had to leave him. I had to break the cycle."

I want to throw up at hearing this. I can feel it kicking around
at the back of my throat, knocking on the door. My stomach is
pushing the acid up. My stomach is saying, *This is too much.*

Kavi disgusts me. He disgusts me more than any other human
being has ever disgusted me before.

Because I am him.

Suddenly I want to drink. The urge hits me like a tsunami. I
don't want to drink in a jovial "Highballs for everybody!" way. I
want to drink to the point where I could undergo major knee
surgery and not feel so much as a pinch.

I sit for a moment, staring straight ahead, eyes unfocused,
unblinking as reality settles over me like a lead dental X-ray cape.

It's not about being an ad guy who throws back a few too many sometimes.

It's about being in rehab or being *fired*.

It's about being an alcoholic.

It's about *me* being an alcoholic.

My lips move when I whisper the words out loud. *I'm an alcoholic.*

Today is one-on-one therapy. This is exactly like seeing a shrink in New York, minus the Barcelona chair and Eileen Gray end table from Knoll. And instead of a dignified father figure with a salt-and-pepper goatee, I have Rae in all her floral-print grandeur.

She's different one-on-one, less intense, more relaxed. I feel like I am visiting a friend. Like we could be sitting at a bar talking, except that there's a ONE DAY AT A TIME poster above her head and her bookshelf is lined with clinical addiction textbooks.

"How are you feeling?" she asks. I tell her that up until the other day, I was ready to check out. I tell her about my Pighead letter and how reading it in front of people upset me. That I'm realizing I don't like to feel things, don't want to feel pain or fear. And mostly, how I can see that I don't drink like a normal person. That I use booze like an escape hatch and also like a destination in itself. I tell her my recent observation of rehab, in terms of how it works. How it sort of sneaks up on you. The way somebody will say some dumb affirmation and then later in group, somebody will say, "I didn't buy that affirmation you said at all," and there will be a heated argument and somebody will be reduced to tears. And how all of this will bring something up inside of you, wake something up. And you have some insight you wouldn't have had otherwise. It's very odd and nonlinear and organic. And yet it's real.

Rae smiles because she knows this is exactly how it works. It is stealth.

She says we need to begin designing a "re-entry" plan for when I leave rehab and go back out into the real world. I think of the space shuttle, burning up as it breaks through the earth's hard atmosphere upon re-entry. This could easily happen to me.

She places her arms on her desk, leans forward. "My recommendation is that you continue with therapy on an outpatient basis after you leave here."

This sounds fine with me, I like the idea of seeing a shrink once a week as maintenance. It's another chance to talk about myself without being interrupted. Plus, a shrink doesn't really know me, so I can present a more balanced picture of who I really am.

"What I recommend is six months of treatment, four days a week. The program I have in mind is called HealingHorizons. It's in Manhattan and we've done a lot of work with them—they're excellent."

I blink. Six months, four times a week?

"Basically, it's a combination of group and individual therapy. It runs about two hours, four times a week." Her facial expression is pleasant. She might as well be giving me restaurant recommendations.

"What about my job, what about advertising?" I ask.

She says only, "You may have to make some changes."

Make some changes? Like what? Move the lamp to the other side of the room?

She takes a piece of paper and a pen and makes a drawing. "Think of a puzzle," she says. She draws a square and then inside of this adds squiggly puzzle shapes, with one missing piece. "So this piece here is you." She draws an individual puzzle piece. "In recovery, your shape changes. In order for you to fit back into the rest of the puzzle, your life, the other pieces of the puzzle must also change *their* shapes to accommodate you."

I have the distinct feeling that this will not happen. That I will end up the misplaced puzzle piece, lost under the sofa. "And if the other pieces of the puzzle don't change? What then?"

"Then," she says, "you find another puzzle to belong to." She leans back in her chair and it squeaks.

And it hits me. The reason for all the metaphors in recovery. Because the bald truth would be too terrifying. What she's saying is that I may need an all-new career and all-new friends.

"Are you looking forward to tonight?" she asks.

I'm not sure what she means.

She must read my face. "The AA meeting tonight, are you excited?"

"Oh, that. Yeah, I guess. It'll be interesting."

"You know," she says, "some people consider rehab to be the ambulance that delivers you to AA. Rehab is a start. It teaches you certain things, you get your first thirty days of sobriety here. But rehab is not a cure, by any means. The real work is done on a day-to-day basis in AA."

"You mean, I'll be going to AA meetings every day?"

"Well, that's up to you, but statistically, those with the longest sobriety tend to go to meetings once a day."

All of a sudden, I feel overwhelmed with the work involved with mental health. Therapy four times a week, AA meetings every day for the rest of my life. "It seems like, I don't know, so much work."

"You found the time to drink every day," she points out.

True. But that was fun. That's why they call it *Happy Hour.* I feel like I'm in prison and have just learned than upon my release, I will be on house parole for the rest of my life, wearing one of those electronic ankle things. Free, but not. I guess I thought that rehab would stop me from drinking like an alcoholic. I thought it would teach me how to drink like a normal person.

●   ●   ●

Today is day twenty. The days have stopped having names and are now numbers. Numbers that indicate how far away I am from my last drink. I've heard rumor that there are people in AA who still "count days" well into the years. So this means that in addition to all the other life changes I may need to make, including friends and career, I must now also live by a calendar with a different principle, like the Chinese. So today, day twenty, would have been just like nineteen except for one thing. A new guy arrived today.

I was in the conversation pit reading last week's local newspaper during one of my rare thirty minutes of free time and I watched the new guy come in and sit in the nurses' station, behind the chicken-wire glass window. He was sitting in the same chair I sat in when I checked in. He looked miserable, his face contorted into a mask of worry, panic, horror. He appeared to be handsome, but neglected.

Since he arrived at around eight, his first exposure to rehab will be the evening Affirmations. The stuffed-animal song and handout. I can't wait.

I finish reading the paper and go to the bathroom to take a leak. When I come back into the room, he's standing next to the coffee table where a coffee machine and a selection of herbal teas are available to all alcoholics, nervously fingering a white styrofoam cup, waiting for the fresh pot of coffee to finish brewing.

"Welcome to hell," I say, taking a styrofoam cup for myself and plopping a Cranberry Zinger tea bag into it.

He looks at me as if I have a stun gun behind my back.

"Er, hello. I'm Hayden." He's a Brit.

"Augusten."

"You'll have to excuse me, I'm just really out of sorts. I'm exhausted and in a bit of a panic over being here. I really can't believe I'm here at all. Frankly, I can't believe I'm alive."

"I know the feeling."

"Where are you from?" he asks.

"Manhattan," I say. I don't say New York City because I don't

want somebody from London thinking I live in one of the outer
boroughs.

"Oh really?" He brightens up a bit. "I'm from there as well."
Then he crashes. "Well, I *was* from there. But I lost my apartment
before coming here. So when I leave rehab, I'll probably have to
go back to London for a while, back to live with my parents."

The coffee's done; he pours a cup. A Brit who drinks bad coffee instead of tea. I like him already. We have twenty minutes
before the evening Affirmations group, so I ask, "You wanna step
outside, get some air?"

"That's a wonderful idea."

We walk outside to the backyard. We are allowed to go no further than down to the edge of the creek, about one hundred feet.
But we don't go that far. We sit at the ratty old picnic table. I get
a little homesick looking at the stars because they remind me of
office lights in skyscrapers.

"How'd you lose your apartment? What happened?"

He takes a sip of coffee, sighs. "To be honest, I lost it because
of crack cocaine. I was seven months behind in my rent, spending
every penny I had on the crack, and I was evicted. Just before
coming here, I was staying at a friend's house, under the condition
that I stop smoking immediately. And, well . . . I didn't—couldn't
stop. So my friend I was staying with, he and a couple of other
friends basically forced me into rehab."

"They forced you?" I ask.

"Yes, they threatened to report me to immigration. See, I've
been here in the states for seven years, illegally. They said that if I
didn't check into a rehab hospital at once, they would have me
deported."

Me too, sort of, I think. Rehab or expulsion from my cushy job.
"So it's crack, not alcohol?"

"Well, no, that too." He looks like a guilty child. A guilty child
in his early thirties.

"So in a nutshell, you're a British illegal alien crack addict

alcoholic, recently evicted from his New York City apartment,"
I say.

He smiles mischievously. "Yes, that just about sums me up at
the moment."

From my vantage point at the picnic table, I can see people
inside filing up the stairs. I catch a glimpse of a floppy blue ear.
"Oh, it's time for Affirmations. Prepare yourself for the unimag-
inable."

He looks at me warily.

We head upstairs to join the others. Hayden sits across the
room from me. Affirmations are as lame as always:

"I'd like to thank Sarah for giving me a hug at group today."

"I'd like to thank the group for accepting me."

"I'd like to thank Paul for brewing a fresh pot of coffee."

Pregnant Paul just gazes at the reflection in the window, like
always. I get the feeling he's here, but not really here. Like he's
pregnant with himself and hasn't given birth yet.

When it's time to sing the song about the codependent plush
toys, I repress an evil smile and just watch.

The instant after the stuffed animals are dropped onto his lap,
Hayden stands up and storms out of the room and down the
stairs. We all gawk at his empty chair.

The counselor says, "Okay everybody, let's continue, let's just
finish our affirmations."

After Group, I walk extra slowly past the nurses' station on the
way to my room. The door is closed and Hayden is standing there
talking to two of the counselors, making exaggerated hand ges-
tures. He looks furious. Both of the stuffed animals are sitting on
top of one of the desks, like confiscated evidence.

Dr. Valium walks into our room, flops on his bed. "It looks
like our new friend isn't pleased with his first hour in rehab." He
smiles wickedly.

"I can't imagine why not," I say.

"It really is an embarrassment," he adds and picks up his copy of *Psychology Today*.

I want to say something to him, but am not sure quite how. "Do you really think you'll lose your license?"

He looks up from the magazine. He takes a breath, then lets it out slowly. "I think it's really possible."

And then I get an anxious feeling. What if I make it through rehab, and they still fire me? They could easily say they got along just fine without me. Word would spread quickly. No other ad agency would touch me.

I sit down on the edge of my bed and consider this. Until now, it hadn't really seemed like something that could actually happen. But if it can happen to a doctor? And to a WASP? And to a flight attendant . . . ?

After a while, Big Bobby comes in, sits on his bed. "Gosh, you guys, what do you think is happening in the nurses' station with the new guy?"

I answer without looking up from my notebook (in which I am writing feverishly), "The fucking stuffed animal thing. He's probably freaked out by it." I have always kept a journal. Before I could write, I had a blue tape recorder that I came to see as a friend whom I could tell anything.

"Gee, that sure is too bad. I hope he gives us a chance." His stomach makes a loud rumble. "Anybody want anything from the kitchen?" he asks.

At breakfast the next morning, Hayden is telling me about his tirade in the nurses' station last night. "I was furious, told them, 'I cannot afford for this program not to work.' I explained that I am very serious about getting off the crack and alcohol and that what I had expected was a professional rehabilitation hospital and not some ridiculous, childish parody."

When I go to butter my toast, it snaps in half. "I don't blame you a bit, I felt exactly the same way." I consider the strange awareness of feelings that seems to happen here. The awareness that all is not Happy Hour. "But it really does get . . . interesting." I think of Rae in her floral prints. "Just give it a couple of days."

"Well, it had better," he huffs. Which is hilarious and I must bite the inside of my cheek to prevent laughing out loud. Hayden is maybe five-foot-two, max. But he does not seem to know this. In fact, he seems to be under the impression that he is six-two and weighs just over two hundred pounds.

"These are delicious," he says of the reconstituted scrambled eggs, the same eggs that sit on my own plate, untouched.

So far, I have lost almost ten pounds. *Why do stars suddenly appear* . . . "You're from London, what would you know."

He laughs, "That's very true, actually. This is far better than anything my mother ever made."

I make a face. "Did you have that nasty, yeasty stuff they spread on toast, what's it called?"

His eyes brighten. "Marmite! Oh yes, I love Marmite."

"You'll enjoy dinner then," I promise him.

For the next week, Hayden and I are inseparable. We sit together on the fireproof loveseats, cocooned in our own world of superiority. We exchange mortifying stories from our sordid pasts. We gossip endlessly about the other patients. No detail is too small to be ignored. When one of the lesbians trimmed her own bangs with nail clippers, we were utterly hysterical. We took it as a sure sign that she was struggling with control issues, destined for relapse.

I don't think I have ever had such a close friend in my life, made instantly like Tang.

Time accelerates with Hayden around. I've stopped watching the second hand on the clock. It's the kind of friendship that's easy to make in elementary school when you're six or seven. You let a kid have your swing and suddenly, he's your best friend. Suddenly, you don't care that you hate math, because you can hate it together. And after school, you want to play together. You never question it. You never say to yourself, *Am I spending too much time with him? Am I sending the wrong signal?*

Then you get pubic hair and everything changes. Pubic hair signals the beginning of your demise. After pubic hair comes high school, college, work. By the time you've started working, you're ruined. And you will never make a friend as completely and easily as you did when you still wiped your nose on your sleeve.

Unless, it seems, you are forced into rehab.

Hayden and I have talked about this very thing. We have marveled at the friendship that has blossomed between us, despite a combined age that would entitle us to a discount at the movies. "And the amazing part is," Hayden has said, "we're not drunk in a bar."

This is true. It is possible to make close, instant friendships while sitting at a bar drinking. But these friendships tend to evaporate at four in the morning when the bar closes, or the next morning when you find yourself sleeping in the same bed.

But with Hayden, it just keeps going. And I can't help but worry that it's some sort of rehab spell. Like, will we still be friends when we're both out of this place? I want us to be friends. I want us to live in the same apartment building, one floor between us like Mary and Rhoda. I feel gypped that I didn't meet him earlier in life, so finding apartments with matching sunken living rooms in the same building seems like something we are owed.

During my last week in rehab, Hayden and I discover a Ping-Pong table folded up in the gym. It was behind a mound of boxes, so we never noticed it before.

"You want to give it a go?" he asks.

"Sure." I haven't played since I was a kid and my grandfather sent us a huge, folding green Ping-Pong table one Christmas. My parents couldn't stand the thing and they kept it folded in the basement, against the wall near the hot water heater. But if you unfolded just one side and left the other side up at a right angle, you could play against yourself, hitting the ball off the opposite wall of the table. I got pretty good, but then it wasn't like my opponent ever did anything unexpected.

After missing the ball three times in a row, I'm finally able to whack it back at him. The Ping-Pong section of my brain wakes up and we fall into a rhythm. "How'd you get so good?" I ask as I bend under the table to pick up the ball I just missed.

"Oh, my father. It's all we've ever done together."

"You're not bad," Hayden says after we've been going steady for a good sixty seconds or so.

"That's because I'm excellent at pushing things away from me."

We play for a few more minutes in silence, actually *concentrating* on Ping-Pong. This is either an achievement for me, or a new low.

He holds the ball up. "You wanna serve?"

"No, you."

He *fwaps* the ball over to me and I *fwap* it back. I'm pretty good at this. If nothing else, I will leave here being able to play Ping-Pong. Possibly even against someone Chinese.

"I'm really going to miss you," he says to me.

I'm leaving here in three days. Which doesn't seem possible, because it feels like I've been here for years. Supposedly, I now have the "tools" that will help me cope on the outside. Tools such as the piece of paper Rae handed out last week in group. It was illustrated with about twenty different faces, drawn with simple black lines and displaying an emotion. Under each face was a caption. *Happy. Sad. Jealous. Angry. Confused. Afraid.* "When you're wondering what it is you're feeling at any given moment, simply pull out this chart and find the face that fits your mood." So it's basically an alcoholic-to-normal dictionary. I found myself carrying the thing folded up in the front pocket of my jeans and referring to it constantly, trying to decide what I was feeling. At the back of the lunch line, I would unfold the chart and find the face that matched my mood: *nauseous.*

"You know what scares me?" I say. "What scares me is how institutionalized I've become. How my whole life is this sick group of alcoholics. It's like some extended, fucked-up family that I have everything in common with. I'm afraid I might not fit on the outside anymore."

Hayden misses the ball. "Fuck," he shouts. "I know exactly what you mean, I never want to leave."

"I'm not ready," I tell him. It's safe here. I can live with fish-cake sandwiches and linoleum flooring. On the outside, people won't call me on my bullshit. I'll be back to getting away with it.

"You're ready," he says.

"How do you know? What makes you think so?"

"Because when I first met you, I wasn't even sure that you were really an alcoholic. I thought maybe you just drank a little too much sometimes." His eyes twinkle. "Now I'm positive that you are, in fact, a raging alcoholic."

"That means I should stay." Is it possible? Have I gotten worse?

"On the contrary," Hayden says, raising the ball into the air as if in a toast. "It means, my dear boy, that you are more real."

PART II

PREPARE FOR LANDING

I am not prepared for what I see when I unlock the door to my apartment. Although I have obviously seen it before, lived with it even, I have never encountered it through the lens of thirty days of sobriety. My apartment is filled with empty Dewar's bottles, hundreds of empty Dewar's bottles. They cover all surfaces; the counters in the kitchen, the top of the refrigerator. They are under the table I use as a desk, dozens of them there, with a small clearing for my feet. And they line one wall, eleven feet long, seven bottles deep. This appears to be far more bottles than I remembered, as though they multiplied while I was gone.

The air feels moist and putrid. And then I see them: fruit flies, hovering at the mouths of the bottles. They form dark clouds at the ceiling above the kitchen sink. And dead fruit flies cover everything, like dust.

Clothing is strewn around the room, carpeting the floor, cov-

ering the chairs, sofa and bed. It looks like the home of Raving
Insanity. It does not look like the home of somebody who makes
TV commercials. There's a full bottle of Dewar's on top of the
stove.

The only word is *squalor.*

An interior design not unlike what I grew up with at the crazy
psychiatrist's house.

Freshly brainwashed from rehab, I carry the bottle into the
bathroom. I hold it up to the light. See the pretty bottle? Isn't it
beautiful? Yes, it's beautiful. I unscrew the cap and pour it into the
toilet. I flush twice. And then I think, why did I flush twice? The
answer, is of course, because I truly do not know myself. I cannot
be sure I won't attempt to drink from the toilet, like a dog.

I have two options. I can just sit here and cry. Which is my
first instinct. Or I can clean this fucking mess. Which seems as
possible as winning Lotto. But this is what I do. I begin cleaning.

I pause only to listen to messages on my answering machine.
The first message is from Jim. "Hey Buddy, you were just kidding
about that rehab stuff, weren't you?" There's loud music in the
background and human commotion so I can tell he's calling from a
bar. I press SKIP and go to the next message. "Augusten, it's Greer, I
just wanted to leave a message for you when you got home."

Greer sounds like she's reading from a script she had written
before calling. I'm fairly certain this is, in fact, the case. Greer is
that way. I once watched her scan her driver's license photo and
twenty pictures of hairstyles, torn from magazines. Then, in Pho-
toshop, she cut and pasted her face into every hairstyle. This was
back when she was trying to decide whether or not she should
have bangs and get highlights.

"Well, welcome home. Not very original, I guess"—forced
laughter—"but I just wanted to say I hope everything went well
and that you're feeling better. I can't remember when you said
you'd be returning to work, so give me a ring and let me know,
okay? Okay then, well, okay, bye."

A message from Blockbuster Video saying I owe eighty dollars for my overdue *Towering Inferno*, and another from Jim, this time sounding hungover and depressed. "Wow, man, maybe you really *did* go to rehab after all. I got a hairy-ass hangover. All I remember are Snake Bites with Coors chasers. Maybe you can teach me some shit you learned. I gotta lay off the sauce for a while."

The rest of the messages play out, and the last one is from Pighead. "Hey Fuckhead, it's Friday and I know you're due back today. I was thinking you could come over and I could make dinner. Maybe liver and onions in honor of your new sobriety." At the end of the message, he hiccups.

The bottles fill twenty-seven gigantic, industrial-sized bags. It takes more than seven hours and by the time I'm finished, I'm manic and drenched in sweat. I go to Kmart and buy Glade scented candles, eleven of them, and light them all at once to fumigate the apartment. After about forty minutes, the apartment reeks of artificial pine scent. I decide now would be a good time to go to an AA meeting.

I dial 411. "What city please?"

"Manhattan," I say, already dreading what I have to say next.

"What listing?"

I clear my throat, remind myself I am talking to a faceless stranger through fiber-optic cables. "Um, the main number for Alcoholics Anonymous." I expect her to either hang up or worse, make me repeat it. *I'm sorry, what was that again?* What *anonymous?*

Instead, she gives me the number and I call. "Yeah, hi, I just got back from rehab and I don't really know where the AA meetings are here in the city."

The guy on the other end of the phone sounds like he could be an employee of the Gap; helpful and good-natured. I feel certain that he's wearing khakis and smells like summer. "What part of the city do you live in?"

"I'm at Tenth and Fifth."

"That's such a cool area," he says before giving me a list of seven different meetings. It turns out New York City is a great place to be a drunk, not only if you want to drink, but also if you want to stop. There are dozens of meetings to choose from. Are you a midget? There's an AA meeting specifically for you, right here in Manhattan. How about an albino midget? A transgendered albino midget NAMBLA member? Yes, there's a meeting, so I have no excuse.

One of the names he mentions is the Perry Street meeting, which I remember Dr. Valium telling me about. The next meeting is at eight, so I decide I'll do this.

It's only a ten-minute walk from my apartment, but I leave immediately. Better to walk around than sit alone in my apartment. I arrive in front of the meeting place in less than seven minutes. I'm walking too fast. But since I have over an hour to kill and Pighead's apartment is five minutes away, I decide to stop by.

The doorman looks too happy to see me and I am immediately suspicious. "How you doin' there, Mr. Augusten?" he says. "Long time no see."

I want to grab him by the lapel of his doorman jacket and say, "What did that Pighead tell you? Whatever he said, don't believe a word: *I've been in Madrid . . . shooting a commercial.*"

But before I can do this, he says, "Oh, your friend, he just now got back from walking Virgil." Virgil is Pighead's scrappy white terrier. Virgil loves me more.

I take the elevator to the fourth floor and make a left. Pighead's apartment is the last one on the right, at the very end of the long hallway. But already I can see he has the door open, because I see Virgil's head sticking out and Pighead's hand attached to the collar. "Go get him," Pighead says and Virgil tears down the hallway, barking and snapping, immediately grabbing hold of my pant leg with his mouth.

I bend down and rub both of my hands across his back really fast. "Virgil, Wirgil, Squirgil, what a good boy, what a very good boy." I run down the hallway to Pighead's door, Virgil yapping at my ankles as he runs alongside.

I walk past Pighead, who's standing in the entryway, and go right into the living room, where I pick Virgil up and throw him onto the sofa. He bounces off and back onto the floor, charging at me immediately. I do it again. Then he runs to the corner of the room and retrieves a rubber carrot, brings it to me and drops it at my feet. He barks. I turn around and throw the carrot down the hallway into the bedroom, and Virgil takes off after it.

"Holy shit," Pighead says when he finally sees my face. "I wouldn't have recognized you."

I take my jacket off, sling it over one of his dining room chairs.

"Don't do that," he says, "use a hanger."

As he walks toward the hall closet for a hanger, I ask, "What do you mean?"

He turns. "A coat hanger? You know, that thing Joan Crawford hit her kid with?"

"No, fool. The other thing. How different I look. Tell me more. Me, me, me."

He rolls his eyes, goes to the closet and hangs up my coat. "You look so . . . different . . . younger . . . and you lost so much weight. You look great." He smiles and looks away from me as if he's shy. He walks into the kitchen. I follow. "Want something to drink?" Before I answer, he corrects himself. "I mean, you know, like juice."

"Oh, Christ. Is this how it's gonna be from now on?" I whine.

He takes two glasses from the cupboard and opens the refrigerator. I notice a bottle of Chardonnay next to the cranberry juice. "Actually," I say, "I'll take some Chardonnay, but only this much." I hold my thumb and forefinger about two inches apart.

Pighead looks troubled. "What, Chardonnay?"

I casually lean my hip against the counter. "Well, we're allowed to have Chardonnay because it's not really alcohol. It's just, you know, wine. And that's okay."

He stands there with his hand in the refrigerator looking back and forth between the cranberry juice, the wine and me.

I grin at him. "I'm kidding, Pighead."

He pours us each a cranberry juice and then carries them into the living room. He sits on the sofa, next to the end table where he sets both glasses and I sit right next to him and rest my head on his shoulder. I mumble something about being confused and happy and sad and overwhelmed and tired. He reaches his arm around my shoulders and moves his head against mine. "It's okay, Fuckhead," he says. "You're still a mess but at least you're not drunk."

Virgil leaps onto the sofa, bouncing onto my stomach, almost knocking the wind out of me. *Bark, bark, bark.* I take his head in my hands and smush his face up.

"Virgil missed you," Pighead says. I look at him, but he's looking at his hands.

"I missed him too," I say gently.

I pick the slobbery plastic squeaky carrot up off the floor and throw it hard, not caring if it hits a wall or a lamp or a painting. Pighead, who has a beautiful, fastidiously decorated apartment, doesn't care either. If a lamp broke, I know it would be okay with him because *I* broke it. But if anybody else broke it, he'd have a shit fit. I know I'm lucky this way.

"What do you want to do for dinner?" he asks.

Pause. "Can't, I have to leave in a few minutes. I have a lush meeting."

"AA?" he asks. "But you just got back from rehab."

Virgil charges back with the carrot, drops it at my feet. I ignore him, and he carries it over near the fireplace and chews, trying to kill the squeaker.

"That's the whole point," I tell him. "Alcoholics go to AA."

"How long do you have to go?" he asks, like I'm on parole, which is sort of the case.

"Every day for the rest of my life."

"You're kidding, right?" he says, eyebrows raised.

I tell him that unfortunately I'm not. I tell him what Rae said about how if you found time to drink every day, you can find time for AA every day.

His eyes become large in actual disbelief.

"Oh, I know," I say. "I was just as shocked as you."

"What's that they say, 'One day at a time' or something?" He takes a sip of juice.

"Yeah, one day at a time. For the rest of my life."

"Jesus."

"Oh, we don't call it 'Jesus' anymore." My head itches so I rub it against his shoulder. "We call it a 'higher power.'"

"Oh no," he says, rolling his eyes. "You've turned 'recovery' on me."

For a moment we just sit there and say nothing. It's so good and comforting to be with him. And yet . . . *and yet*. A sense of loneliness, and something else that is more frightening but that I cannot name. "Pighead?" I say.

"Hmm?" He turns to me.

This time I'm the one who turns away. I examine the cuticle of my thumbnail. "Nothing."

"What?"

There's so much I want to talk to him about. Need to talk to him about. But I'm not even sure I know what it is I need to say. It's an odd feeling. Well, *all* feelings are odd to me because I'm not accustomed to being aware of them. But this feeling is especially odd. It's like when I was a little kid, I never wanted my parents to leave the living room and go to bed until I was asleep first. I needed to know they were there, otherwise I couldn't fall asleep.

"I have to go," I tell him, getting up from the couch.

"But you just got here," he says.

"I know. But I have to go. I just stopped by." I am happy to see him, therefore I must leave. It's weird, like there are magnets at play.

He straightens a book on the coffee table. "Well, it's nice to see you haven't changed all that much. 'So long. I have to go. Everything's more important than you, Pighead.' As usual."

It's not difficult to hear the hurt in his voice. "I have to go," are probably the four words I use most with him. The thought that normally accompanied these words was, *Because I need a drink.* Now it's because I need to go *talk* about needing a drink. It's like alcohol gets in the way even when it's out of the way.

The room is small, no larger than the average suburban kitchen, though it's not bright yellow with spider plants hanging from colorful baskets in the window. It's dark and grim because the front window of what could have rented out as a tiny but chic Perry Street boutique instead features a donated curtain that blocks all the light out. In the center of the room against the wall are a small podium and a tall chair behind it. In a horseshoe configuration around the podium are about fifty folding metal chairs—the chair of choice for recovering alcoholics. Above, an old ceiling fan turns, just barely. The bumpy walls are covered with thick beige paint that can be no fresher than twenty years. When beige was new. When it was "the new white."

"What you see here, what you hear here, stays here," says the chairman of the meeting. The single overhead light has been dimmed, and the meeting has officially begun. He goes through the AA preamble. The AA preamble is the same at all AA meetings, everywhere. Just like Big Macs. It outlines the purpose of AA, which is to help people get sober, and it explains how there are no dues or fees or politics. It ends with a few questions.

"Is anyone here today new to the Perry Street meeting?" he asks.

I raise my hand.

In rehab, we had specific lectures about raising our hands. "In meetings, always raise your hand to share. Volunteer for service.

Get a sponsor. Do ninety meetings in ninety days. Don't just fade into the wallpaper." In AA, one must not be wallpaper but a colorful wall hanging.

"My name is Augusten, I'm an alcoholic and this is my first time at Perry Street." People clap encouragingly. I'm an albino seal and I've just caught a beach ball on the tip of my nose and then bounced it through a hoop of fire.

The chairman then reads off AA announcements from the notes he holds in front of him on pink index cards. A Sober Singles dance next Friday night at St. Lutheran's Church; more volunteers are needed to man the phones at the main AA office; would anyone like a free kitten?

I catch a glimpse of a cute guy sitting in the back, off to the side. He has cool sparkly silvery hair and these incredibly bright blue eyes. He looks exactly like Cal Ripken Jr. And at once I am very comfortable. I decide that this may become my "home group," the AA meeting I attend regularly.

On the wall directly across from the podium is a large, framed poster, listing the Twelve Steps of Alcoholics Anonymous. But the Twelve Steps are misleading. It's not like assembling a bookcase from Ikea, where once you've finished with the last step, you get to put all your books on it and then all you have to do is dust it once a week. Here, when you've finished with the last step, you go back and do the first step again.

"Is anyone here counting days?" the chairman asks. Until I have ninety days of sobriety under my belt, I'm supposed to "count days."

I raise my hand. "Augusten again," I say. "And today is day thirty."

Not only applause, but a couple of whistles plus "Congratulations" from a few people around the room. I scan the faces. Just normal people. Normal *New York* people, which of course means freaks. Nobody is wearing a primary color, most of the men have pierced eyebrows and long sideburns called "chops," and the majority of the women wear suburban 1970s hairstyles with irony. Everybody looks like they're about to appear on MTV's *Total Request Live*. But then I am in New York City at an AA meeting downtown on Perry Street, which is one of the "it" addresses. If I were in a Tulsa AA meeting, I might see a Sears sweatshirt or two.

"Our speaker here today is Nan. Let's give her a warm welcome," the chairman says.

People clap absently. I crave a cigarette.

Nan rises from her folding metal chair in the first row of the horseshoe, walks to the podium. She's a striking woman, all bone structure and pewter hair. She impresses me as someone who tosses Caesar salads in a hand-carved teak salad bowl. I bet she reads Joan Didion in hardcover.

"I'm a little nervous here today, but I'm just going to do it. I'm just going to speak and not think about it."

In rehab, it was called "thought dropping." When your addict is saying, "It's eleven A.M., let's go celebrate with gin and tonics!" you drop the thought—push it out of your head.

"Well, today is my ninety days."

A thunder of applause. You can't help but feel a sense of excitement from the vibrations alone. Ninety days is significant for an alcoholic. It implies you are seriously on the road back to sanity.

Nan blushes and smiles, while averting her eyes.

Nan "shares." She's forty-seven, started drinking when she was sixteen. "I was expelled from the cheerleader squad for being intoxicated during practice. Can you imagine?"

A few people laugh softly and nod their heads. One man nods his head vigorously as if *he* knows the pain of being forced off the cheerleading squad all too well. But then, this is the West Village.

Nan grew up in Greenwich, Connecticut, moved to New York when she was eighteen. She got a job as the personal assistant to this very eccentric and notorious senior editor at a fashion magazine. Two years later, Nan was a fashion editor herself. "I was twenty, I was hot, I was like, get the hell out of my way."

I'm thinking, *Me too.*

"And fashion, you know, is a crazy business . . . parties, drinking, parties, coke, parties, more drinking. And this was my life, for twenty years. But you know, it was everyone's life. Or so I thought. I didn't have blackouts or do crazy things. No drama, no missing work, nothing."

I notice that her long red nails are chipped. I like that. It says something about her priorities. In rehab, I learned that being sober has to be your number one priority. Then a tiny seed of doubt enters my mind. Does it really say she's just barely holding it together?

"After a while I realized I was always the first one with a drink and the last one to leave the party. I mean, I knew I was drinking too much. I felt like it was no big deal because, you know, nothing had ever happened to me. And oh, you know. Let me just tell you that time passes. I went on like that all through my twenties and thirties." She stops talking, takes a sip from the tall Starbucks cup in front of her. "People bitch about Starbucks but I think it's the best," she says.

People laugh. Starbucks owes every alcoholic in America a few free rounds.

"Starbucks is my higher power."

People laugh harder.

She clears her throat, places both arms on the podium. "Okay, right, so last year, I'm in the shower one morning and I'm thinking about what I have to deal with that day. You know, like I have a meeting with Michael Kors, a lunch with the buyer from Bloomingdale's, etcetera, etcetera; just work stuff." She takes her pinkie finger and swipes it beneath her right eye. "And all of a sudden, I feel this lump in my breast." Her voice becomes small, as though she's just stepped over the threshold into a church or temple. "It was a big lump. It was a *mass.*"

The blades of the ceiling fan continue to turn, oblivious.

"I think, Well, this is nothing. That's what I tell myself. Nothing at all. A callous. That's actually what I told myself. Can you imagine, a callous on my breast? I mean my sex life is just not *that* good." When she says this people laugh openly, grateful for the valve.

"But even my powers of denial aren't that powerful and I gently reminded myself that my mother died of breast cancer, my grandmother died of breast cancer. . . ." Nan starts to cry, she just loses it. She covers her face with her hands and I watch her head bob against them as she heaves her tears out. But then just as fast, she regains her composure, swipes a tissue that has magically appeared in her fist across her eyes. "Sorry about that. So anyway, you know, now I totally *know*. I go to my doctor, he sends me to an oncologist. They do a biopsy and surprise surprise, it's breast cancer. More tests, more doctors, more bad news. It's not just in my breast, but in both breasts—as well as my liver, my stomach, my lungs and my lymphatic system." She lets out this great sigh.

Somebody's pager goes off.

"See, it was just like that," Nan quips. "Your beeper goes off one day and there's nothing you can do. Your time's up."

People laugh as though this were a much funnier joke than it is. The terminal cancer-ridden alcoholic is able to joke about her own mortality thanks to AA, and this lets us off the hook. She knows how we fellow alcoholics hate feelings. I love Nan.

"When he told me I had maybe four months to live, my very first thought was, *I'm going to go get sloshed at Old Town Pub.* But then I thought, *I am not going to die a drunk. I am going to try to live the best I can.* And that means as somebody who is sober. You see, even though back when I was drinking I thought nothing bad ever happened to me, something did. Time passed. A lot of time passed. In bars, at parties with people I didn't care for. It was always the drink. It wasn't about love or reading the Sunday paper in bed. Or housebreaking a puppy. Or anything that people call 'life.' It was about drinking. So actually, something bad, very bad, did happen to me. I wasted my life. And now, what little I have left, I want."

I think she's spectacular. I think I'm pathetic and shallow. If I were her, I would be at Old Town right now, I am absolutely certain. I would be so drunk, I wouldn't even know I was there.

"But today, I have ninety days. Maybe tomorrow I will have ninety-one, maybe the day after—ninety-two, I don't know. I'm already living off borrowed time. But you know what? I'm sober today and I would rather have today, this one day sober than a whole lot of days drunk."

The room applauds. Applause is a constant thing in AA. It's how we buy drinks for each other.

She smiles, her eyes moist. After she's finished, people raise their hands and she calls on them.

Somebody says, "Nan, your story really made me grateful for my own sobriety. I have fifteen years, one day at a time, and, well, I think you are so brave."

Nan smiles. Calls on someone else: me.

"Hi, Nan," I begin. "I just got back from rehab and it's weird. It's like, I'm, uh." I can't think of what to say. As soon as I opened my mouth to express my thoughts, my thoughts dissolved. "I mean, you know. I guess I just feel raw and like all opened up. I was thinking as you were speaking, you know. That if I were you, I'd already be drunk. I don't have your courage. Or your appreciation for life, I guess is what I mean. I mean, I'm really feeling good about being sober and everything. But I don't know if I could deal if, you know, something bad happened."

Nan asks, "How many days did you say you have?"

"Thirty."

"Congratulations, that is so fucking great. But I can tell you that at thirty days, I was a mess. At sixty days, I was getting better. And today, I really have this sense of sobriety. I really would rather be here, at Perry Street, than out there." She motions with her head to the outside. "Thirty days ago, if I heard my story, I'd feel the same way you do. Keep coming back."

I want whatever it is that she has. Looking around at the faces in the room, I notice a certain amount of peace. These people don't look strung out. They don't look desperate. Nobody has tremors that I can see.

We join hands and repeat the Sinead O'Connor serenity prayer. Followed by a chant: "Keep coming back it works if you work it so work it you're worth it."

My feeling at the end is that AA is utterly amazing. Complete strangers getting together in rooms at all hours and saying things that are so personal, so incredibly intimate. This is the kind of stuff that happens in a relationship after a few months. But people here open up right away, with everyone. It's like some sort of love affair, stripped of the courtship phase. I feel bathed in safety. I feel like I have this secret place I can go and say anything in the world, about anything I feel, and it's okay. And this makes me feel grateful to be an alcoholic. And this is a very odd feeling. This is like what my friend, Suzanne, says about childbirth—that it husks the soul.

Back home, I sit on the sofa of my newly clean apartment. I'm still blown away by the mess I encountered. Like stepping right back into my old life. How could I have lived like that? How could I have not seen it? The problem is, I'm a slob to begin with. So when you combine alcohol with a slob, you just end up with something that would appall any self-respecting heroin-addicted vagrant.

The next day, I go to the gym. It's been over a month since I've worked out and I'm depressed to see that instead of being able to do curls with the forty-five pound weights, I struggle with the twenties. This shouldn't matter to me. *I'm not drinking* is what should matter. But the fact that I've deflated depresses me and makes me want to drink. I gained one thing and lost another. *Just shut the hell up, asshole,* I tell myself. *Get your priorities straight.*

While I'm doing tricep kickbacks, my face ready to burst capillaries, a handsome guy doing squats smiles at me. Nods his head. I immediately look away, feeling very much like damaged goods. Because even though I'm in public like a normal person now, I am still removed from society. I imagine how our coffee conversation might go.

Squat Man: So, tell me about yourself.

Me: Well, I just got out of rehab. And went to the first of the AA meetings I will have to attend for the rest of my life.

Squat Man: Hey that's great, man. Good for you. Listen dude, I gotta run. Nice talkin' with ya. Good luck. Ciao.

Like cubic zirconia, I only look real. I'm an imposter. The fact is, I'm not like other people. I'm like other alcoholics. Mr. Squat can probably go out, have a couple drinks and then go home. He might even have to be talked into a third drink on a Friday night. Then on Saturday morning, he might have a slight hangover. I, on the other hand, would have to be talked out of a thirteenth drink on a Monday. And I wouldn't wake up with a hangover. Just a certain thickness that only after rehab, only after waking up without this thickness, did I realize was a hangover. A comfortable hangover, like a pair of faded jeans or a favorite sweater with too many fur balls on it.

I go down to the locker room. In the shower I think about how I'm a drunk that doesn't get to drink. It seems unfair. Like keeping a Chihuahua in a hamster cage.

Today is my first day back at work. It's my moment of dread. I make sure I am there by nine. At a quarter past ten, Greer knocks on my door even though it's open. "Knock, knock," she says softly, smiling, leaning her head into the door. I feel like I'm in a sanitary napkin commercial and she's about to discreetly ask, "Kelly? Do you ever feel . . . you know, not so fresh?"

"Hey," I say, getting up from my chair.

Greer is wearing a smile, as opposed to having one. "Give me a hug," she says, outstretching her arms in a huge, grandiose arch.

We never hug. Even though we've worked together for years, we just never hug. I was raised by an angry, unaffectionate alcoholic father and a manic-depressive, narcissistic mother, which explains why I don't hug. Greer is from a "good" WASP family in Connecticut. They owned bluetick coonhounds and she vacationed in Switzerland. Which explains why she doesn't hug, either.

We hug, stiffly. She tells me, "You look *great*, so trim and healthy. I wouldn't have recognized you." Greer is beaming. When she beams, the skin on the bridge of her nose wrinkles in a funny way because of the two very subtle scars leftover from her nose job. ("It wasn't a *nose job*, it was rhinoplasty. I had a bulbous nasal tip. That's a medical *condition*.")

We sit, I at my desk, she in the chair next to it. She crosses her legs, adjusts the gold bangle bracelet on her wrist. "So . . ." she exhales. "Tell me everything." Then with a gossip-columnist grin, "Meet anybody famous?"

"Um, just Robert Downey, Jr., he was there."

Greer's legs fly into an uncrossed position and she leaps at me, slapping both hands on her thighs. "Oh my God, you are kidding!" she cries. "Robert Downey, Jr.? Why I am just so *not* surprised. I was reading in *People* last week . . ." She continues her story. I wait for her to catch up. It takes a moment. Then she sinks back into her chair, recrosses her legs. "Oh, I should have known. I am so gullible. Stupid Greer." She knocks the palm of her hand against her left temple, careful not to disturb her hair. "Okay, so how was it . . . really?" she asks.

Do I tell her about the girl who needed her lover to cut her with razor blades? Or maybe the stuffed animal ritual? Perhaps I should talk about relapse triggers. Should I say, *I'm transformed, I see it now, I get it*? I feel overwhelmed by insight and knowledge, yet I also feel like I can't explain everything to her. Or anybody. Like people say after they tell a really bad joke, you just had to be there.

"Honestly, Greer, it was great, it really was."

I scratch my elbow, which probably means something to body language experts. "I don't have the energy to go into all the details now. It was too intense and complicated, but—"

"I understand, I understand completely. Don't feel you need to talk about it," she says, cutting me off. Then she smiles, raising just her right eyebrow. "Wanna know what's going on around the office?" she says, unable to contain her enthusiasm.

It's a bit of a letdown that she doesn't press me for details. I wouldn't mind grossing her out with Kavi stories. "Sure, there must be a ton of work."

Greer smiles. "You're going to be *so* excited. We're pitching the Wirksam account. Wirksam beer from Germany, can you imagine? I mean, I know it's not Beck's, but how cool!" Her face lights up, sixteen-hundred-dollar laser-whitened teeth gleaming.

"Wirksam beer?" I ask. "Hmm." According to my rehab feeling chart, I am feeling worried and concerned, but also hopeful and excited. Possibly slightly panicked, though I don't recall a face for this.

"What??!!" Greer wants to know. "You don't seem . . ." She searches for that elusive word. ". . . excited."

"Well, I am, you know. It's just Wirksam is beer and beer is alcohol and, well, I just got out of rehab."

Her Edith Bunker face appears. "Ohhhhhh," she says, getting it. Then something in her head clicks. "Yeah, but beer isn't alcohol. It's just . . . beer. I mean, right? That's right, isn't it?" She smiles the guilty smile of somebody who has just dropped off her purebred Basenji to the Humane Society because it chewed her bedskirt—innocent without the right to be.

"No, beer *is* alcohol. It counts," I say.

Now Greer is wearing this *I just shot my parents by mistake* face. "I'm sorry, yes, yes, of course. Oh my God, I really hadn't thought of it like that."

I wave my hands. "It's okay, it's fine. I'm not saying that it's *going* to be a problem, just that I have to be careful."

"Oh, we'll be very careful," Greer promises. "Very careful."

I've never seen her look so bizarre. The vein on the side of her forehead seems to actually be pulsating. It's awkward to be around her, because I feel like she's walking on eggshells. Like in one of those cheesy interracial movies from the seventies where nobody ever mentions that the white girl's boyfriend is black, but everyone is highly aware of it. Then somebody says *watermelon* in a sentence and everyone sort of gasps. That's how I feel.

"I'm going to make a latte run, you want one?" she asks nervously. "Never mind, I'll get you one. A decaf," she says before I have a chance to answer.

My first day back and already there's something boozy to deal with. Writing about beer isn't drinking beer, but it's certainly romanticizing it. I see the green glass bottle sitting on the white sweep, lit from behind, reflectors placed on either side to catch every glistening drop of moisture on the bottle. Unfortunately, it's not much of a leap to then see myself licking the bottle caps, drinking the flat beer, making a pass at the photographer's assistant and being fired for falling on top of the Hassleblad.

I will have to be careful. I will have to be more than careful. I will have to act as if I am in a hot zone, working with Ebola.

At a little past five, I decide that I have had enough for the first day and I take a cab home. Leaving at five in advertising is like leaving at eleven A.M. at normal jobs, so I feel a little guilty, like I'm slacking off. But all the way home in the cab, I notice how much brighter the colors of the signs out the window look, how much grander the buildings are. And when the cab bounces over a huge pothole, I seem to remain in midair just a little longer.

I am in possession of this cool new thing: my sobriety.

And it's an actual high.

The cab flies down Second Avenue, making all the green lights. And then I see a yellow coming up and I think we're not going to make it, but we do, just in time. We make it and this gives me a rush because making all the lights like this feels predestined, and to miss a light now would be like bad luck, a curse. I survived work, I'm going to an AA meeting tonight and I'm not drinking. I don't even *want* to drink. Everything feels right.

And I don't even feel like I'm talking myself into it, which for me is always an occupational hazard.

"You must be Augusten," the woman in the floral print dress and Reeboks says to me. "I'm Wendy." She extends her hand. What is it with alcohol counselors and floral prints?

I rise from my chair in the reception area of HealingHorizons. She has no grip. She lays her hand in mine like she's handing me a baby trout she just caught and doesn't know what to do with. I think, *Her father wanted a boy, so he didn't bother to teach her about grips.*

"Hi, Wendy, nice to meet you."

"Follow me, then." She smiles.

She smells like hair conditioner. She smells like her floral print dress. I suspect a cover-up of some sort. But then, alcoholics are suspicious.

Once inside her office, she takes the seat at her desk and points me to the chair beside it. There's a framed poster on the wall across from me that reads WILL YOU *PLEASE* LET GO OF YOUR WILL!? She also has a large bookcase filled with various manuals: *Managing Codependence, Twelve Steps One Step at a Time, When Children of Alcoholics Aren't Children Anymore, If You Want What We Have.*

For the next fifty minutes, we go over my "plan." Group therapy Tuesdays and Thursdays, one-on-one every Monday. I sign a consent form that states I will not become romantically involved with anyone from group therapy, that I will not come to Group intoxicated and that if I am unable to attend either Group or one-on-one, I will give at least twenty-four hours' notice.

"So how are you feeling, settling back into your life?"

I smile broadly. The new me is open and expressive. "Tentative, but hopeful, really hopeful." I've learned to always list more than one emotion when asked. It's more believable.

"That's good," she says reassuringly. "It's okay to have some mixed emotions. And I'm glad you admit that you feel tentative." She smiles at me and there's a long silence in the room. My hands start to sweat slightly. I'm not sure why. I think it's because I'm thinking I should say something. But I'm also thinking that therapists believe silence is okay. So I am actually not being silent, but manipulative and controlling. Once again, an alcoholic specialty.

"How was your experience at Proud Institute?" she asks.

She's the first person to say that name since I've returned. "It was very intense," I tell her. "At first, I wanted to leave. My first impression was not a good one."

"But you revised your opinion?"

I nod my head. "Yeah, that's an understatement. I never expected it to be so intense. It was like emotion, emotion, emotion half of the day. And facts, facts, facts the other half. It was like *Jerry Springer* meets medical school. I mean it's not like I had some great moment of truth or anything. More like a lot of little ones, gradually. Although I did really realize I'm an alcoholic, so I guess that's happened."

"I've heard that from many, many people."

This makes me want to ask her if she's an alcoholic. That she's "heard" it implies she hasn't experienced it herself. I don't want a therapist who has only textbook knowledge. I want a therapist who lost a leg in the war. Someone who has been there. And this doesn't seem unreasonable to me. Every woman I know goes to a female gynecologist, after all. They don't want some *guy* poking around in there.

"So, what made you go into chemical dependency counseling?" I ask, as if I'm interviewing her for a position at my Scarsdale facility.

"What makes you ask?" she asks back.

"I guess it's not my business, but I was just wondering if you have personal experience with addiction."

"Would it make a difference with your program whether I have or have not?"

I feel trapped. If I say, *Yes, my mental health is possibly connected to whether or not you are an alcoholic,* then I am not taking responsibility for my mental health. If I say, *No, it makes no difference to me,* she'll wonder why I asked in the first place. So I give her an advertising copywriter answer; I give her a weasel. "It was just a thought that passed through my head. I'm new to this 'emotions' stuff, so I'm making an effort to say just exactly what enters my mind. Right or wrong, good or bad, relevant or not." I shrug and smile.

"I think that's a great idea," she says. "For you not to self-edit is exactly right." Then she says, "So, have you been to AA yet?"

I think, *I have to be more careful with what I say.*

I come home and find myself feeling less than positive. Feeling that I just want to disappear. I feel disconnected, or like I am on PAUSE. I'm restless, but not energetic. Depressed? I think back to the feeling chart. I decide I am borderline panicked, but also I feel homesick or something else; lonely. Then I get it.

I miss alcohol.

Like it's a person. I feel abandoned. Or rather like I've walked out of a violent, abusive relationship and want to go back because in retrospect, it wasn't really all that violent or abusive. They told me in rehab that this happens. That out of the blue your moods can change. They also said it would be like dealing with a death in the family.

I turn on Channel 18, the Discovery Channel. Zebras. The announcer says, ". . . the female zebra is winking her vulva to attract a mate." Sure enough, it winks.

Then the boy zebra mounts the girl. And I think, *Why do they call it 'hung like a horse?' It should be 'hung like a zebra.'* Its penis was at least half the length of its body. The zebras fuck.

It occurs to me that my sober life now includes watching animal pornography.

Depressed, I shut the TV off and go to sleep. I dream about winking zebra vulvas and swinging zebra penises all night long.

I wake up feeling relief that I am not dreaming anymore. Also, this slight feeling of being high, realizing I'm not hungover. This is one of the more pleasant side effects of not drinking.

I spend the day trying to live in the present at the office. Things that would have annoyed me before, I now let pass over me. I practice acceptance. I return phone calls. When I am asked to write body copy for somebody else's ad, I say, "Sure." As opposed to saying, "Get the hell out of my office."

For lunch, Greer and I walk to a salad bar. I create a salad from dry spinach leaves, raw broccoli florets, zucchini slices as thin as matchsticks, and a small scoop of low-fat cottage cheese. I am eating like a girl, trying to accelerate the loss of my booze gut. I'm amazed by how quickly I was able to lose most of it. Now, it's mostly just loose skin. The actual gut is mostly gone. I do a hundred situps every day and go to the gym four times a week, as required for a Manhattan guy who is into guys. If you're gay and live in New York and don't go to the gym, eventually they come for you. The Gym Rats from Chelsea come in their Raymond Dragon tank tops and haul your ass into the back of a Yukon. You wake up hogtied in a bathroom stall at a Red Lobster in Paramus.

A sign around your neck reads, DO NOT DRIVE ME INTO MANHATTAN UNTIL I HAVE PECS.

Greer eyes me with contempt when she sees my lunch. She has also made a salad, but hers is topped with crumpled bacon and blue cheese dressing. "How can you deprive yourself like that?" Greer wishes she could deprive herself like this. She is very tall and thin as it is. She does not have to worry, but she worries. She obsesses.

"It's easy," I tell her. "If I can't have alcohol, not having anything else is a breeze."

I'm learning to appreciate the differences between brands of bottled water. Evian is too sweet. Volvic is crisp, clean. Poland Springs is also good. But Deer Park tastes like plastic.

We take our lunches back to work, go into Greer's office and eat them. "I've noticed a change with you already, and you haven't even been back all that long," she says.

"Like what," I say, forking dry spinach into my mouth, machinelike.

"Like you're less angry." She stabs a large chunk of bacon with her fork, then rolls it against a morsel of blue cheese.

"I feel . . . transformed in many ways," I say. "I realize it's about letting things go, and not adding more things." And the fact that I realize this surprises me. I hadn't really expected to realize anything or change in any positive, meaningful way. But somehow, something sunk in.

"What do you mean, letting things go?" Greer asks.

Because she is asking questions, I feel almost like a minister, like I need to preach and convert. "Well, by getting rid of the alcohol, it's like I have lost this thing that took up so much of my life and caused too many problems, directly and indirectly. You know, the butterfly thing."

"What butterfly thing?" she says.

"You know how when a butterfly beats its wings in the Amazon, this sends a mote of pollen through the air which causes the wild boar in wherever to sneeze which creates a breeze which, etcetera, etcetera, etcetera, all ends up affecting traffic in LA or something. I forgot how it works exactly."

"Oh, yeah," Greer says. "There was a Honda commercial a few years back like that."

I roll my eyes at her Greerness. "I just feel like I have less baggage and so, I don't know, I'm able to just accept things more, not have to fight them. Don't fight the river, go with it."

"God, you do sound transformed." She dabs the paper napkin against the corner of her mouth. Then she abruptly looks down at it. "Speaking of the rain forest," she says. "Poor napkin."

As we finish our lunches, I feel this little flame inside of me. This proud little flame, because even though it's new, I do feel transformed. The technical term is Being on a Pink Cloud. I hear the only trouble with Pink Clouds is that eventually you fall off.

After work, I head straight to HealingHorizons for my first Group. For the first fifteen minutes, it's exactly like rehab. Because I'm new, they go over the rules of the group, all of which I already know: no crosstalk, no handing tissues to someone if they cry, "I" statements. We go around the room introducing ourselves, saying a little bit about our lives, how long we've been sober. But after fifteen minutes, the door swings open, this guy walks in and everything changes.

The first thing I notice about him, the first thing *anybody* would notice about him is the plain fact that he is what a magazine might describe as painfully handsome. He's got jet-black hair, husky-blue eyes, a strong nose, a strong chin, dimples—all of it. Yet, he's a little rough around the edges; five, maybe six o'clock shadow, tousled hair, rumpled clothes. But he looks sloppy almost as if a fifteen-hundred-dollar-a-day prop-stylist made him look this way. He apologizes for being late as he makes his way over to an empty chair by the window. His voice is deep, low-country South Carolina. "I've had an awful day," he begins, taking over the room. But nobody seems to mind. In fact, everybody is looking at him, spellbound. So am I. Every few seconds his eyes twitch, a nervous tic. I have the exact same nervous tic. This is truly appalling.

Foster is his name. He's thirty-three, a crack addict/alcoholic who doesn't need money and thus has too much free time on his hands. He has a small, vague job for just this reason. He's living with a physically abusive alcoholic illegal alien from London named Kyle. And from what I gather, he's trying to get the guy to move out. "I almost used last night," he says. "After work, I got off at two A.M., I was just dreading going home to him. So I went up to Eighth Avenue and I was going to score some crack. I was out of control and I was going to do it. But then, this hustler I know, the guy I was going to buy the crack from, was arrested right before my eyes, just as I was about to come up to him." Foster exhales, tosses his head back. I look at his Adam's apple, the dark razor stubble that shadows his neck. "It just really knocked the wind out of me."

He runs his fingers through his hair. He doesn't seem to actually look at anybody in the room, make eye contact. Just shifts around in his seat, fidgets. He's in his own world.

The moderator of the group, Wayne, asks the room, "Would anybody like to give Foster any feedback?"

An older man to my left says, "I'm glad you didn't use, Foster. I'm really glad you didn't use."

Foster mouths a quick *Thanks* and slumps lower in his chair.

For a moment, the room is silent. Watching him. I mean, handsome people are always interesting to watch. But a handsome person in crisis is riveting.

"You know," Foster begins with almost a manic level of intensity, "I just want go kayaking in the Florida Keys, get a black lab, grow tomatoes, have a life. I don't want all this craziness. I don't want this insanity. I'm really sick and tired of it." He pounds his fist on his thigh.

His eyes dart around the room. He glances over here, over there and then at me, and then on to someone else, but he sort of skids into a double take and turns back to look at me. He stares at me for what feels like a very long time and I think, *Do I have something hanging out of my nose?*

"Hey, I'm sorry I was late. What's your name?" he asks as he gets up out of his chair and comes over to me, hand extended.

"Augusten," I tell him, discreetly wiping my hand on my jeans before taking his hand to shake it. My heart is racing. He is thrilling.

"Augusten," he repeats. "Augusten. What an interesting name. You mind if I call you Auggie?"

"Auggie is fine." I repress the urge to smile at my delight over having just been given a pet name by this man.

He smiles back. "Great," he says. "Welcome to Group."

He sits back down and Group continues. For the next hour and a half, I am aware that he is watching me.

When Group is over, we all pile into the same elevator and nobody says a word. That's the strange thing about elevators, it's like they have this power to silence you. I've just been in group therapy where people will reveal the most intimate details of their lives to complete strangers, yet in the elevator nobody can say a word.

Outside, people exchange *good-byes* and *see you soons*, and head off in different directions.

I make a left toward Park Avenue and I can feel Foster a few beats behind me. *Talk to me, talk to me, talk to me,* I am psychically commanding him.

But he doesn't. At Park, he heads north and I head south.

I walk the ten blocks home thinking about Group, specifically this Foster guy. I realize I'm excited for Thursday, the next Group. I realize Foster is the reason why.

I go straight to Perry Street AA. Tonight, the speaker is talking about how people in recovery are always looking for these big, dramatic miracles. How we want the glass of water to magically rise up off the table. How we overlook the miracle that there is a glass at all in the first place. And given the universe, isn't the real miracle that the glass doesn't just float up and away?

THE BRITISH INVASION

Hayden calls from rehab, collect. I accept the charges.

"I'm leaving tomorrow," he says in that British lilt that I miss as soon as I hear.

"Really? What are you going to do, where are you going to go?"

Silence. Then, "Well, I really don't have anywhere to go, except home to London, but I'm not ready for that yet. So I was wondering . . ." He drifts off. "Well, I was wondering if maybe I could stay with you, just for a little while, just until—"

I cut him off, unable to contain my excitement. "Yes, I would love it."

"Really?" he asks.

"Come immediately. It'll be like a minirehab."

It's decided that he will arrive tomorrow night, at eight. After we hang up, I walk around my studio apartment, grinning like a crazy person. It's a tiny apartment, but no smaller than the rooms at rehab, and three of us fit into those at a time. Hayden can sleep on the sofa, like a pet.

He can curl up at night with the stuffed animal I will get for him.

At work the next day, we're informed that we are finalists in the review for the Wirksam beer account. This means that instead of pitching against seven other agencies, it's down to three.

"I have a really good feeling about this," Greer confesses. Then, "It's really too bad about Fabergé."

Our perfume client has decided not to launch a new perfume. The account has gone into remission. I feel spared and am relieved that I don't have to work on that account. I want to be as far away from Fabergé eggs as possible.

"Yeah, bummer," I say sarcastically.

At work, Greer has a copy of *Entertainment Weekly* on her desk and I thumb through it. It's amazing how many of the celebrities in there remind me of Foster from group. I'm hit by a pang. A pang of what, exactly, I'm not sure.

"I don't like Meg Ryan," Greer announces.

"Why?"

"I just don't buy her 'I'm so together' bullshit. I think she's really a very angry person inside."

"Oh . . . kay," I say. "We're not *projecting*, are we, Greer?"

"Oh, fuck off," she says.

Good. That's the Greer I know and love.

I glance down at my desk drawer and there's something sticking out, so I open it. The drawer is crammed with pages torn from magazines. "What the?" I say as I pull the pages out, unfold them. It takes me a moment to see that the pages were not just randomly torn out. They are beer ads. "Did you do this?" I say to Greer.

"Do what?" she says, leaning forward.

I unfold one of the ads, an ad for Coors, and show it to her. "This. Did you stuff all these in my drawer?"

"That's weird," she says in a way that makes me know she's innocent. "Why would someone do that?"

I crumple them up and shove them into the trash can. I try to dismiss it as some sort of weird joke, but I can't shake the creepy feeling. Somebody went to a lot of effort to pull those ads from magazines. Somebody put some real time into it.

It's like something I would do myself in a blackout.

Hayden's plane is delayed six hours. He arrives at two in the morning. We have a late dinner at a twenty-four hour restaurant in the East Village and then stay up until five, talking maniacally. Plotting, planning our sobriety. It's amazing how drunk you can be without alcohol.

It's unclear how long Hayden will stay. At least a couple of weeks. I'm thinking even a month or perhaps for the rest of my life. The only thing is, we made this agreement: if he relapsed, I have to ask him to leave. I can't imagine him relapsing, because he's so determined. And I know that I certainly won't. Once I put my mind to something, that's it. Of course, that was the whole problem in terms of cocktails.

I feel incredibly euphoric tonight. This *must* be that glorious Pink Cloud, God-rays shining through. With Hayden's suitcases opened next to the sofa, and the sofa turned into a makeshift bed, the room feels highly occupied. I'm glad I'm not alone; instead of feeling cramped, I feel secure. At around five-thirty we crawl into our respective beds and sleep.

My alarm clock goes off at nine and wakes us both up. "Do you feel hungover?" I ask Hayden groggily.

"I most certainly do," he admits.

"I don't mean tired, I mean—"

"I know exactly what you mean," he interjects. "I feel like I drank a bottle of wine. I even feel guilty."

"Exactly!" I say, relieved that he feels it too. Relieved that I am not the only one who is so unaccustomed to happiness and the feeling of impending punishment that follows.

I climb out of bed and twist, trying to pop my back. "I have Group after work, so I won't be home until like seven-thirty. If you want, we can go to the eight o'clock Perry Street meeting."

"Great," he says.

"What are you going to do today?" I ask.

He smirks. "Oh, I don't know. Maybe relapse." He laughs. "Actually, I want to go speak to someone at Carl Fisher about perhaps doing some freelance music editing."

I ask him who Carl Fisher is.

He tells me that they are a huge and famous publisher of classical music, that he's worked with them before. I had forgotten that Hayden was not only a crack addict, but also a classical music editor. I think, *Please don't look at my CD collection: Madonna, Julia Fordham, one well-hidden Bette Midler.*

There's nothing to do at work but wait for beer news. So Greer and I make the most constructive use of our time by thumbing through magazines, making long distance calls and talking about other people.

"Is he cute?" she asks when I tell her Hayden has come to stay with me for a while.

I throw a pencil up at the suspended ceiling like a dart and it sticks. "No, it's not like that at all, there's absolutely no physical chemistry between us. We just click, you know, in other ways." I tell Greer about what I heard at AA the other night, about the glass of water.

"God, that's really insightful," she says, trotting her paperclip pony across the top of the stapler. "It's like really appreciating what you have, what's in front of you." She gazes out the window. "I need to remember that. I seem to fly off the handle too easily. And all my books say anger is really bad for your health."

Aside from collecting crocodile handbags from Hermés and Manolo Blahnik slingbacks, Greer is an aficionado of self-help books.

"I wish *I* were an alcoholic. I mean, you're getting all this really good therapy and all these insights from those alcoholic meetings."

I do feel a little smug. But then my compassion kicks in. "You could be an alcoholic too," I tell her.

"No," she sighs. "I wouldn't be a good alcoholic. I'd be the good *wife* of an alcoholic. *I'm* codependent. That's why you and I get along so well." She looks at me earnestly. "I'm glad you're an alcoholic though," she adds. "I mean, I'm glad you're getting all this therapy, because I feel like I'm getting it too, secondhand from you."

I smile at her like, *You moron.*

"No, I mean it, I'm practicing the same 'letting go' thing you are. I already feel like things are bothering me less. You're really inspiring to me. I even have a sticky note on my refrigerator at home: LET IT GO."

Then I realize what's happening: Greer is shape-shifting. She is a puzzle piece who is reshaping herself to accommodate the newly reshaped me. More or less.

At Group, I talk about work. How it's manageable, how I don't feel obsessed with it. Actually, I explain, it's the opposite. Then I tell everybody about how Hayden has come to stay with me for a while. I explain how we met in rehab. The group consensus is that this could be a very good experience, but to make sure we've established boundaries.

Foster speaks in sweeping, affirmative statements about how he's going to ask *his* Brit to leave. He's very confident, high-strung.

The group encourages him. "Yes, you should," they say. It seems that Foster has been trying to get rid of the Brit for the six months that he's been in Group. It also turns out that Foster has been in and out of rehab four times.

Three times I catch him looking at me, then looking away. I feel this strange, invisible connection with him. Like a current. I wonder if I am imagining it. I also wonder if there is any significance to the fact that last week, he was wearing a long-sleeved denim shirt and today he is wearing a tight white T-shirt.

Outside after group, I head off toward Park, walking quickly so I make it to Perry Street on time to meet Hayden.

Foster appears beside me. "Hey, Auggie, wait up," he says, passing me a slip of paper with a phone number written on it. "I just wanted to give you my number, you know, in case you ever need to talk." He winks. Or is it a twitch?

Alcoholics are always giving their phone numbers to each other. In fact, in rehab, I learned you're supposed to ask for people's phone numbers, in case you need to call somebody. And sure enough, I already have a collection of ten phone numbers from people I don't know at Perry Street. I got six numbers my first night. "In case you need to talk, call anytime," people say. Alcoholic friends are as easy to make as Sea Monkeys.

"Okay, great—thanks," I say, slipping the number into the front pocket of my jeans. "I appreciate it." I try to sound normal, casual. An experienced phone-number recipient, simply working the program.

"See ya next week then," Foster says, smiling as he heads into the street, arm extended, a taxi stopping immediately, as if on cue.

As I walk to the Perry Street meeting I can feel the slip of paper in my pocket. It seems to contain a heat source.

Hayden's waiting outside with two large cups of coffee. He hands one to me. "What happened?" he says, smiling, waiting.

"What do you mean?" I ask, taking the lid off the coffee, blowing some of the heat away.

"I don't know," he says. "You just look so happy."

I laugh too hard. "I do?" Coffee sloshes over the edge of the cup onto my hand. "I don't know, I guess it's just the Pink Cloud. Wanna head inside?"

"I suppose. Oh, by the way," he says casually as we're taking our seats, "I never would have pegged you for a Stevie Nicks fan."

I glare at him.

All through the meeting, I pay no attention to anything anyone says and instead sit there, silently concocting reasons to call Foster.

After Perry Street, we find a place around the corner from my apartment that has a Ping-Pong table, so we go there and play. We find a rhythm and actually keep the ball going for a good five minutes at a time.

Ping: Hayden thinks he'll get some work from Carl Fisher.

Pong: I had a slow day at work.

Ping: Hayden went to the library and checked out some books.

Pong: I think I'm really attracted to a crack addict in my group therapy.

Dribble, dribble, dribble, the ball bounces off the table onto the floor. "What are you talking about, what crack addict?"

It seems best to play this casual. "It's nothing," I say, leaning over to retrieve the ball. "It's just a feeling, you know. It'll pass."

He eyes me suspiciously. "You know better than this, Augusten," he says, his British accent lending his words an extra helping of authority.

"I know, I know," I say. "Nothing's going to *happen*, it's just this weird thing. He's a mess, I would never get involved with him, besides there is NO WAY he would ever be attracted to me. He's just friendly."

We leave, head home.

"I'm going to keep my eye on you," he warns.

When Hayden's in the bathroom, I slip the number out of my pocket and stash it safely in my wallet. It gives me a little thrumming sensation in my chest knowing it's there.

There's a message on my machine. "Hi Augusten, it's Greer. Listen, since tomorrow's Friday and nothing's going on at work, let's just take the day off, a mental health day. Call me if that's okay with you."

Hayden and I spend the evening reading. He reads poetry. "God, I'm not sure reading Anne Sexton is such a good idea in early sobriety," he comments.

I read a paperback novel, but must read each page twice because my mind won't focus on the words. At ten, we turn off the lights and go to sleep. I lie awake for at least an hour, replaying the moment Foster handed me the phone number.

And then in a moment of shining epiphany, I realize I didn't actually *see* him write the number down. Which means he must have written it down before Group. Which means at least once, he has thought about me *outside* of Group. Which means that whether consciously or subconsciously, this could have affected his choice of what to wear to Group. Which means that the tight white T-shirt could very well have been meant for me. Sometimes people compare gay men to teenage girls and they are correct, I realize. I think the reason is because gay men didn't get to express their little crushes in high school. So that's why we're like this as adults, obsessing over who wore what white T-shirt and what it means, *really*.

"Are you asleep?" Hayden asks softly.

I mumble, as if I am half-asleep. Best to keep my obsessions to myself for now. Besides, nobody in rehab said there was anything wrong with having a little fantasy.

• • •

"I don't know, I just feel lousy."

I'm talking to Pighead on the phone. I called him to see if he wanted to do something since I have the day off. "Do you have a fever?"

He hiccups. "No, it's just that these . . ." He hiccups again, midsentence. "Hiccups won't go away." Then he confesses, "I have a small fever, my head feels fuzzy."

I'm at his house within fifteen minutes, and he looks awful. Pale and sweaty and the hiccups are almost constant. "I think you should call your doctor."

"I already have," he says. "She's out of town, her message center is trying to get ahold of her so she can call me back."

Virgil is hyperventilating, running from room to room, as if there's about to be a thunderstorm. "Can you take Virgil out for a walk? I haven't taken him outside yet."

It's nearly noon. Pighead always walks Virgil at around seven, before work. Even when he's on vacation from work, like now.

I walk Virgil and the instant his paws hit the curb, his leg goes up and he pees. He pees for what feels like twenty minutes. I walk him around the block and I realize I am feeling a little bit of panic. And then I realize that the reason I am feeling this way is because I saw something in Pighead's eyes that I have never seen before: fear.

Back inside the apartment, Pighead swears he's fine and that he just needs to rest. He tells me there's no reason for me to hang out. That he'll call if he needs anything. I leave. The whole way home I have an uneasy feeling I can't shake.

Hayden's pouring boiling water into a mug when I come back to the apartment. "That was fast. Is your friend okay? Want some tea?"

I lean against the sink. "I don't know Hayden, it's strange. I mean, Pighead never gets sick."

"But you said he has AIDS."

"No, he's HIV-positive, but he doesn't actually have full-blown AIDS. I mean, he's been positive for years, and nothing—not even a cold."

"Well, it could just be a cold or something. But you need to not be in denial that it could be"—he hedges—"it could be something *more*."

The word is heavy, leaden and falls on the floor between us making such a loud sound that neither of us say anything for a while. I don't allow myself to even imagine that possibility.

Finally, I say, "They have new medications for AIDS now. It's not like it used to be. People live with it." As I say this, I recognize in my voice the same tone I use when I'm talking a client into an ad he doesn't want. I'm selling.

Hayden smiles, blows on his tea.

"Too hot?" I say.

He nods his head. "Oh, by the way, your undertaker friend called you."

"Jim? When?"

"While you were over at Pighead's. Sorry, I forgot to tell you."

"That's okay, I'll call him later."

"He said he really needs to talk to you."

A craving strikes. Before, I would have said I wanted a drink. I see now that what I crave is distraction. I don't want to think about Pighead and his hiccups. I speed-dial Jim. "What's up?"

"I met somebody," he says. Jim is always meeting somebody. His somebodies usually last for a week. Or about as long as it takes for him to finally confess what he does for a living. Whichever comes sooner.

"Oh yeah, what's she like?" I ask.

"She's great," Jim says. "A computer programmer. And she's *stacked*."

They met at Raven, a very dark and moody goth bar in the East Village that tends to attract people who are nocturnal and consider Diamanda Galas to be easy listening.

"Have you guys gone out . . ." I want to say, *in daylight yet?* But instead I say, "to dinner or anything?"

"Yeah, we've already made it past the three-date point. And guess what?" he says excitedly. "She knows I'm in prearrangements."

"Jim, does she know what *prearrangements* means?"

"Yes," he answers, annoyed, "she knows."

I imagine a woman with pale skin, long black hair and black fingernails who wears black lace and is thrilled to have landed herself an undertaker. I see a black hearse sailing along a highway upstate, tin cans flying behind, a sign in shaving cream on the back window: JUST MARRIED! "Sounds great," I say.

"We're getting together tonight for drinks at this new place. I was wondering if you wanted to join us, so you can meet her."

My first reaction is fear. I recall something spoken to me in rehab: *If you walk into a barbershop, sooner or later you'll get a haircut,* Rae had said. *So don't go to bars. Don't even think about it.*

"Jim, I'd love to meet her. But I really don't think I should be going to a bar."

Hayden looks up from his book.

"Well, it's not a bar really, it's a restaurant. They have a bar, but it's basically a restaurant."

Hayden watches me, his eyes saying, *whatsgoingon???*

I'll feel like a horrible friend if I don't go. And as long as I'm aware of what I'm doing, I know I'll be okay. "What time?" I ask Jim.

Hayden's mouth opens, his eyes widen in disbelief.

"Eight."

"Okay, give me the address."

"Are you *mad?*" Hayden asks after I hang up.

"It's not a bar, it's a restaurant."

"A restaurant with a bar," Hayden argues.

"Look, I'll be fine. I'll walk in, meet this goth girl, have a seltzer and then leave."

Hayden has turned into a mistrustful parent. He doesn't even need to use words, he can use *looks* alone. There will be no drive-thru McDonald's for me tonight.

The restaurant is in Soho, on Wooster Street. It's easy to spot, because its fabulousness can be seen from a block away. Two huge French doors open out onto the sidewalk, and long, rich, red velvet drapes hang from each door and billow in the warm summer evening breeze. Inside, it's so dark my eyes need time to adjust. For a moment I stand there in this unknown void. Gradually, it reveals itself to me. An expansive bar begins near the door and stretches back into blackness for what is probably miles. Low Moroccan tables are peppered throughout the converted loft space and the only light comes from small votive candles inside blue glass orbs on the tables and along the bar. Behind the bar, colorful liquor bottles are lit from below like fine art.

They look breathtakingly beautiful. Seeing them, I am filled with longing. It's not an ordinary craving. It's a romantic craving. Because I don't just drink alcohol. I actually love it. I turn away.

Two women sit cross-legged on tapestry cushions at one of the tables, each with an exotic blue drink before them. Cigarette smoke curls up from their ashtray like a cobra. In the corner, I see a tall man in a suit whispering into the ear of a woman who looks like a young Kathleen Turner. Four gigantic, thick-bladed ceiling fans barely spin above my head. I realize that in Manhattan, this is the year of the ceiling fan. I could be in Madagascar, circa 1943, in a bar reserved for spies.

Jim is standing at the bar, talking animatedly with a woman, their backs to me. Relieved, I make my way slowly over to them, careful not to accidentally trip on one of the cushions, the low tables or some other unseen, impossibly exotic design element. This is the Kingdom of Heaven and I am only allowed to visit briefly. Sit on the floor, not a cloud.

"Hey, buddy," Jim cheers as he sees me. "Holy shit, you look totally different, you look awesome." His eyes are wide with vodka. I haven't seen him for over a month. I have never seen him when I'm sober. In the hundred-watt bulb of sobriety, he reminds me of a train wreck.

He aims me at the tall, attractive blond woman next to him. "Augusten, Astrid—Astrid, Augusten." We shake hands. Her hand is moist and cool, not from nerves but from the drink she is holding.

"Shit, man," Jim says, giving me the once-over for the second time. "I gotta say, the way you look—hell, I wouldn't kick you out of *my* bed." He breaks into laughter and gives Astrid a playful wink. She laughs too, and takes a big swallow of her cocktail.

Jim forgets that two years ago, he in fact *didn't* kick me out of his bed. We had been out until four in the morning when the bars closed and ended up at his apartment. When we woke up the next morning, we were together in bed, naked. We were both so horrified by the situation that neither of us ever spoke of it again. I am tempted to remind him now, but refrain.

The bartender glides over, as if propelled by silent jets attached to the heels of his Prada shoes. All bone structure and musculature, he's a head shot that can also mix drinks. "What can I getcha?" he asks, using just one corner of his mouth. I am sure he has stood in front of his mirror for many hours saying this exact phrase, using this exact side of his mouth. If you asked, I bet he'd describe himself as *A few degrees left of cool.*

A Ketel One martini please, very dry with olives, I want to say. "Um, just a seltzer with lime," I say instead. I might as well have ordered warm tap water or dirt. I feel that uncool. And suddenly, it's like I can feel how depressing alcoholism really is. Basements and prayers. It lacks the swank factor.

"You guys okay?" the head shot asks Jim and Astrid, pointing at their drinks.

"We'll have a couple more, same thing," Jim says, giving Astrid a sideways glance that tells me he might have found his female drinking buddy after all.

"Done," the head shot says with a polished *kewl*ness that brings to mind images of nipple rings, Sudanese beatnik poets and quality nightlife.

Jim turns to me. "So I was just telling Astrid here about this family I'm dealing with at work."

Thank God. A good undertaker story will take my mind off this place. "Yeah, what's going on?" I ask.

Jim reaches for his glass, sees that it's empty and looks at the bartender. I know exactly what he's thinking. He's thinking, *Can't you shake that thing any faster, Pretty Boy?* "Anyway, like I was telling Astrid, I'm handling the arrangements for the daughter of this rich, snotty-fucking Park Avenue family." He pauses while the bartender sets the drinks down on the bar. Both Jim and Astrid take immediate, thirsty sips. "And get this," he says wiping his mouth on the back of his hand, "the mother actually asks me, 'She will be safe in your building, won't she?' Man, I just looked at her like, *Huh?* I wanted to say, 'No, I'm gonna dress her up in black fishnet stockings and red split-crotch panties. And then I'm gonna prop her up in my minivan and have her turn tricks for horny bums on the Bowery who are into girls with chilled and distant attitudes.'"

Astrid lets out a loud chortle and links her arm through Jim's, sloshing liquid out of both of their glasses.

I laugh politely. I feel uptight, stiff. The phrase *social lubricant* comes to mind and I realize this is what I want, social lubrication. Cocktails. My mouth is dry and I take a sip of seltzer.

"I don't get it," he continues, shaking his head. "They're just gonna plant her in a former landfill cemetery in Queens. And they want to know about her *safety* at the funeral home?" He contorts his features into a mask of disgust. "I mean, in two days this girl is gonna be under six feet of smelly earth with old Delco car batteries and used condoms resting on top of her. Shit. The stuff people worry about."

I realize for the first time that part of what bonded Jim and me in the first place was that our jobs were a major reason we drank.

Jim turns to Astrid. "Hey, babe, you've been awfully quiet," he says, placing his hand on her lower back.

I learn that Astrid is twenty-nine, Danish and once dated a guy who claimed he once slept with Connie Chung.

Jim kisses her cheek and then orders another round.

This is my cue: *exit, Augusten, stage right.* "I gotta take off you guys, I've got some work to do." I turn to Astrid. "It was really nice to meet you."

She looks at me as if she has just seen me for the first time. Jim looks stunned. "Hey, you leaving?"

"Yeah, I just wanted to pop by and say hi," I say, resting my glass of ice and lime on the bar. *I've gotta get out of this place now.*

"Okay, well, thanks for coming, buddy. I'll call you next week." Then immediately he turns away from me and starts talking to Astrid.

"Cool," I say, slap him on the shoulder. As I leave, I notice the head shot talking to an Asian model who is standing at the bar, probably fresh from a go-see. This makes me feel as cosmopolitan as skim milk. *And I am somebody.*

"I really wanted to drink. I didn't. I didn't even come close, but just being there, in that atmosphere, it was just like, powerful. It was the first time since I've been back that I really felt the alcoholic terrorist in my head." It's Monday and I'm sitting in Wendy's office, confessing. Part of me feels guilty telling her this, like I'm breaking a confidence. Part of me didn't want to admit that I wanted to drink with Jim and Astrid.

"I don't think it's a good idea for you to go to bars, but I'm glad that you're being honest about how you feel, that you're not just keeping this inside of you." Then she asks, "Did you go to a meeting afterward?"

I tell her I didn't. I came home and talked with Hayden about it until midnight.

"Next time something like this happens, it's a good idea to force yourself to go to a meeting."

Meetings are the Hail Marys of alcoholics. You can do or *almost* do anything, feel anything, commit any number of non-sober atrocities, as long as you follow with an AA chaser.

"After I cut off his penis, I sautéed it in rosemary butter and ate it."

"But did you go to a meeting afterward?"

"Yes."

"I wouldn't worry about it, then."

Wendy asks how things are going between Hayden and me. I tell her it's great to have him around, how he takes his sobriety very seriously, how we're both really good for each other. We spent the entire weekend going from AA meetings to movies to Ping-Pong.

She asks me how Group went last week. I tell her that I thought Group was very helpful. She says she thinks I'm doing well, that I'm "rising to the challenges of sobriety." I nod and think, *I'm actually getting away with this.*

As I'm standing in the hallway, waiting for the elevator to take me downstairs, I hear behind me, "Auggie?" I turn to see Foster walking toward me. "What are you doing here?" he says.

"One-on-one with Wendy," I tell him. I wish I had a longer answer. One that would take at least forty-five minutes to explain. In private.

"I just had my one-on-one with Rose. What a coincidence," he says, shifting all his weight onto one leg and smiling at me.

"Yeah, funny," I manage. My heart is racing in my chest.

The elevator arrives and we step inside. Foster breaks the elevator law by speaking. "So, ah, what are you up to now?" he asks.

I watch the numbers illuminate as we sink. "Oh, I don't know, probably hit the gym."

The elevator stops on the fourth floor, but nobody gets on. He sticks his head out, looks both ways, shrugs and pushes the DOOR CLOSE button.

We both look ahead and neither of us speaks until we reach the lobby. As we walk toward the main entrance Foster says, "You wouldn't wanna go out for some coffee, would you?" Adding, "I mean, unless you gotta hit the gym right away."

In as calm a voice as possible, I answer, "Yeah, sure, why not?" I don't obey my first impulse, which is to jump up and down like a six-year-old and cry, *Can we? Can we? Can we?*

We walk to French Roast on Sixth Avenue and Eleventh. We take a table outside and order cappuccinos. There's a light breeze that seems to have arrived via FedEx for this exact moment from a resort hotel in Cabo San Lucas.

"So, Auggie," he asks me in his slow, thick drawl, "what's your story?" He settles back in his chair like he intends to stay there for a while, like whatever I have to say is bound to be fascinating.

I love summer because the sun takes so long to set. The gold light is coming at us almost horizontally. I notice the dark chest hairs that peek out from the V of his shirt collar actually glisten. His eyes are so clear and blue that nothing but clichés enter my mind.

I smile, confident that the side lighting will accentuate the cleft in my chin.

He smiles. Cocks his head slightly to the right. Full dimples.

I look away. Look back.

Our cappuccinos arrive.

He's surprised to learn that my Southern parents divorced when I was young and that my mother gave me away to her psychiatrist when I was twelve and that I lived with crazy people in the doctor's house and never went to school and had a relationship with the pedophile who lived in the barn behind the house.

I'm surprised to learn that less than two months ago, he was in a crack hotel with a piece of broken bottle glass pressed against his neck. And that he knows, for a fact, he is unlovable. And he's afraid to kick the Brit out of the apartment because he's worried the Brit will kill himself.

"But in Group, you were saying how he hits you, screams at you all the time." Even I wouldn't put up with that shit. I'd deport his ass. "He sounds just awful."

"I know, Auggie, he is awful. But I'm all he has. If I kick him out, where will he go?"

Fresh from rehab, I answer, "That's his problem. He is his own responsibility, not yours."

"Naw, he *is* my responsibility, in a way. He doesn't have any money." Foster scratches his collarbone and his biceps becomes the size of a large mango.

"Are you in love with him?" I ask impartially, sipping.

"No, I'm not in love with him. I never was. We were just two messes that got together and stayed together." He laughs bitterly. "That's me, a big ol' mess." He takes a sip from his cappuccino and asks, "So what about you? How's your relationship going?"

"I'm not in a relationship," I tell him.

"But . . . I could have sworn you said something about some guy named Hector living with you?"

"Hayden," I correct. "And we're not boyfriends, I met him in rehab. He's just staying with me for a while before he goes back to London."

Foster gives me a little smirk. "You *sure* there's nothing going on?" He wipes some foam from his upper lip, then licks his finger.

"You think I wouldn't know?" I say. Although in the past, it's possible I wouldn't have.

He laughs. "Sorry, it's none of my business anyway." He strains his neck to the right and there's a crack, then he cracks it to the left. He looks at me. "But you *are* single?"

"Yeah, I am single. Unlike you." There's faint hostility in my voice and I regret it instantly. It gives me away.

He scratches his chin and smiles so slightly that a person wouldn't notice unless that person were transfixed by his lips.

The waiter arrives with a book of matches and lights the candle at our table. I'm in the middle of horrifying myself, telling Foster all the details of my life. My crazy, psychotic mother, my mean, drunk father, my advertising career, how I used to have a wake-up service call me on my cell phone just so it would ring when I was out to dinner at a fancy restaurant in Soho with friends. When cell phones were new and the size of baguettes.

He flicks the light switch behind his blue eyes. "So what do you find attractive in a guy?" As he asks this he slings one arm over the back of the chair next to him.

I gaze at the arm like a dog watching bacon and stammer. "Oh, you know. Hard to say, really."

"Gimme a hint," he says.

"I hate this question—okay—I guess, somebody with a lot of substance; someone who's funny and smart and reads and is crazy but not too crazy." Then I add, "I sound like a really bad personal ad here."

He laughs. "What about physically? What physically draws you to a guy, what qualities?"

I reach for my coffee, see that it's empty. Foster catches this and he picks up his mug and pours the contents of it into mine. "So?" he says.

"This is embarrassing," I begin. "I have this really shallow . . . attraction . . . to furry arms." I space my words out so that the fact can be diluted.

He laughs in a way that reminds me of a huge, fragrant glass of red wine. His laugh is expansive. He nods his head. I feel like some straight guy on a date with Pamela Anderson who has just told her, *I love big nipples.*

As he laughs, he casually unbuttons the cuffs of his shirt, rolls up his sleeves and then rests his furry arms on the table in front me. "I'm not laughing at you," he goes on. "I'm laughing because I also have this really specific thing I'm attracted to." He's grinning wickedly.

"What's that?"

A breeze passes over the nape of my neck. I feel stoned, like I've smoked a joint.

"I've got this . . . *thing* . . . you could say, for guys with cappuccino foam on their upper lip." He winks or twitches again.

Without taking my eyes off his, I swipe my index finger above my lip, then pull it away and look: cappuccino foam, of course. "Is that right?" I say, probably bright red. I'm drunk from the attention.

"That is very right," he drawls in a way he has to know is sexy.

"Can I get you something else?" the waiter asks.

"No, that's okay," I say. I glance at my watch because I've seen people do it in movies. "I guess I should head home."

"Okay, Auggie," he says with something that my feeling chart might lead me to believe is hopefulness, sadness and disappointment. I get the feeling he would stay here all night.

I reach for the check, but he snatches it up. He glances at it and reaches into the pocket of his jeans. He pulls out a crumpled twenty-dollar bill and tucks it under the candle so it doesn't blow away.

We get up from the table, go to the corner. We stand there for a moment just looking at each other. "See you at Group tomorrow," he says finally.

I want more of him. In the same way that if he were a martini, I'd want a few more rounds. "See you tomorrow. Bye."

We both wait to see who will walk away first. He does. But then he pauses and turns back. And it hits me that I haven't felt this infatuated with anybody since Pighead. It was a feeling I never wanted to lose. And to feel it again, even in this tiny, embryonic form, is wonderful.

We leave in opposite directions. He goes home to his British alcoholic boyfriend. I go home to my British alcoholic/crack addict roommate. As I walk, I say to myself, *These feelings are for Foster, right? They're not still for Pighead, are they?* I answer myself that the feelings are indeed for Foster. I'm certain of it. Almost one hundred percent certain.

I haven't felt romantic toward Pighead for years. The way it started with us, you'd think we'd be a blissful, nauseating couple by now, finishing each other's sentences and making our friends not want to be around us. I was intoxicated by his suits, his smell, the way he threw language around like it was a volleyball. Pighead, the investment banker, always had an answer for everything and could argue you into believing anything.

We always had to have dinner at the "it" restaurant. We always drank the "it" drink. We went to clubs where extremely handsome people danced, and we danced with each other. We had sex, we went home to our separate apartments and then we had phone sex.

Pighead could never be caught, and this made me try. But then I got sick of trying. And then he got sick and all of a sudden it was like, "Okay, you can have me now." Except I didn't want him by then. It had been too much effort to get over him.

All I had to do was picture him on the beach at Fire Island, in those bright orange trunks, talking to the guy who was a dancer, while I stayed behind, walking the dog, letting him pee in the shrubs. Pighead actually had the nerve to get the guy's phone number. "What's the fucking problem?" he said. "We're not married. We've had this discussion, Augusten. I love you but I don't want to feel trapped."

So naturally, I spent months trying to kill him with my thoughts.

And then he was diagnosed and suddenly, a new Pighead emerged who was unafraid of commitment, who said things like, "Let's build a life together." To which I responded, "Do you think I should wear the black jacket or the brown one on my blind date tonight?"

On Tuesday, I'm standing at the urinal at work taking a leak when I hear the door to the men's room open, then Greer shouting, "Augusten, are you in there?"

"Yeah, what is it?" How annoying of her.

"You need to hurry up, Pighead is on the phone. He's calling from the hospital."

THE DANGERS OF CHEEZ
WHIZ AND PIMENTO

I don't understand. You said the hiccups went away. When I called you on Sunday, you said you felt fine. You said it was some twenty-four hour thing." I'm sitting in my office, stabbing a pen into a pad of yellow stickies. Panic has made me angry. Greer is hovering in the doorway.

"I was fine. But then last night, they started again. They didn't stop all night. I called my doctor this morning and she told me she wanted me to check into St. Vincent's for some tests."

"How long are you going to be there?"

"Just a couple of days. She says."

"Well . . . what . . . what are they doing, what tests? What do they think it is?" I ram the tip of a bent paperclip under my fingernail, making it bleed. Nobody goes into a hospital for *hiccups*.

"They don't have any idea. They've been—*hic*—sucking blood out of me all day long." He pauses. I can hear him breathing. Then another hiccup.

"Well, I'll come over right after work."

"No, don't bother. There's nothing you can do."

In a way I feel rejected that he doesn't think there's anything I can do. But I feel an almost greater relief that he doesn't expect this from me. And I'm ashamed. I ask, "What about Virgil?"

"My brother's taking care of him."

"What about work, weren't you supposed to go back today?"

"I said I had a family emergency."

I can hear something in the background, voices, commotion.

"I gotta go. They want to me to go downstairs for an MRI. Look, I'll talk to you later, okay—bye." There's strain in his voice and hearing it rubs my heart a little raw. I want to protect him from the doctors. I don't want the doctors taking his Valium.

I hang up the phone in slow motion, just sit there for a minute. Finally, I look at Greer. "I don't know what's going on. Neither does he."

Greer sits in the chair across from my desk, her legs tightly crossed. "Well, is he okay?" she asks.

"I don't know," I say.

She gives me a look she has never given me before. I don't like that this moment warrants a new look.

Foster told the group he kicked the alcoholic abusive illegal alien Brit out of his apartment. He gave him a check for ten thousand dollars and instructions to get out of his life and stay out of his life. When asked why he finally made this big move, Foster looked at me for one brief though ninety-proof instant before looking away and saying vaguely, "I just realized what I might be missing."

I talked about Pighead. Not that there was much to say. "Is *lost* a feeling?" I asked the group.

"I'm sorry, Auggie," Foster says once we're outside on the sidewalk.

"Thanks," I say. I feel small. A Disney dwarf miscast in *Terminator 5*.

"I wish I knew you better," he says softly, "so I could give you a hug."

"You don't have to," I tell him. Pause. "Know me better, I mean."

Foster opens his arms and I move into them, rest my head on his shoulder. He doesn't hug me like I've seen alcoholics hug each other after AA meetings. He doesn't hug me like a crack addict I have known for three group therapy sessions and one meeting over coffee. Foster hugs me like he has known me all my life.

He doesn't pat my back or pull away after four or five seconds. He hugs me tightly and takes deep, slow breaths, almost like he is teaching me how to breathe.

"I'm afraid," I say into his shoulder.

"Of what?" he asks.

"Of everything."

"You know what you need?"

I can feel it coming. He's going to say, *A blowjob*. He's just another pig, after all. Just another typical gay guy who wants to get his rocks off, disguised as somebody I can imagine myself caring about, despite the fact that I can't.

"What?" I ask, not wanting to know.

He gently pushes away from me so he can see my face.

"You need a Cheez Whiz and pimento sandwich with potato chips. And not the low-fat baked chips either, the real ones."

Foster's apartment is on the forty-seventh floor of an East Side high-rise only a few blocks from my office. It's a beautiful space, furnished with boxes and bookshelves overflowing with books, dust rabbits—not bunnies—and various pairs of khakis strewn about. We obviously have the same decorator.

His machine is blinking and he walks over to it. "Oh God, now what?" he says, punching the PLAY button. "You have fifteen new messages . . . first message today at . . ." Foster pushes STOP, then ERASE. The machine, an old-fashioned cassette-tape version, whirrs into motion.

"That's Kyle. Ever since I kicked him out, he calls me twenty times a day asking to move back, and then asking for more money when I tell him to leave me alone."

"Man, I'm sorry," I say, understanding completely what could lead a person to stalk Foster.

He goes into the kitchen and opens the refrigerator, pulling out the ingredients of the Southern white trash sandwich.

"Can I use your phone?"

"Sure, go ahead," he says with his head in the refrigerator.

"You . . . are . . . where?" Hayden asks like the parent I have turned him into.

"I'm at Foster's apartment. We're just having a little sandwich and talking some."

"You're at the crack addict's apartment? *Having a little sandwich*?" he says. From the tone of his voice, you'd think I'd just told him I was hanging out at a playground wearing a NAMBLA T-shirt.

"Anyway, I didn't want you to wonder, worry about where I am. I'll be home soon."

I hang up before he gets the chance to guilt-trip me.

Foster appears from the kitchen with two sandwiches, each with a little pile of Ruffles next to them. "You can't eat Cheez Whiz and pimento sandwiches off china; you have to use paper plates," he says, sliding the plates onto the coffee table. I'm sitting on the sofa. He sits in the chair.

Foster talks about Kyle. How crazy Kyle is, how he hopes the phone calls stop soon. He talks about how much he wants a dog. How he misses South Carolina. He tells me about his job as a waiter at Time Café and how even though he doesn't need the money, the job keeps him occupied at night, which is when he most wants to smoke crack. Foster talks so much that I have finished my entire sandwich, plus almost all the Ruffles, before he has even finished half of his. His knee bobs up and down really fast. His eyes twitch. Suddenly he looks less like a rough-around-the-edges movie star and more like a crack addict.

And for some strange reason, I find this incredibly comforting. He's such a distracting mess, that I'm able to get outside myself. Like watching a really strange art film at the Quad Cinema on East Thirteenth.

"Do you wanna talk about Pighead?" he asks finally.

I swallow a potato chip. "No."

"That's okay," he says.

I smile and eat another chip. I don't want to talk because talking makes things real.

"You know, the minute I walked into Group, that day when I was late, I saw you immediately."

I swallow, but when I do my throat makes a noise. A little gulp sound. It was loud enough for him to hear.

"I saw you immediately, too," I say. "I mean, obviously I saw you too because you came in late." I am as articulate as a log of petrified wood. With as much common sense.

There's this long and uncomfortable silence where we both make an effort not to look at each other. The phone rings. "Aw, damn it all." He reaches for the receiver. "What do you want, Kyle?" he growls. He rolls his eyes. "No, Kyle."

Silence.

"I said *no.*"

More silence. "Good-bye, Kyle." Foster hangs up the phone and then reaches behind him and unplugs it from the wall. "Sorry, where were we?"

We were at the part where we start making out and you tell me that you've been lying all along. That you're not really a crack addict mess.

That you really are as sweet and warm as you seem and that your movie-star good looks have nothing to do with the real you.

"I don't know. I can't remember. The sandwich was great though—thanks."

"You're very welcome. You feel better, a little?"

"I feel a lot better, I really do. The feeling passed, the panic."

"Good."

"I should get going."

"Aw, already?" he asks, puppy-dog style. Even if he is a crack-addict mess, I feel fairly certain that this is the only time in my life somebody who is better looking than Mel Gibson will hint for me to stay a little longer.

"Well, soon," I amend.

"Good," Foster says. "Soon is better than now."

He excuses himself, says he needs to change his shirt. The tag on the back of the collar is driving him nuts, he'll be right back, do I mind?

"I don't mind," I say. Instead of, *Can I do it?*

He disappears down the hallway. A second later, I see him walking back, carrying a white T-shirt. He goes into the bath-room, flicks on the light. I can see his reflection in the medicine cabinet mirror which for some reason is open, creating this bee-line to my retinas. I don't think he can see that I'm watching him. And I do watch him. I watch him lean into the mirror, I suppose quickly checking his nose for blackheads. I watch him unbutton the white shirt, take it off, drape it over the shower curtain rod. His muscular chest has a spread of black hair across it. A trail of hair leads straight down to the lip of his jeans, a perfect line. His abs contract as he slides the T-shirt over his torso. This is a guy that even a straight guy would watch. Would pay nine-fifty plus another seven dollars for popcorn and a small Coke to watch.

He flicks the light switch off and comes romping back into the room. This time he sits on the couch, but at the far end away from me. "Much better," he breezes.

The arms of the white T-shirt are stretched tightly across his biceps. His nipples poke through the cotton. I can see a shadow of the hair underneath.

"You wanna see my photo album?" he asks.

"Sure."

He stands up, goes to the bookshelf, comes back and sits right next to me. His knee is touching mine. He opens the album across our laps. As he flips the pages, he explains the pictures: Aunt so-and-so from somewhere, Uncle what's-his-name, Cousin this and that, etc. I don't hear a word he is saying because I am watching his hands, his arms. I'm caught up in the hair that covers his forearms and tapers sparingly to the middle of each finger. Basically, I am a frat boy at a Nymphomaniac Supermodels Anonymous meeting.

I haven't felt this attracted to anybody in my entire life. It's like every cell in my body is magnetically drawn to him. My mitochondria want to make friends with his mitochondria. And as soon as I become aware of this powerful attraction, I remember something from when I was thirteen.

After Bookman raped me, he became my friend. We used to go on walks every night. After a week, he told me I had turned his world upside down, that he realized he was in love with me. He said he was sorry for what happened that night when I came over to his apartment to look at his photos.

After midnight, he would sneak into my room and we would have sex. His mouth tasted like walnuts. There were always tears in his eyes when he looked at me. "So beautiful, you are so beautiful."

I was thirteen and he was all I had. I hated school, never went. I spent all my time with him. And he became insane with obsession.

After two years, it all boiled over. "I'm either going to kill you or myself." He went out to get film for his camera one night, and never came back.

Nobody ever heard from him again. Everything I had, as much as I hated it, him, was instantly gone. It all seemed so normal at the time.

"Auggie, are you okay?" Foster is asking me, looking concerned.

"What?"

"Are you okay? You seem so distant. I hope I'm not boring you with the photos. I'll put it away." He closes the album, gets up and puts it back on the bookshelf.

"No, I'm sorry, it's not that, it's something else. I was just thinking." Strange, but ever since I stopped drinking, my brain sometimes hands me these memories to deal with. It's like my fucked-up inner child wants attention, wants me to know he's still in there.

"About what? What were you thinking?

"I don't want to talk about it, just old stuff. Some memory, it's nothing. One of those pictures I saw made me remember something. I sorta spaced out for a minute, I guess."

He sits back down on the couch next to me. "C'mere," he says, pulling me into him, his hand stroking my head. "Don't think," he soothes, "just close your eyes."

Uh-oh.

I waited by the phone all day long, every day, for more than a year. Every time it rang, I was sure it was him. I reread the love letters he had written to me, each in perfect penmanship on white lined paper:

"I believe you are God. Not a mythical Greek god, not the idealization, but the essence, the truth, the only God. And yet, you continue to abuse me, try to destroy me with one glance from your jewel eyes, one of your winning smiles, thrown to somebody else but me. I am insane for my love for you, yet you beat it and beat it and beat it down. You make every effort to crush me. At thirteen, you have already lived many lifetimes and you use your wisdom of your past to toy with my emotions, you create me, I exist for you and only you. And I hate you now. I hate you for abusing your power."

Foster's hands move from my head to my chest. He spiders his fingers over me, pressing gently. I can't believe this is happening.

I can't let this happen. I'm not supposed to date somebody from group therapy. There is almost no worse crime a recovering alcoholic can commit. Second would be cooking the head of another alcoholic in wine.

"I need to get going now, I really do." It feels impossible for me to sit still another moment. Better to leave than be left.

"You going to be okay?"

"Uh huh."

We stand. I place my hand on the brass doorknob, turn and pull. Nothing happens. He reaches over and twists the deadbolt; the door opens. For an awkward moment, we stand there.

He gives me a hug. I don't fight it.

"You smell good," he tells me.

"You do, too," I say, reduced now to single-syllable words.

The hug goes on longer than casual hugs do.

"And you feel good, too."

"So do you."

We both feel it, it would be impossible not to. But neither of us will mention it.

I pull back and say, "Okay, see you later. Thanks for the sandwich and everything."

"I'm glad I got to be with you some."

I walk down the hall toward the elevator bank. I turn back in the direction of his door, and he's still standing there, watching me. I want to run back to him and tell him everything that was going through my mind. But I don't. I leave. He's a crack addict from my group therapy. I can't have these feelings about him.

In the cab home, I feel like I have been sniffing glue all night. High and guilty. The fumes of him still trapped in my nose.

"It's obvious what you're doing," Hayden says. He dunks and redunks the chamomile tea bag in his mug. "You're defocusing."

To "defocus" is to focus on someone else, or something else other than your sobriety. Your sobriety should, at all times, remain your number one priority. Alcoholics instinctively defocus. I am a perfect example. With three hundred bottles of Dewar's in my apartment, all I could see was the wall. Now all I can see is Foster.

"I know. I mean, I think that's part of it."

"I don't like the sound of this at all, you getting involved with a crack addict from your group therapy. That's really addict behavior."

"We're not involved," I say in my own defense.

"You told me he was hugging you on his couch."

"Because I was upset. He's a nice guy."

"Look, I'm not here to make judgments, but I just think this is, well, crazy."

I wish Hayden would vanish in a cloud of smoke. "Hayden, you're gonna have to stop with this mental health stuff. Or I'll have to take a cheese grater across your face."

"You're obsessing on him," he says, unfazed.

This is true, I am. "I am not," I say.

"This is your addict talking. Your addict needs something to fill it up. Your addict is hungry. It's trying to feed." He sounds as though he is describing the plot of a science fiction horror film.

"I'm just upset about Pighead being in the hospital. Foster was only being nice, helping me out. That's all."

"What do you mean? Pighead is in the hospital?"

I want a beer. A six-pack. And then I want to go out for drinks. "Yeah, hospital. He called me at work today. His doctor checked him in. They're doing tests, that's all I know. Hiccups that won't go away."

"Dear God, I'm sorry. Is he okay?"

"I don't know. They're still trying to find out what's wrong. I mean, yeah, he's *okay*, I'm sure he's okay. They just need to figure out this hiccup thing."

Hayden looks at me with utter compassion; the long-lost son of Mother Teresa.

For some reason, the fact that Pighead is in the hospital lets me off the hook with Hayden. And then, this awful feeling. I feel *happy* that Pighead is in the hospital, deflecting the attention. And I'm a monster again.

Think of your head as an unsafe neighborhood; don't go there alone, Rae once said.

My office door is unlocked. Immediately, this makes me suspicious. I always lock my door. And if I don't, the cleaning lady does. I throw my stuff on the sofa and go over to my desk. There is a yellow sticky note on my computer screen. DRINKS. ODEON NINE TONIGHT—BE THERE. Beneath this is another line: (ONE GLASS OF WINE NEVER HURT ANYBODY.)

I pick up the phone and dial Greer's extension, but she's not in yet. I walk over to the bookcase, and I notice that the storyboards we did for the Pizza Hut pitch have been rearranged. These are boards we presented last year, and we just keep them because we never got around to throwing them out. As a result, I've been staring at this pan of Deep Dish pizza for the past twelve months, and now it's gone. I thumb through the boards, and it's clear that somebody has been snooping. It then occurs to me that this is something Rick would do. Rick would look through our old Pizza Hut boards because he needs ideas. And sometimes you can take an idea from one place and use it somewhere else.

Ideas come easy to me. But this is not so for Rick. He struggles. I can write a script—and a really good one—in a few minutes. I've created campaigns over tuna sandwiches with Greer. But Rick needs to fester for a while. He needs days, sometimes weeks. And even then, he often doesn't come up with anything that great. Usually something he's recycled from some old issue of *Communication Arts* magazine.

And all of a sudden I can picture him in my office after I have left for the day. I can see him fingering the boards. *That faggot. He thinks he's so good. He's just a fucking lush,* he would say. And then he'd leave the sticky note.

"I can't believe you got here before I did," Greer says, suddenly standing in my doorway, winded from her brisk walk from the train.

"Check it out," I say, gesturing toward the computer.

She walks around the desk and looks at the note. She leans in to read it. "Maybe somebody has a crush on you," she says, looking up.

"A crush?" I say. I pull the Pizza Hut board back out and place it in the front. I stack the boards neatly against the wall.

"Well, yeah. Maybe somebody likes you." She smiles slyly. "Maybe it's that new account guy," she says. "You know, the one with the goatee."

"Greer, this isn't about a crush. It's somebody being a jerk."

Greer plucks the note off the screen. "Why do you always have to be so cynical?" she says. "Maybe it's not some big joke. Maybe somebody really does want to meet you for drinks. Maybe you should go."

I tell her about the storyboards being examined.

"That's ridiculous," she says. "The cleaning woman probably moved them to dust. God knows you never clean in here."

"I think it's Rick," I say.

"Rick? Why would he do something like that?"

"Think about it, Greer. The beer ads, the fake concerned looks, and now this. You and I both know what a pathetic loser he is. He's not above doing something like this. He's looking for ideas to steal."

Greer considers this. "I don't think Rick is creative enough to think of something like this," she says. "I mean, Rick's a jerk. But a harmless jerk."

I'm not so sure. So all day long, I keep an eye on him. I watch him for signs of guilt. We pass in the hallways, and I make eye contact. He makes eye contact back and smiles. But he doesn't look away, which to me would implicate him. I'm tempted to confront him, but if he didn't do it, I really would seem like a crazy alcoholic faggot.

I also make sure to walk past the new account guy's office at least twice, just to see if he looks up. I walk casually, as if out for a stroll. Just to see if by some far-flung chance, Greer is right, that the note is for real and the guy really does have some sort of crush on me. But the third time I walk by, he looks up from his desk. "Can I help you with something? Do you need me for some reason?"

I step into his office. "Um, I was just wondering if you have the competitive beer reel," I say.

He smiles. "Nope, not with me. But I could get a copy for you. I'll make sure somebody drops it by your office."

I notice a framed picture of a beautiful woman on his desk. She is on the beach, laughing into the sun, the straw hat on her head about to blow off. "Never mind," I say.

"You sure?"

"Positive."

Later, when I tell Greer that the note wasn't from the account guy, she says, "That picture doesn't mean anything. It could be his sister."

"Greer, even if his sister were Christy Turlington, he wouldn't have a shot of her like that on his desk. Trust me. It's his wife or his girlfriend."

"Maybe," Greer suggests, "he's confused. Maybe he's engaged but doesn't really know if he can go through with it. Maybe it's like some sort of sexual-orientation cry for help."

"Oh my God," I say.

"Well, it's possible. I mean, maybe he's got all this family pressure, and all this pressure from the girl, and maybe he just really needs somebody to talk to."

"Greer," I say, "you are in the right business. I have never met anybody so skilled at creating mountains out of molehills."

Greer looks pleased with herself. "You're not the only one with a bookcase full of advertising awards."

"My name is Augusten, and I'm alcoholic," I announce to the room. "And today I have ninety days."

The alcoholics at the Perry Street meeting applaud. I'm sitting at the podium because today I have ninety days of sobriety and in order to "work my program" I need to "qualify." I glance over at Hayden, who smiles at me.

I'm amazed by how nervous I am, how dry my throat suddenly is. Even though I make a living talking in front of people, presenting advertising campaigns to CEOs, I'm terrified and speechless. My hands are almost dripping with sweat. I can't think of how to begin, what to say. My mind is filled with two-ply facial tissues. Yet, my mouth somehow switches to autopilot and words come out of me, like involuntary farts. I talk about how it was when I was drunk. I begin with the Fabergé egg exhibit, then being forced into rehab by my boss. I talk about rehab, and then coming back into my life, sober.

And I'm obsessed with a handsome, hairy-armed crack addict from my group therapy, I don't say. I say I feel grateful for the people in my life, grateful for my sobriety, one day at a time, etcetera.

"You were spectacular," Hayden tells me afterwards.

"How so?"

"You were so honest and substantive. Just no bullshit," he says, slapping me on the back.

"Really? I seemed normal?" I ask.

"Of course. You were great."

"What a relief. I had no idea what I was saying. I was actually thinking about how my chest hair is growing back after having shaved it all off."

Hayden turns sharply, *"What?"*

"Well, I thought maybe of bleaching it for the summer. But then I thought how awful it would be to have roots. Chest hair roots. That would be really humiliating. The blond chest hair might look good and natural like I go to the Hamptons on the weekends. But as soon as the roots started to appear, it would be like, 'Oh, that's very sad, he's obviously looking for something and just not finding it.' "

Hayden stares at me with mock horror. Or maybe it's real horror. "You absolutely terrify me. The depth of your shallowness is staggering."

"Let's go get Indian," I say.

At the restaurant on First Avenue and Seventh, I tell Hayden that I think asshole Rick from work is fucking with me.

"I thought your boss's name was Elenor," he says, biting into a vegetable samosa.

"Rick is her partner. They work together. Good cop, bad cop."

"You said work was going well. I don't understand."

I tell him about how last week, I got into work and somebody had crammed beer ads from magazines in my desk drawer. I tell him about the sticky note.

Hayden is aghast. "That seems hostile," he says.

"Rick's a fuck. He's a homophobic closet case and he hasn't got an ounce of talent. He just hitched his wagon to Elenor years ago and she's too busy to notice he's as dumb as a box of hair."

Hayden takes a long sip of water. "You have to keep an eye on this Rick person."

I intend to.

• • •

"Come over to my apartment at six and we'll walk to Group together," Foster tells me on the phone.

I hurl my body into a cab and head uptown. Each block has tripled in size since the last time I was in a cab. I can't get there fast enough.

He opens the door wearing a towel around his waist and half a beard of white shaving cream on his face. "C'mon in, I just have to finish shaving, then we can go."

I stand in the doorway of his bathroom as he shaves; steam from the sink fogs the mirror. The towel is short enough that I can see the muscles in his legs flex each time he shifts the weight from one leg to the other. Thick muscles, covered with tan skin and black hair. He's a hairy guy, circa 1970 when guys didn't bother with electrolysis or waxing. Foster is physically retro. He watches me as he shaves, glancing from sink to skin to me, smiling. "Are we going to be okay, or are we late?" he asks, scraping the blade across his face; the sound of a butter knife against sandpaper.

"We're okay," I say without bothering to look at my watch.

Foster pulls the towel off from around his waist, revealing a pair of white boxers.

I think: *Is it okay for one member of group therapy to see another member of group therapy in his underwear? Am I crossing a boundary?*

He rinses his face over the sink, then stands up and takes a towel, presses it against his face. "All done," he announces. He brushes against me as he walks by. "Oh, sorry," he says, grinning. "Clumsy ol' me."

I follow him to the bedroom. "Should I wear these . . ." he asks, holding out a pair of black jeans, ". . . or these?"—holding out a pair of khakis.

"Neither," I say.

He raises just one eyebrow. Something that I know (from Greer, of course) takes hours of practice in front of a mirror.

"Okay," he says flatly, letting both pairs of pants fall to the floor. Then he saunters over toward me, smiling. I pretend to back away.

"I meant you should wear sweatpants," I say, laughing.

"Is that what you meant?" He raises his arm up, brushes his forearm against my cheek. "Fur," he says.

I move my hands around his waist, press him against me. He wraps his arm around me and somehow manages to move us over to the bed where we collapse.

"How'd you get this?" I say, pointing to a small scar under his chin.

He rubs it lightly with the tip of his finger. "I cracked up my pickup truck when I was in college, smacked my face on the steering wheel."

His earlobe fits perfectly between my lips. I'd forgotten how it feels to kiss somebody. Back when I was in love with Pighead, I always felt like he didn't want me to kiss him, but that he let me anyway. This is different. Mutual makes all the difference. And then I realize I'm kissing somebody from my outpatient group therapy.

"Foster, this is crazy. What are we doing?"

"You said you liked crazy guys."

"I know, but not, you know, crazy guys I'm in group therapy with."

I make an effort to rise; Foster pushes me back down. "Stay," he says.

I stay, lie back flat. I close my eyes. He rolls over on his side, puts his arm over my chest.

"What are you thinking?" he asks.

Wendy's face is in my head, along with the consent paper I signed at HealingHorizons, stating that I will not become romantically involved with any of the members of the group. "Nothing," I lie.

Foster kisses my neck. "Know what I'm thinking?" he asks.

"I don't know if I want to know."

"Yes you do, I guarantee. So ask me." He gives me a shake.

"Okay. Foster, what are you thinking?"

"Gee, Auggie, how sweet of you to ask. I was thinking that I can't wait to see people's reactions in Group when we walk in this afternoon, together, late."

"Shit. C'mon, let's go."

Foster is laughing and I'm pulling him up from the bed by his arm, shoving the khakis at him.

"I'll walk in after you," I plot.

He slides his pants on, buttons them. "Aww. Where's your sense of adventure?"

We take a cab downtown, Foster clutching my index finger in his hand the whole way. It's a sweet gesture because he does it without thinking, while he looks out the window. Before we walk into Group, I check my watch, see that we're fifteen minutes late.

We open the door, the talking pauses and all heads turn. Foster walks in first, whispering, "Sorry, sorry, go ahead."

I take a seat on the opposite side of the room from him, despite the fact that the chair next to his is empty. Peter, one of the alcoholics in group, continues where he left off before we came in. I look at Peter, giving him my complete attention. Then, I briefly sneak a look at Foster. And Foster, the idiot, is smiling widely, staring not at Peter but directly at me.

This evening Hayden and I were walking on Perry Street heading home from dinner and I was wondering out loud which apartment Linda Hunt lived in because I read she lived on Perry Street; used to see her walk her dog. In fact, the first time I saw her I was squatting down scooping up Virgil's shit into a Zip-Loc baggie and she was standing there, almost face-to-face to me, and she asked how old my dog was. The one time a celebrity, an Oscar winner no less, speaks to me, I am hunched over, collecting feces off the street.

As we were walking, a man in a wheelchair, parked on the sidewalk in front of his brownstone building, said something to us. I ignored him, assumed he wanted money. I walked on, then noticed Hayden had turned around, stopped. They were talking. I didn't hear what they were saying because I was further ahead, frowning back at him. I was annoyed that he was talking to an older man in a wheelchair. Hayden waved me over and said, "This gentleman needs our help. He's been waiting for somebody strong to come along."

I'm strong, so Hayden volunteered me. The man focused his attention on me. I looked between them, impatient and annoyed.

Finally, the man in the wheelchair said, "Thank you for offering your help. If you could just get me up the stairs and unlock my apartment door."

He produced his keys, fumbling with them with his semiparalyzed hands, looking for the correct key among the many. I was thinking, *You don't need to show me the key now; you can show it to me at the door if I can't immediately figure it out.* Since I was now going to help him, I wanted to do it as quickly as possible. I wanted it to be over. "Just wait one minute while I park my wheelchair over there by the stairs," he said.

After his wheelchair was in position he hit a switch and turned the motor off. Then he asked me to pull the chain out of the pack on the back and fasten it to the railing of the stairs.

I forced a smile, although I felt conned. I reached into the bag and found the chain, then I secured the chair. All the while he sat, watching me. "Careful," he said. And "Be gentle, please." I wanted to say *Shut the fuck up.*

When I was done he asked me to carry him. "Just pick me up under my knees while I . . ."

I couldn't hear another word he said because suddenly I knew

I would be holding this man, carrying him up the stairs to his apartment. I heard "Like a baby. Just like a baby," and I felt ill. I felt like I was visiting my mother.

My mother had a stroke ten years ago that left the right side of her body paralyzed, left her in a wheelchair. I thought about how I can never bring myself to visit her. And when I did, last time must have been over a year and a half ago, I could never bring myself to stay long. From the moment I walked in the door to her apartment, the need hit me in the face, thick like an odor. Would I change a lightbulb? Then roll her across the bridge. Then buy canned tuna. Then unscrew something, affix something or bring something to her and set it in her lap. Always turning something on or off, moving something from one side to another. As if she needed me to do these things, me specifically. As if she had been saving them up for me to do. Like they were gifts. Love. Dead birds she had caught and killed with claws, saved while I was away and dropped, all together in a mound on my doorstep for me to appreciate. Of course, they were such small things to do, but they each felt so impossibly large and uncomfortable to me.

I feel dirty when I visit my mother. I feel that her intimacy is exposed. Her nightgowns are so thin that her flesh shows through them. Her need is like a vagina. And I do not like to see it.

Her apartment isn't as clean as our home was growing up. When I was a child, our house was immaculate; one dust mote on the teak dining table would be cause for a complete spring cleaning.

Like holding this man tonight, I've had to hold my mother, not carry her but hold her. I guess it's called *hug* her. Or help her into a restaurant, hot-faced in shame. Looking around at the other people in the restaurant. Ashamed that my mother alone required two people to do the activities of one.

Furious, underneath of course, for giving me away to her lunatic psychiatrist when I was a little boy. And now paralyzed, needy, she has the nerve to crave?

I don't go to see her because I don't know her body. My

mother in someone else's body. A paralyzed woman's body. Like she traded her own former lifeguard body in for one that was limp and frail and hungry. I resent her because I feel like she did this on purpose, made an impulse decision and now regrets it. Like it was a way of drawing attention, once again, back to her.

Of course this isn't true. Hers simply broke, like a car, and she can never get a new one. A capillary burst in her brain one night while she was sleeping and when she woke up her life as she knew it was gone, like a dream. My mother lives inside a paralyzed woman's body. When I hugged her, visited her, I was doing it to a stranger. I visited a body, like a medium that is a cripple and can fluently channel my dead mother. I feel particularly uncomfortable when I have to use her bathroom because it smells of something other than bleach or Soft Scrub. So does the kitchen. These rooms smell of paralysis. They smell of the handicapped.

My mother, who seemed to feel it was entirely okay to let a pedophile fuck me up the ass for three years when I was a teenager, this woman may not expect anything from me. She has not earned the right to expect me to change one lightbulb in her apartment. She gave me away when I was twelve, and she does not get to have me back.

But I did help the wheelchair man. I carried him all the way up to his apartment, four flights. He was light and silent like a bag of laundry. I delivered him right to the door. I had to reach into his pocket for the keys. It felt obscene, an invasion, my fingers against the heat of his dead leg. Yet he didn't seem uncomfortable in the least. As if he were accustomed to invasions. Welcomed them maybe, or at least tolerated them. As I deftly slid each key through my fingers, hunting for what looked like an apartment key, he directed, "Not that one, not that one, the brass one, the round one," until I had found the correct key. As I slid the key into the lock, I braced myself for what his apartment must be like. I expected a horrid, putrid, paralyzed smell to escape from the room like a big, bounding dog.

I opened the door and the apartment was stunning. It was large, artful and spotless. A Frank Gehry chair, beside a le Corbusier sofa. Bookshelves floor to ceiling, packed. Photographs on the wall, black frames and white mats. Photographs of him, before. Handsome, with friends, beachside. A computer and a fax and a glorious fireplace filled not with logs but with lilacs.

He asked me to take the change out of his pockets and put it on the counter. "No, not that counter, the other one, with the rest." I set the change down, next to some other money. I thought, *I could take his money*. I could steal the small Picasso sketch that was framed and autographed. I could take his life. I could kick him and he would be defenseless. He lives on faith. Good faith. He thanked me and I smiled, told him it was nothing.

I was uncomfortable in my clothes all the way home, as if something of him wore off on me. I was afraid to touch my face, afraid of the transfer of molecules. I was thinking of a little girl I knew growing up, Annie, how she was playing in the yard and got dog shit in her left eye when she was four and caught a parasite that blinded her in that eye. I felt like some of his vulnerability, some of his need, some of his dependence, had attached itself to me.

He and my mother are like clams without shells. Clams and snails and lobsters without their shells. Vulnerable and exposed.

I e-mail my mother every day. She feels cut off if we don't e-mail. Tonight, when there is no message, I feel oddly uncomfortable, disconnected. I wonder why she didn't write. But I don't wonder too deeply. I don't consider that she might have fallen. Or had a seizure. Or another stroke like the one that took away her left side. I don't think of her being hungry. Or depressed. I think of her as illuminated words on my computer screen, sometimes misspelled, but always there. Able to file away in her own little folder. And it's sequential, our relationship. It's never one on one. It's one after the other. Time and date stamped. I'm removed from her not just by miles and cities, not just by computer, but also by time. I call fairly often, but I don't send her any money even though a little of mine would be huge for her.

Is this punishment?

It just feels too difficult to find the stamp, make out the check and mail it off. Like when you have a dream where you're trying to run underwater. I'm not committed to my mother. I treat her with the same regularity I feel she treated me.

Sometimes I fantasize about having a mother who wears a pleated navy skirt, crisp white shirt and a pale blue sweater draped casually across her shoulders. Her tan leather bag doesn't rattle with prescription bottles when she tosses it on the seat of the car. And this version of my mother can be made happy with something from the Macy's catalogue instead of the Physician's Desk Reference. She would have a shoulder-length bob.

"Would you mind helping me with these bottles?" she would ask. My mother would have been to a farmer's market in Hadley. She would take long baths in goat milk. "I just love what it does for my skin."

When I hand her my report card, all A-'s, she would say, "You know, it might not seem like much, but that extra effort, that extra ten percent, could mean the difference between Princeton and Bennington." Then she would smile at me in a way that suggested a private in-joke. "Bennington, darling. Think about it. Lesbians."

Even in my fantasy, I would hate my mother sometimes. I would think she was petty and materialistic. I would complain. "You've already had your eyes done once."

And she would reply, "No. That's not accurate. They weren't done correctly, so this counts as the first time."

My mother would date men who own franchises.

"But you've always loved a Blimpie," she would say, trying to convince me.

"He's a pig, mom. He scratches his butt and then smells his fingers. I've seen him do it. Plus, his fingers are hairy."

She would go on monthly pilgrimages to New York City where she would return loaded with bags from all the shops on Fifth Avenue. I would, from a distance, come to view Manhattan as a mall without a roof. I would not romanticize it. I would make a mental note to avoid it forever.

So when I turned eighteen, I would apply to USC. My mother would be aghast. "Good God, you can't be serious. The University of Southern California? Have you been smoking pot? What can you be thinking? What are you going to major in, fast food preparation technologies? Surfing?"

I would say, "No, mother. Entomology."

She would hate that I used this word because she wouldn't know what it meant and would feel I was only using it to be showy (I would be a bookworm). "Well, if you want to be a doctor, I don't know why you wouldn't stay out East."

"Entomology is bugs, mom. It's the study of insects."

She would freeze, nail polish brush midair. "What?"

I would look at her. Then I would shrug. "What?"

"Bugs?"

"Yeah. Entomology. Bugs."

She would replace the brush into the bottle and screw it tightly. She would blow on her nails and her eyes would meet mine. "How can I phrase this so I don't hurt your feelings, damage your youthful enthusiasm? Hmmm. Okay, I've got it. NO."

I would tell her it wasn't her choice, it was mine.

She would remind me it was her money.

I would say I'd get my own money.

She would ask how.

I'd say from getting a job and saving.

She'd say that I must be out of my mind and that she was going to take me to a therapist. She'd say, "If you don't agree to see a therapist, I'll cut you off without a dime."

I would not agree. I would storm out of the house, furious.

We wouldn't speak for a week.

And in the end, I would go to Princeton. Because in so many ways, my mother would have been right. And it would make her so much happier, could make life so much better if I just agreed. So I would agree. And because the future of bugs isn't exactly promising, I would agree to at least try prelegal studies.

She would buy me a Rolex.

I would be wearing it on the first day of school.

Of course, I probably would have turned out to be an alcoholic lawyer who hated my mother for overprotecting me, so I guess it all averages out in the end.

CRACK(S)

Are you okay?" Hayden asks from the couch, his doggie bed.

"What?"

"I said, are you okay?"

"Oh, yeah. I'm fine. Why, do I seem weird?"

"Because you don't look well at all."

I close my notebook, clip my pen to the cover. It's true, I am very unwell. "Can we talk?" I ask. "I think I need to talk."

"Of course," he says, dog-earing the page and closing his book. "What is it?" He's concerned. "Is it Pighead?"

"No," I say. Now that I've asked if we can talk, I don't want to talk. "Maybe it's just my Sunday night dread. I hate Sundays, I don't want to go to work tomorrow."

Hayden waits for the truth.

"I need a cigarette," I say, getting out of bed and going over to the kitchen counter for a Marlboro Light.

"I'll have one too," Hayden says, and he also gets up, goes to the pile on top of his suitcase and takes a Silk Cut from the pack. Our lighters go off at about the same time. Two addicts, in sync. Exactly like college girls who get their periods at the same time.

"It's Foster," I say.

"Oh, God. You didn't sleep with him?"

I exhale, blow smoke into the room. "No, but it was close."

"When?"

"Last Thursday, before Group. I went over to his apartment to pick him up." I feel guilty, confessing.

"You know, it's not that I think this Foster is a bad person or anything," Hayden begins. "But I do think it's risky for you to become involved with anybody so soon." He's sitting on the couch. I'm sitting across from him at the desk.

"I don't know what it is. I'm fucked up."

Hayden goes to the stove and lights the flame under the kettle. He takes two mugs from the cupboard and puts a tea bag in each.

"Why am I so needy?" I ask. "What's the matter with me?"

Hayden turns to me. "It's not bad to be needy. It's not bad to need love."

"I think I love him."

"Maybe you do."

"But I'm not sure if I love him, or if I'm obsessed with him."

"Have you talked to Wendy about this?"

I look at him. "What? Are you kidding? I'd get thrown out of Group if they knew."

"I think you should talk to her. I think you should be honest with her. You'll feel better."

I feel so frustrated and angry. Angry at Hayden for suggesting I talk to Wendy. Angry at myself for being in this position in the first place. Angry at Pighead for scaring the shit out of me with his fucking hiccups.

I begin pacing back and forth, like a zoo animal. "Nothing is enough, nothing is *ever* enough. It's like there's this pit inside of me that can't be filled, no matter what. I'm defective."

"You're not defective. You're an alcoholic," he says, as if this is neatly explains everything. Which, of course, it does.

I go over to the bed, lie down. "I just need to sleep. I'm tired is all."

Hayden pours the hot water into the mugs, brings one over to me. "Tea improves everything. Tea is what you're missing in your life."

As I lie there, I think about how if I don't talk to Foster on the phone at least once a day, I start to feel panicky. Last night on the phone, he told me he wishes he'd never tried crack in the first place. "It's a feeling you just don't want to have." He also said he feels he leads a useless life. "I should be doing something, like you."

"I hate what I do," I told him.

"Yeah, but you're good at it and you make a lot of money."

"You have a lot of money," I reminded him. "Far more than I'll ever have."

"I know, but I didn't do anything to get it except be born. Besides, what do I do with it? Do I have a beautiful apartment? Take weekend trips to Paris? No. It sits tied up in mutual funds and I spend the dividend checks on cocaine and expensive underwear."

"What do you mean, you spend it on cocaine? You're not using, are you?"

A slight pause. Then a correction. "No, I mean, that's what I *used* to spend it on. Now it's just expensive underwear."

I think of his inexpensive white Hanes boxers but let it slide. "Foster, do you think this is weird between us?"

"Well, of course. That's why I like it."

"No, I mean, this in-between thing of ours. It's like all the hugging and affection and everything, but we don't have sex."

"You will let me know the moment you'd like to change that fact, I trust." I imagine his crooked smile.

"No, I mean I have mixed feelings."

"Auggie, look. I know we're not supposed to see each other. I know it's this big no-no, but I like being with you, I *love* being with you. More than anybody else I have ever known. And that's the truth, it is."

"No major life changes for at least a year."

As I lie on the bed I think that Foster is bar, bartender, cocktail, cocktail napkin, lime wedge, salt, tip and two Xanax all in one.

I'm worried that all of the inner mess that was channeled into alcoholism is now channeled into other disturbing rivers. That I've drained the lake to flood the city.

Somebody from Group relapsed last week. His name is Bill and he's in his late fifties or early sixties. He's been with his boyfriend for over thirty years, moving out of his parents' house into his lover's when he was in his twenties. He's a solemn man who never smiles, not once. He struggles. His hair is silver and I expect it has been since he was thirteen. He's a retired investment banker like Pighead and reminds me of Pighead. There's something about how he tries so hard to understand things. And the way in which he takes his life as a series of steps. Like he is following a formula or directions.

He had been named executor of a will a few months ago and was in the house this week and there was scotch in the kitchen, in the living room. He said he avoided the bottles, knowing they were there. And I thought how I wouldn't avoid the bottles. I would hold them up to the light and think about how something so beautiful can take so much from a person. I'd want to hold the gun that nearly killed me. But I guess he avoided the bottles, the rooms they were in. And then he got into an argument with a woman, I'm unclear who. And he drank. And then he went home and his lover smelled alcohol on his breath. He said they had a quiet night. And I could imagine it. He said they ate dinner together. And I could hear the knives scraping against the plates. I could hear water glasses being set down on the table. Both of them sitting there, steeping in failure. And I was thinking how horrible that must feel. How doomed I would feel if it had been me sitting there telling people that I relapsed. And would somebody say, "I saw it coming, I have to say"? Or would it be a surprise? It would be a surprise to me.

Thirty years with the same man.

My nasty German beer client wants an advertising campaign based on German heritage. "Ve vant to be ze authentic Cherman beer. Ve vant to own Cherman heritage." I swear I hear his heels click together beneath the conference room table.

"German heritage?" I repeat, making sure I hear him correctly, that I'm not presently attending an off-off-Broadway satire. His dark brown, almost black eyes become smaller as he squints at me, his eyebrows pinching together into one.

I think, *They would have gassed you in a heartbeat. Black hair, black eyes. You look like a Gypsy. You could even pass for a Jew.*

"Do you not understand vat I have just said? I believe my English is not so bad." He retrieves a small steel nail clipper from his jacket pocket and begins to clip his nails over the table. Half moons scatter everywhere.

"No, no, I heard you . . . I just wanted to make sure, you know, I understand what you want . . ." I say, trying to be diplomatic, professional, ". . . without getting into all the Nazi stuff."

His face goes red instantly, a mood ring dropped in boiling oil. He slams the clipper down on the table. He glares at me with pure hatred. I can feel him picturing me hanging by parachute straps in a German high-altitude simulation booth, sans the air-mask. "I am so sick and tired of you Americans associating modern Germany vith . . ." He pulls out his mental German-to-English dictionary. ". . . zat unfortunate time in our past. That vas many years ago. *I* had nothing to do with that, *modern Germany* had nothing to do vith zaat. It just happened; bad things happen in war times."

Barnes, the redheaded account guy, Tod, the junior media planner, Greer and I all exchange a look. Our creative director, Elenor, was fortunate enough to have a maxi-pad meeting in Cincinnati. Asshole Rick blew off the meeting to go to a movie.

"Ve haf been vith so many agencies over ze years; ve have tested campaigns, changed agencies, and vatched our sales decline. All ve vant is a *solution*," he nearly spits. Both of his fists rest on the table before him.

I want to say, *You fucking Germans and your* solutions. Instead, I say, "Okay." Later in my office, I sit at my computer. German heritage. Hmmm. I make a list of all things German:

cuckoo clocks
lederhosen
leather underwear
Doberman pinschers
graph paper
white lab coats
expensive, precision-engineered automobiles
showers
ovens
uniforms
peculiar facial hair
assorted schnitzels
sauerkraut
twins
sunlamps for reviving unconscious, cold-water survival
    experiment subjects
techno music
pharmaceuticals
SS officers

involuntary train rides
razor wire
rocket scientists
dentists

I look at my list and realize I'm in trouble with this German heritage thing. This is not, as they say, a rich area. I lean back and exhale, rubbing my eyes. When I open them, I notice the bottle. It's small, the kind they serve on airplanes. A small green bottle of gin, tucked between two books on the shelf.

Rick.

It's got to be Rick. And suddenly, I'm anxious. I walk over to the bookshelf and take the bottle down. I hold it in my palm. I look for more, but it's just this one. And the thought occurs to me that I could uncap it and drink it right down. And that's exactly what I would like to do. Because I'm sick of thinking of German beer ads and I'm sick of Rick's weirdness. I take a deep breath and toss the bottle into the trash.

I just bought black leather pants and a midnight-blue velvet shirt to wear at some future, unknown event. I didn't try anything on in the stores, I took them, red-faced, to the counter and paid with cash. Then I came home and put them on, the shirt unbuttoned nearly to my waist, the collar back off my neck. I looked like Sex. I looked like something that might have a scent strip attached to it that you can peel open and rub on your wrist. I took the clothes off and folded them and put them on the top shelf of the closet, the one that I never open by the front door.

I went to a movie with Foster and while I was sitting there in the dark looking at the screen I thought, "I have black leather pants and a midnight-blue velvet shirt in my closet." This fact could never be known by looking at me. You might think I own flannel shirts from Eddie Bauer, worn Timberland boots, Nikes caked with mud, T-shirts with editorial-house logos on them. You might even think I own an Armani suit. But you would never guess the truth. The recent truth.

Then last night, I saw a giant rawhide bone at a pet store. A novelty bone. Much too large for any real dog. I bought it and went over to Pighead's to give Virgil his new bone. He was euphoric, had no idea where to begin chewing first. Pighead called me this morning and said, "So now, it's the bone he runs to, not me or his water. The bone."

And it occurs to me: if I wore the black leather pants and the midnight-blue velvet shirt, and carried Virgil's new giant dog bone, I could get into any club in Manhattan.

It's Saturday, noon, and I've been chain-smoking and drinking coffee alcoholically since seven this morning. I've had two pots. I feel electrified, like I've been blow-drying my hair in the bathtub. I'm completely manic—singing along loudly to the radio, but to different songs than they're playing. I'm like somebody who has just decided to stop taking important psychoactive medication. I'm so crazy this morning that Hayden couldn't stand being around me and went out for a walk.

I go downstairs to buy green apples. I'm picking them up and they're covered with black grit. The little Indian man who guards the fruits and flowers outside grins and says almost toothlessly, "Is dirt . . . from the cars . . ." and he points to the street. I buy Jolly Ranchers instead.

I want to feel calm and at ease. Like someone who lives in Half Moon Bay, California, and makes hummus from scratch. Instead, I feel like I'm a contestant on some awful supermarket game show where I've got sixty seconds to hurl my shopping cart down the aisles, piling it with as much as possible before the buzzer goes off.

"Fill it with expensive meats!" the studio audience is screaming at me. "*Chutneys!!*" they shriek. "No, stay away from the bathroom tissue!"

My eight A.M. call to Pighead woke him.

"Get up! Do something with me!" I was manic.

He said no, told me to go back to sleep and then he hung up on me.

Then I called Jim, but he didn't answer. No doubt he's in bed with Astrid, screening his calls: no single people or recovering alcoholics.

Maybe I should get a puppy. I would love to have a dog, except that alcoholics aren't allowed. *No major changes for your first year.*

But now that I have all this free time, drinking time, I need something constructive to do with it. Like housebreaking. I always had dogs when I was a kid, but since I've been in New York and drinking, I never had time. You can't just have a dog, then tie it to a parking meter outside Odeon every night while you're inside getting hammered, slyly watching Cindy Crawford pick at a plate of mixed greens.

I hate having feelings. Why does sobriety have to come with feelings? One minute I feel excited, the next I feel terrified. One minute I feel free and the next I feel doomed. I think about lobotomies. Are they are like nose jobs, can you just go and have one? Or do you need a doctor's recommendation?

And lately, I get annoyed with AA, because even though I've been going every day, I haven't really made any close friends. Or actually, any friends. It seems much easier to make friends in bars. I have to keep reminding myself that these AA people are exactly like bar people—they *are* bar people—except their bars have all been shut down. And I have to admit, this makes them less interesting to me.

I need a hobby. Sober people have hobbies. But my hobby can't involve a major lifestyle change. Something like Feed the Children. I could collect letters from malnourished orphans.

The bloated face of Sally Struthers filled my television screen recently. Her chin was trembling and she looked to be in physical pain, as if wincing from a sharp punch. But, strangely, she also looked hungry. Because I watch television with the sound off, I had to hunt for the remote to hear what she was saying. That's when I heard her begging for me, personally, to send her cash so that she could Feed the Children. Cut to little Anna, a shriveled Indian girl with jewel eyes. Back to Sally, this time walking. Turning sideways so that she could fit through the alley between two mud-cake homes.

Well, somehow I felt that if I sent Sally a donation, she would open the envelope herself and squeeze the cash into the hip pocket of her elastic-waist jeans. She would then treat herself at Pizza Hut, using my envelope to dab pepperoni grease from her chin. I imagined her maybe having garlic cheese bread on the side and a salad of iceberg lettuce topped with blue-cheese dressing, Bacos and croutons. She would do her eating alone, eyes never leaving the table. Her chin would tremble as she chewed and chewed and swallowed hard, against the threat of tears. After leaving her tray on the table for someone else to clean up, she would moan as she climbed into her 1981 Cadillac Fleetwood. It would be an effort to close the door. She would then place both hands at the top of the wheel, and pressing her forehead against the backs of her hands, begin sobbing right there in the parking lot. Then, blinking back the tears, I see her starting the car, swiping her plump little pinkie beneath both eyes and driving away. Maybe she drives down La Cienega or Pico, hunting for a Taco Bell drive-through window. Paper sack in hand, she enters her apartment, which I picture to be on the second floor of an anonymous motel-style apartment building in West Hollywood. Here, she plays videotapes of *All in the Family*. The ratty curtains are drawn and she's eating a Burrito Supreme while her lips move along with the dialogue on the show. Shredded cheese falls out of the bottom of the burrito onto her bosom.

Then I imagine her padding barefoot into the kitchen, leaving the Taco Bell wrappings on the sofa, and opening the fridge just to look. I imagine her grunting as she squats down in front of it. She opens the salad crisper drawer and finds two slices of Oscar Meyer olive loaf, drying out and curling at the edges, in the yellow, plastic package. I see her rolling them up together into a tube and placing them between her lips like a cigar, nibbling her way to the end while her eyes scan for more, more, more of something.

"I'm very proud of you," Pighead says as he pours dog food into Virgil's bowl. "You've really turned your life around in terms of this not–drinking thing."

I lean against his granite kitchen counter, and my elbow knocks over a few of his prescription pill bottles. A couple of them roll onto the floor. "Shit."

"It's all right," he says. He places them back in order, then bends over and picks up the ones that rolled in front of the stove. He checks their labels and adds them to the others, setting them in their proper places.

And the pills do have a precise order on his countertop. There is almost a military strictness to their arrangement. Pighead, the millionaire banker at thirty, is incredibly gifted at removing variables.

There are pills for the morning, for the afternoon, before bed. Dozens of pills. So many that nobody should have to take them alone. I should know each pill. I should help him more. And yet I'm paralyzed.

"I'm sorry," I tell him, meaning it.

"For what?" he says, leaning against the counter across from me.

"I'm just sorry."

"Augusten," he says, moving to my side. "I love you very much. And I will always love you. And not a day doesn't go by that I don't beat myself up for not realizing how much I love you, sooner. Back when you were in love with me."

"But Pighead, I—"

"It's okay. I understand why you had to move on. And I know you love me. As a friend. And I'm grateful for that."

I might cry, but I don't. "How come I'm not a better friend? Why do I always run away from you?"

"Because you're afraid of losing me."

I start to say something. I get out this much, "But—"

He hiccups convulsively. "Shit," he says, frustrated. "I just wish I knew what the hell is causing them."

"Can't they just chop out your hiccupper?" I ask.

"They can't find it," he says.

Then he looks at me like, *you fuckhead*. And I look at him back like, *you Pighead*.

After work today, I go to Sophia, my usual Greek barber at Astor Place, and she says, "Same thing?" And I say, yeah. *Same thing* being short on the sides, flat on top, natural in the back. And then she does something she's never done before. She starts buzzing the clippers over my ears, and way, *way* down my neck. And I'm thinking, *This is really bad. It's starting. The hair-where-you-don't-want-it stuff*. And when she is done with the hair on top, my head looks shiny, like a baby crowning. My bald head saying *here I come* through the ever-thinning hairs on top. If I had thick hair, I would probably just buzz it off like the rest of the fags. And I wouldn't care, because then it would be by choice.

At the barbershop while I was waiting, I read a quote by Michael Kors in *Vogue*. "I love Calvin Klein's reissue of his original jeans, but my feeling is, if you wore them the first time around, you have no business wearing them now."

Before reading this article, I bought two pairs. I have the bag with me.

I leave Astor Place and wish I had some cocaine.

• • •

We're in a cemetery in Mystic, Connecticut. Foster rented a car and picked me up. We stopped for take-out fish and chips at a shabby place called the Clam Shack and now we're sprawled on the grass, eating the crispy, greasy things out of large cardboard bowls. Foster is wearing khakis, loafers without socks and a white T-shirt. Over this he has a green pinstriped Brooks Brothers button-down, opened. The fish and chips are making me sick, so I set them aside. Foster is leaning back, propped up on one elbow. He looks exactly like a Julia Roberts co-star.

I lay my head on his thigh.

"I've missed you," he says.

I don't say anything. I don't want him to know how much I've missed him, too.

"I know we talk on the phone all the time, but I don't see you enough. I want to see more of you. I want to see you every day."

I roll over on my side, still using his thigh as a pillow. There's a swan on the lake in front of us. I point at it. "We should catch it and cook it."

Foster laughs. "Let's catch it and put it on a leash and give it to that friend of yours, Hayden." He becomes animated. "Couldn't you just see little Hayden walking that big ol' swan around the streets of Manhattan? He could name it Addiction. It could sit on his lap in AA meetings and bleat away. From what you've told me about him, I think Hayden would love a little pet."

I smile into his leg. "Foster, what is it you like about me?" I stare at the blades of grass before me, afraid to know the answer. Afraid because I want to know the answer.

"What I like about you is that I've never met anybody like you in my life. You've got depth and you're funny and you have a sweet, good soul." A breeze from the water passes over us. "And I admire your strength."

"I don't have any strength," I inform his leg.

He puts his hand on my head and his touch is warm and soft, his fingers intelligent. "Oh yes, you do. You're a survivor. You have strength in your sobriety, and making it through all you've made it through." His hand moves to my stomach. He slides it under my shirt and rests it there. "And you're the handsomest man I've ever seen in my life."

What's scary is his utter conviction. "That is such a lie, Foster."

"No, it's not."

I can tell by his voice that he means what he says. This makes me want to pay his rent for life.

"So what do you like about me?" he asks.

"Oh, lots of things. I don't know. I feel comfortable with you. You're very easy to be around. You're warm and giving and kind and smart. You make me laugh. You make me sandwiches."

"And I have furry arms."

"That too."

"You know, Auggie, all my life, people have liked me for my looks. It's always the same thing: sex, sex, sex. One of the things about you, is that you're not like that. You don't just dive into sex."

"I can't. I signed a piece of paper saying I wouldn't." I imagine the document I signed when I joined Group being faxed to my office, the words BECAME INVOLVED written in red marker at the top. I imagine Elenor waving the document in my face. "You fucked somebody in your group therapy?" And she fires me.

He rubs his hand around on my stomach. "There is no piece of paper that would stop you from doing what you wanted. I know that much about you."

I feel flattered that he presumes to know anything about me at all. It makes me think maybe someday, he would know what book I would like, what foods I would hate, what movie I would go see. It makes me imagine things happening at a future point in time that involve a dual credit application.

"I just know you're not with me because of how I look. You're interested in the *me* part of me. I can feel that," he says.

"No, I'm not. It's only because of your looks."

He takes his hand out from under my shirt, places it on my forehead. "Thanks, Augusten, I was hoping you'd say that."

We drive on to Providence, Rhode Island. Foster still has this swan thing in his head and is driving very slowly down residential streets, making me check people's lawns for a plastic swan or swanlike bird that he can steal. "All we have to do," he says, "is jump out real quick, take the swan and stick it in the trunk."

We don't see any swans, so Foster drives to the coast. It's late in the afternoon, past four, the beach is empty. "Let's take a quick nap," he says. "Get caught up on our sitting around."

He parks along the side of the road. We make our way down, over the bluff. How long has it been since I've seen sea grass? The ocean? How long has it been since I've seen the ocean sober? I have a sudden longing for a Cape Codder.

At first, the water is so cold that I can't even stick my toes in it. My mother and I have taken a holiday at the Bay of Fundy in Nova Scotia. She's on the empty beach writing in a notebook beneath the overcast sky, and I am trying to make it ankle-deep into the water. I move in gradually, with much foot-stomping. And eventually, I am able to swim in the frigid water. I swim in circles, dog-paddle. I lose all sense of time and space. The icy water seems to hypnotize me.

"Augusten, come out of that water!" my mother yells from the shore. I paddle back toward her.

"Good God," she says, "you're blue." She checks her watch. "Jesus. You were in there for over an hour."

I feel so happy, loose and warm, like I could fall asleep right there, standing up, dripping onto my mother's fresh page. I never lost time like that before. I never lost time like that again.

The shore is rocky, littered with pieces of smooth driftwood. The sand is not fine and soft, but coarse and blended with broken shells. Foster rolls the cuffs of his pants midway up his calves. He slips off his loafers, carries them with two fingers hooked inside the heels.

I take off my sneakers, then my socks. I ball the socks up into one of the shoes, and roll up the legs of my jeans. I head for the shoreline.

Foster drops his shoes next to mine and follows me. I step onto the wet sand, feel the cold water being sucked away from beneath my toes. A wave rolls in, splashing all the way to my knees. I inhale deeply, close my eyes.

From behind, he wraps his arms around my body. His legs and chest are pressed up against me and I can feel his erection pricking up against my butt. Yet there's something oddly unsexual about this embrace. It's sensual, I guess. That's the difference. The sensation of looking out and seeing nothing but water and the distant horizon, coupled with feeling so close to him, makes me feel like I have taken a hit of NyQuil. I lean my head back against his shoulder. He kisses my neck. Runs his fingers across the stubble on my cheek. I turn around. And I can see it right there on his face.

He's in love with me.

His lips taste like sea salt. In the back of my mind I hear myself whisper, *Well, I guess one glass of wine couldn't hurt.*

There's no traffic on the way home. The sunroof is open and I have my head in Foster's lap, looking up at the sky. It's so clear and black, with tiny pricks of white everywhere. You don't see stars in the city. It's easy to forget they even exist. The last time I saw stars was in rehab. These look very different from the rehab stars. And immediately, I know why. Stars should not be seen alone. That's why there are so many. Two people should stand together and look at them. One person alone will surely miss the good ones.

Foster's right hand never leaves my chest. He drives the whole four hours with his left arm.

I don't think we say a single word the entire way.

It's after one A.M. when I finally reach the door to my apartment. I try to sneak in quietly, so I don't wake Hayden. But as soon as I close the door, the light next to the sofa goes on. Hayden's blinking at me, fresh from sleep. He raises himself to his elbows. "God, I was just having the most awful dream about you," he says. "I dreamt that you were being carried away on a stretcher."

All week, I am at the office until after eight. I cancelled my group therapy and have totally blown off AA meetings. To be honest, the meetings are just not doing much for me. I mean, they're depressing. Why talk about not drinking all the time? Why not just *not drink?* Besides, my life is too stressful now to deal with AA. And anyway, I'm fine. I'm going crazy, yeah. But in terms of the not-drinking thing, I'm fine. Fine, fine, fine.

And it's not just my life that's crazy. Greer is on the verge of a nervous breakdown. "God, I should have been a gynecologist," she keeps saying, over and over like a crazy person. Sometimes, I actually think Greer is the perfect candidate for complete mental collapse. On Tuesday, I caught her looking into her compact mirror, with both hands pressed against the sides of her head.

"What are you doing, Greer?" I asked.

She didn't look up, just kind of cocked her head to the side and continued to stare at her reflection in the mirror as she said, "Wouldn't it be strange if you had no ears?"

Yesterday, we presented our second round of beer ideas to Elenor.

"Whatcha got for me, guys?" she asked as we stood at her doorway.

Greer crossed her legs at the ankles, leaned against the door. "Ready to see some more beer work?"

Elenor mashed her cigarette out in her overflowing ashtray. "Yeah, yeah, sure. Come on in. Sit." She motioned us over to her couch.

I sat on one end of the sofa, Greer on the other. Then Greer looked at the space between us, rolled her eyes and scooted closer to me. She rested the storyboards facedown on her legs.

Elenor tapped at her Mac. "Hold on a second there, guys. Just finishing up."

Greer picked a framed picture up off the glass coffee table. "Is this your daughter?" she asked.

Elenor answered without taking her eyes off her computer. "That's my Heather."

"She's adorable. I didn't know you had two children."

"I don't," Elenor said.

Greer set the picture back down. "I could have sworn that you just had her, like a few months ago."

Elenor stood and came over to the chair in front of us. "Three and a half years ago," she said, sitting.

"I cannot believe it's been that long." Greer turned to me. "What happened to the past three years?"

"UPS, Burger King, Credit Suisse . . ." I said.

Elenor laughed. "Yup. That's advertising. All blends together after a while."

Greer sat motionless, somewhat stunned by this time-compression event.

Elenor reached for her phone. "I'm just gonna pull Rick in here," she said, holding the phone to her ear. A moment later she said, "Get your ass in here, I'm about to look at Wirksam with Greer and Augusten." She hung up.

Great. The asshole has to be here too.

"Hi, Greer," he said as he entered the room.

"Hmmmmm," Greer said back coldly. Greer is the only other person who sees through Rick's Nice Mormon act to the black, charred soul underneath.

He smiled at me and took the seat next to Elenor, crossing his legs.

"How are you feeling, Augusten?" he asked.

I smiled and said, "I'm great, Rick. Thank you so much for asking."

He closed his eyes briefly and smiled tightly. "You're welcome," he said, except no words came out. He just sort of mouthed the words.

"Anyway," Elenor said. "Let's see some work."

We took Elenor through the storyboards. "This campaign would take place in real bars in modern Berlin," Greer began.

"Uh-oh, do I smell a travel bug in this room?" Rick said in his annoying, high-pitched perky voice.

Greer ignored him and continued. "And the bars would be filled with really hip, eccentric characters. Dwarfs, albino waitresses, cross-dressers."

Before we were able to even take them through the whole storyboard, Elenor interrupted. "I don't want to get into the whole weird Germany thing. I can just tell you they're not gonna go for that. I mean, it's totally true, the Germans are all perverted, but they'll never go for it. Sorry."

I looked at Greer. "Let's show her the next one."

Greer pulled the next campaign out. "Okay, no weird Germany. How about playing off all the other German imports. Like Claudia Schiffer, BMWs, Albert Einstein."

"That could be cool," Elenor said, nodding.

As Greer led her through the visuals, I read the copy out loud.

A look of concern spread across Elenor's face. "It's too much like Apple. Got anything else?"

We presented our German perfectionist campaign, which made both Elenor and Rick think of concentration camps.

"What else?" Elenor asked, lighting a cigarette and then chewing on her lip while she exhaled through her nose.

Greer coughed. "We were looking into this direction of old

German stereotypes, like milk maidens and lederhosen. Making them new and hip."

"Sort of a 'Germany isn't what you think' kind of thing," I said.

"I like that concept," Rick said as I held up the picture of the blonde with double braids.

I studied his annoying face, the ponytail years out of style, the Diesel jeans that no forty-four-year-old should be wearing. He struck me as sad, if not pathetic. I silently willed him under a bus, soon.

"What?" he said pleasantly, catching me staring at him.

"Nothing."

"Listen guys," Elenor began, "I don't think we're there yet. Keep working. We really want to push the envelope on this one. Think outside the box. Think Nike."

Greer forced her mouth into a smile. "Okay. We'll keep going."

"I agree," Rick said. "Keep going. But I'd stay away from anything that's gonna cause problems." He clasped his hands in his lap. "And stay away from the whole *New Germany* thing, that's just not a safe space to be thinking in."

Elenor glanced at Rick, puzzled. As if to say, *What New Germany thing?*

I looked at Greer. We hadn't presented our New Germany campaign. We decided between us that it was wrong. The New Germany campaign existed in only two places: in our heads, and in my backpack in the form of loose sketches.

"Rick," I said, "how do you know about the New Germany campaign?"

He sat a little straighter and blinked. "You just presented it."

"No we didn't," Greer said quickly.

Rick looked at Elenor who was looking at Rick, waiting for his answer. "What do you mean?" he said.

"How did you know we did a New Germany campaign?" I

said. I folded my arms across my chest. My heart was pounding, I was furious.

"Well, I just, you know, I just mean *in general*," he said clumsily.

"You fucking asshole," I said. "You went through my god-damn backpack. You went into my office and you looked at our work."

"Hold on there a minute, Augusten," Elenor said.

I turned to her sharply. "He's been rooting around in my office. He's been leaving nasty notes and moving my stuff around. He stuck a bottle of booze on the bookcase."

"Oh, that's absurd," Rick said. "Augusten, you're tense. You're really being paranoid. I know you've gone through a difficult time, but no one is out to get you. Really."

Greer glared at him and he seemed to shrink into the sofa.

"You're pathetic," I spat. "I see through you, you know. You don't fool me at all."

Elenor said, "Okay, let's just move on." She rose from her chair. "I can't sit here all day and listen to who took whose crayons. We've got a lot of work to do."

Greer and I moved to the door. "When do you want to see another round?" I asked.

"Oh, I don't know. Tomorrow morning?"

I checked my watch: it was almost six.

In the elevator, Greer stabbed the lobby button. "I hate those two," she spat. "I can't believe we have to work all night again. They are so full of shit. Nike! They don't want anything cool. They want some awful jingle."

"I wish Rick would get gang-raped by a bunch of Muslim garbage collectors," I said, fuming. Now I knew for sure. The magazine ads, the bottle and now this.

The doors opened and Greer stormed through the lobby. We walked to the coffee shop next door and ordered two large coffees. In the elevator on the way back up to our office, Greer turned to me. "God, her ugly little daughter must be horribly spoiled and obnoxious."

"I can just imagine," I said. "And ad people are so full of shit. 'Push the envelope.' It's like, they think something is cool and edgy if they've only seen it a couple of times before."

"Exactly. I'd like to push the envelope right up her cunt," Greer hissed.

After work one night, I call Foster. I either have to see him every day or talk to him on the phone. It's come to that.

"C'mon over," he says.

When I get to his apartment, I'm shocked by how awful he looks; ragged and red-eyed. He hasn't shaved for days. "What's the matter with you?" I ask him.

He walks over the sofa, sits. "I just haven't felt good this week."

He's smoking crack, I think. "Are you using?" I ask.

"No," he says.

Foster has two clocks in his living room. One on the fire-place mantel and another on the table next to the sofa. Both clocks are set incorrectly. And he knows exactly *how* incorrectly. The clock on the mantle is one hour and four minutes slow. The one on the table is five minutes fast. So when you ask him the time, his eyes dart back and forth between the two clocks while he does the math in his head. Although he could have not one but *two* clocks that are each set to exactly the correct time, this does not happen. It would be too easy. Better to struggle. Better to *work* for the time and sometimes get the math wrong and arrive an hour late.

I ask him if I missed anything interesting in Group this week. "Nah, nothing much," he says. Something is off with him. Or maybe it's me. Maybe he doesn't like me anymore. I test the theory by leaning back against him.

He folds me into his arms. "Ahhh, that's exactly what I needed," he drawls. "I missed you so much, more than you can know. I hate your work, Auggie."

I figure, as long as there aren't any scented candles burning, this can't be considered *romantic,* and thus in violation of the "no romantic involvement" clause I signed.

He reaches over for a book on the coffee table. "Here, let me read you a little Dorothy Parker. That'll cheer us up." He gives one of his utterly comforting Southern laughs. His laugh is made of porch swings and lemonade. He begins reading, and I close my eyes. I realize I have not been read to since I was little kid. My mother used to read to me all the time. As he reads, he kind of wraps those thick legs of his around mine. I picture my therapist Wendy asking me, "So what do you and Foster do?" And me replying, "Oh, we talk on the phone, hang out."

What are the odds of me finding another movie-star handsome, literate, sweet, loyal, masculine, independently wealthy and single guy who seems to be crazy about me? Crack is only five letters, I remind myself.

Last week after my road trip with Foster, Hayden asked if we'd slept together yet.

"No, we haven't," I said, the truth.

"Just be careful," he said. "Just know what you're getting yourself into."

"What do you mean?" I asked.

"I mean, if you're going to sleep with the mobster then fine, sleep with the mobster. But don't pretend that's a Stradivarius he's carrying around inside that violin case."

We haven't slept together. But we've napped.

The weekend goes like this: Hayden paces around the apartment, frantic and edgy, because of an opera he's editing freelance, which he calls "incomprehensible, impossible."

I pace around the apartment wondering why Foster hasn't called me. Why, when I call him, which I have been doing constantly, he doesn't answer. I've left messages, I've spent large chunks of time psychically directing him to make my phone ring. Nothing. Why is it not difficult to imagine him smoking crack in a hotel room somewhere?

Hayden goes to four meetings on Sunday. I go to none.

Out of sheer anxiety and general mental dysfunction, I shave off my chest hair and see a Gus Van Sant movie at the Angelika. I go to the gym twice. I almost have a washboard stomach now. It's a five-pack, not quite a six-pack. I take care of it like I'm taking care of Foster's pet. I consider it his.

By Sunday night Hayden's calmer, having made progress on the score.

And I'm worse. At group on Tuesday, there's no Foster. And the reason there's no Foster is, as Wayne the group leader explains, because "Foster has quit therapy. He called one of our staff on Monday and explained that he's been using for a month and that he's not ready to stop."

My first thought: *Evisceration—swift and complete.* My second thought: *So that wasn't salt I tasted on his lips at the beach. It was crack.*

After Group, I go to the nearest pay phone and call him. I let it ring a couple dozen times. No answer.

"Guess what?" I tell Hayden when I come home, furious. "Foster quit therapy. He's been smoking crack for a month, in secret."

"Je-sus," Hayden says slowly. But I detect something in his voice. Awe. Envy?

I call Foster again; still nothing. I am insane, that's all there is to it. What was I thinking? Falling for a crack addict from my group therapy? A guy who can't even set a clock? A man who, while stroking my hair and telling me everything is perfectly fine, was going out at night and scoring crack?

All of a sudden Hayden says, "I need to go for a walk. I need some air." And before I can ask him what the problem is, he's out the door.

I rummage around for a snack. I choose the wrong thing. There is no worse taste in the mouth than chocolate and cigarettes. Second would be tuna and peppermint. I've combined everything, so I know.

"I'm sorry, Auggie. I'm sorry I let you down."

I'm sitting on Foster's sofa, because I took a cab up to his building and tipped the doorman fifty dollars to let me in. Then I took the elevator up to his apartment and pounded on the door until he answered it, groggily.

"Why?" is all I can think to say.

He says nothing.

I look at him, sprawled back on his sofa. A raging crack addict, group therapy dropout disguised as a Banana Republic ad. His toes wriggle in his socks and my first thought is, *I want to snip them off with hedge trimmers.* Not only does he not deserve to wriggle his toes, he does not deserve to *have* toes. He deserves to have stumps. He cannot be trusted with toes because they enable him to walk and thus seek out the company of crack dealers. Kathy Bates's character completely understood this concept in *Misery*.

"I hate you," I tell him. "I really, really hate you." I lean my head against his chest. "You're bad for me." I am channeling Hayden. What I really feel is, *You are perfect for me.*

He kisses the top of my head and I pull away. "You look horrible, Foster," I tell him. And he does, for him, look horrible. He's fallen rock-bottom to a nine-and-a-half in the looks department. I turn away. It's an effort.

The coffee table is strewn with debris; cigarette butts, dirty glasses, old newspapers, his asthma inhaler. I fantasize about sticking a safety pin through the opening of it and *ppppfffffssssssssst,* letting all the medicine out. So when he reaches for it in the night, it won't be there, like the sobriety he had amassed. It will be gone. And as he wheezes and turns blue, I will point out the irony. "See, Foster, one must never take for granted those things which keep us alive."

"Don't hate me, Auggie," he says, in his best puppy dog voice, which unfortunately is a very good puppy dog voice.

"It's a little too late for that, Foster." Kick the puppy.

"Auggie, answer me honestly. Do you hate me?"

Long, contemplative sigh. "No, I don't *hate* you, Foster." I don't tell him that what I feel is far beyond mere hatred, and well into another state of mind that only a handful of people on the FBI's Most Wanted list ever experience. Those people and perhaps Jim.

"It's so easy for you, Auggie, so easy. You go to rehab and *BAM!* you come back and that's it—you don't drink anymore. You don't even go to meetings anymore. That group therapy just wasn't working for me."

"Well, how could it work, if you were high all the time?" I'm disgusted with him. And me. "Look, you know what? Go ahead and smoke all the crack you want. Hang out with your hustlers or your dealers or whatever it is you do." I stand up to leave. "But *know* exactly what it is you're giving up."

He leaps up off the couch and grabs a hold of my arm. "Auggie, please."

"Please *what*, Foster?"

"Please don't walk out of my life."

I could kill him, I really could. "Give me one good reason why not."

"Because I love you."

Uh huh. "Yeah, but not as much as you love other things. Like crack, for example." I pull my arm away and turn back toward the door. I tell myself, *Just keep walking. Go to the door and turn the knob. Don't look back at him. Don't do it. Go with the flow of mental health.*

"Auggie," he says.

I stop, still facing the door. "What?" I say angrily.

"Would you please turn around and look at me?"

I don't budge.

"Auggie, please?"

I turn around and face him.

"Please don't give up on me."

"What difference does it make if I give up on you? You've already given up on yourself." This seems like the right, dramatic thing to say. I am a movie of the week.

And then something in him *engages*. Some internal machinery. And very slowly, he walks toward me, head slightly down, shining ice-blue eyes looking directly at me. His jeans are rumpled, his T-shirt half untucked. I back away, until I'm up against the door. Inches from my face, he cocks his head slightly. Then he moves his lips so close to mine, they just barely touch and he whispers,

"One

more

chance."

Had I known beforehand that this would be the night I actually slept with him, I'm sure I wouldn't have come in the first place.

WHAT'LL IT BE?

I make it home sometime after midnight. Hayden is lying on the sofa reading Elizabeth Berg. "Well, hello there," he says as I walk in the door.

"Hey," I say, trying to sound casual, hoping he won't ask where I've been.

"I almost relapsed," he says, resting the book on his chest.

"What!?" I shout.

"You know, when you told me that Foster has been smoking crack for a month, it just triggered something in me. And I swear I could actually smell crack." He looks a little crazy. "And I wanted it."

"What did you do?" The idea that he came so close to relapse is fascinating and also appalling. I simply cannot imagine myself coming anywhere close to relapsing, no matter how awful things become.

"I went into a bar and I ordered a glass of wine."

"I can't believe I'm hearing this."

"And then I got up from the bar right away and went straight to a meeting."

Relief.

"But I'll tell you, I was mighty close."

"Hayden, I am so glad you didn't relapse."

And then without missing a beat, Hayden asks me with his most British of British accents, "And where were *you* this evening?"

Hayden is aghast that I not only went uptown to confront Foster, but that on top of it, had sex with him.

"We didn't technically have sex," I say in my own defense.

"Well, you either did, or you didn't. Which is it?"

"Yes and no," I say.

"Augusten . . ."

"Okay, I know this is going to sound strange, but I didn't look at it."

Hayden looks at me like he's not sure he really wants to understand what I mean. "You didn't look . . . at what?"

"I didn't look, you know, at his *thing.*"

"At his penis?" Hayden says, a word the British should never say out loud.

"Yeah. I didn't look at it. So technically, I've never seen him fully naked and this means, we couldn't technically have had actual sex."

Hayden takes the book off his chest and sits upright on the sofa, looks at me with his mouth agape.

"And besides, Hayden, even if you do consider it sex, I haven't crossed any boundaries because we're not in the same group therapy anymore."

Hayden laughs, rolls his eyes. "You make it sound like he switched over into another group. The reason you're not '*in the same group therapy anymore*' is because your little boyfriend quit group therapy so he can smoke crack cocaine full-time."

"But I love him," I say in all my pathetic glory.

Hayden stands up, pulls a Silk Cut from the pack. "If—just for a moment try to imagine—if this Foster character wasn't as you say *devastatingly handsome*, if he looked just average, would you still be in love with him?"

His question really takes me by surprise, because I'd never even considered that. Yet the answer comes immediately: "No. I don't know. Yes. No."

Hayden lights his cigarette, blows the smoke smugly into the air. "You see? Your pathological shallowness is going to be your demise."

All of a sudden, I feel like an emotional paraplegic. I feel that all of my gains and insights are based on control and denial. I'm worried that I'm so profoundly sick as to appear healthy and together.

Once I actually placed a personal ad asking for somebody who was paralyzed or without arms or legs. I did this while very drunk, but I did it. I thought that maybe this way, I could get a really good person that nobody else wanted. I'm like Greer's mother who at Thanksgiving dinners always announces to the table, "That's okay, I'll eat the neck."

Had I placed a personal ad to meet Foster, this is how it might have read:

> Handsome and naturally masculine recovering alcoholic with 5 months sobriety and thinning hair. Sexually inhibited, gym-body, chain-smoker. Enjoys reading, photography and listening. Seeks substance abuser with criminal record, current abusive boyfriend, and untreated medical conditions for permanent relationship. I'm very sincere, honest, fun to be with, affectionate and have a large disposable income. You needn't have phone service or a steady job. Hairy arms a big plus. I like to try and fix things.

"Foster is consuming you. He's become your drug. You never see Pighead anymore," he says. "Pighead is your closest friend, yet you never see him. Or call him. It's just work. And Foster."

I take two Advil. Not because I have a headache, but because they're the only thing left that I can take.

I'm sitting in Wendy's office, confessing. Hayden guilt-tripped me with slogans from rehab: *secrets make you sick, your addict will do anything to get a drink, get your will out of your way.* Shame oozes out of me as I tell Wendy about eating fish and chips in a cemetery with Foster. About the kiss on the beach. I even tell her about his clocks. "My relationship with Foster has progressed. Well, maybe *progressed* isn't the right word," I tell her. "It's metastasized. I went over to his apartment to tell him that this just wasn't working. And something happened and we ended up in bed. Or, on the floor, actually, right in front of the door. But that's how close I was to leaving."

Wendy nods, the kind, compassionate therapist. Then she says, "I'd like you to read something." She reaches behind her, scanning the bookcase with her fingers. From in between a couple of books, she pulls out this thin booklet and hands it to me. I read the title: *The Codependent Woman's Survival Guide.* I read the title again. It still says the same thing. "Don't pay any attention to the title," she says. "It's not just for women."

No, of course not, I think. *That's why they put the* pink *type on a baby-blue background. So guys will see the blue and think, hey—that's for us too!* I feel like she's handed me a tampon. I drop the booklet on the floor. "I don't think it's just my shallowness," I tell Wendy. "I think part of the reason I'm attracted to Foster is *because* he's such a mess. I mean, the people I have loved in my life have never been easy to love. I'm not used to normal. I'm used to disaster. I don't know, as messed up as he is, he's also sort of exciting, sort of a challenge. I'm accustomed to working for love."

Wendy licks her lips and gives me a large, enthusiastic nod.

"What, am I onto something here?" I say.

"Yes, I think you are."

I decide to run with it. "Well, the thing is, part of me believes that love is more valuable when you have to work for it. Like taking a clunker of an old car and really fixing it up so it's a *restored classic*. As opposed to just running out and buying a new Lexus."

"Question?" she says, crossing her legs. "Which car would you depend on to get you to work day in and day out? The clunker or the new Lexus?"

This is so pathetic. Like looking in the mirror and noticing that your mole has changed colors. I can't believe I need to ask someone with a doctorate in psychology whether or not my attraction to this man is unhealthy. Like Wendy's going to say, "Well, as long as you realize it, I don't see why you can't just go ahead and date him. As a matter of fact, I know this great Thai place . . ."

What I really want is to sit next to someone under an L.L. Bean blanket on the beach in the fall and drink coffee from the same mug. I don't want some rusty '73 Ford Pinto with a factory-defective gas tank that causes it to explode when it's rear-ended in the parking lot of the supermarket. So why do I keep looking for Pintos?

I'm standing here looking around my apartment realizing that I bought all of my furniture while either hungover or drunk. Tables that are too low. Surfaces that need to be polished constantly. "Oh, that's fine, I'll just dust them every day." All this stuff bought for somebody's else life, with somebody else's lifestyle. What compelled me to purchase a two-hundred-dollar Ted Muehling butter dish when I don't cook or even eat in the apartment? I bought it for the person I wanted to be. Bookshelves that don't hold enough books? "I'll buy fewer books." A twelve-hundred-dollar video camera, which I never use. Adirondack chairs for my summer house. Which I don't have. It will work. I will change. I will shrink to fit the too-small sofa.

Hayden comes home, sees me standing in the middle of the room staring at the table beside my bed. "What's the matter, is there a rat?" he asks with alarm.

"No, I was just thinking about how at one point, every decision I made in my life was somehow influenced by alcohol. And now, I feel so far away from alcohol that I can barely remember what I was like. Sometimes, I think 'You must be in denial. You must want to drink so much and are so close to the bottle that you cannot even allow yourself to admit it."

"I don't think that's true," Hayden says. "I think you've made a choice. I think the reason you're sober and the reason it's not difficult for you to remain sober is because you're doing it for you."

"Shit, do you think I could possibly be that healthy?"

"I think you're healthy in certain ways, and I think you're a pathetic disaster in others. Oh, speaking of which," he adds, "Foster called while you were in Group, asked you to call him back."

Foster answers on the first ring.

"I went to a Narcotics Anonymous meeting and I got an interim sponsor. I just wanted you to know. Plus," he continues, "I cleaned the entire apartment and called a real estate broker about maybe getting some small little thing on the coast, maybe even Providence. He's also looking into bed-and-breakfasts for me to buy."

I say nothing.

"Auggie, are you there?"

"Yeah, yeah, I'm here. I'm just . . . listening."

"I want to make a fresh start . . . you really have no idea how powerful your influence was on me . . . and I really want to change my life . . . maybe even finally do some writing . . . maybe get a puppy . . . you'd love a puppy . . ."

"Don't get me wrong here, Foster. I'm really glad you're so . . . motivated . . . and everything, but you sound a little, I don't know, hyper?"

He laughs into the phone. "Well, I must have had ten cups of coffee today. Plus a couple of Xanax."

"You're taking Xanax?"

"My mother's a nurse, Auggie. She sends it to me."

"Well, I'm really happy to hear all of this, but I have to run. I'm supposed to meet Pighead for dinner, and I'm already running late."

I call Pighead. "Can I come over? Do you have any hot dogs?"

I'm at his apartment in ten minutes.

"Oh Sport, what are you doing hanging out with this man? He's totally unstable. Hand me that spatula," Pighead says.

"Why does he have to be so sweet and weird and handsome?"

He rolls the hot dogs around in the skillet; the butter crackles. "I'm sweet and weird and handsome. And I don't see you banging down *my* door."

"I know. But you don't have enough psychological problems for me. I need somebody with more damage."

"HIV isn't damage enough for you?"

I hit him on the shoulder. "You know what I mean."

He turns and looks at me. "No, honestly, I don't know what you mean."

I look for the pepper. I ignore this comment.

"I think you're obsessed with this guy and—well—you just deserve somebody who's not addicted to deadly illegal narcotics. Grab a couple of plates."

"Any more hiccups?"

"So far, nope."

"And they still don't know what caused them?"

"Not a clue."

I walk into the dining room. "Where's the remote?"

"Where it always is."

"No it's not."

"Oh, okay. Maybe it's on the—"

"Found it."

As we sit at the table, watching TV and ignoring each other, I think, *This is such an amazing relief. To just sit here and not have to talk somebody out of some criminal activity.*

On the way home, I walk past a wine bar. It's bright, with clean lines, modern and utterly appealing. It's not dark like an ordinary bar, but flooded with light. *Why couldn't I have a glass of wine now and then?* I wonder. *Why must I be so extreme?* And in the back of my mind, I'm also thinking that if Foster gets to smoke crack, I should get to drink wine. I walk on, telling myself how much better my life is sober.

The nasty German client finally bought a campaign. It was our least favorite campaign, of course. Unoriginal, uninspired. It is, what we call in advertising, a "montage" commercial. Instead of a concept, it contains only happy shots of attractive people leading active lives. There is a puppy in one shot. And of course, nobody actually sips the beer, as this is illegal to show. He felt it would be "more than satisfactory." He especially liked that we didn't have to fly to Germany to shoot it, but could spend a hundred thousand dollars less and shoot it in LA.

"It'll be a relief to get away," I tell Greer.

"I know. Let's try to eat healthy," she says. "Let's treat it like going to a spa. I really don't want to end up hanging around the set eating all those M&Ms and corn chips all day."

Basically, this is what commercial production is all about. The director shoots the commercial, the client dresses "casual Friday," worries constantly and pesters the agency, and the agency ignores the client and hangs out at the craft service table gorging on cocktail weenies and cookies. The craft service table is a magic, magnetic thing.

"We'll take the fat pills," I reassure Greer.

"Thank God for chitosan," she says.

Both of us swallow fat-absorb pills with religious fervor. Greer owns stock in the company that manufactures them.

"I need to get out of New York," I tell her. "Too much stress."

"I'll bring along some books. *Seven Spiritual Laws of Success* for me and . . ." She thinks. "*A Setback Is a Setup for a Comeback* for you."

Two days go by without a word from Foster. I will not let myself go to his apartment again. When he's good, he's so good. He makes me laugh harder than I ever laughed when I was drinking. He's so warm and loving and attentive and sensitive. But then all of a sudden, he's *gone*. Missing in action. It really is like he's seeing somebody else. How can I compete with crack?

Why would I want to?

He told me, *I love you*. Then he called me all manic saying how much I'd changed his life. And now, nothing. So I'm going up and down, my mood completely dependent upon his sobriety or lack of. He's like this incredibly beautiful Van Gogh painting with slashes all through it. True, it's a Van Gogh. But look at those slashes.

I can see the person he could be, the person he almost is. And I want that person. I want to love that person. I want *that* to be the person who tells me I'm hogging all the covers. I can't stand one minute looking at the stars out the sunroof and the next minute wondering, does he have a broken bottle pressed against his neck?

And here's the part I don't admit to anybody, even Hayden: part of me wants to see him using. I want to know what he's like. I want to know *all* sides of him. I want to see if he looks more content when he's with me or his crack.

When Hayden walks in the door, he looks suspicious. Guilty. I immediately think, *You've relapsed.* "Augusten, we need to have a talk."

Here it comes.

"I'm going back to London."

Because this is the last thing I expected him to say, I make him tell me again.

"It's time for me to get back to London. I've been here for more than six months. And there's a project waiting for me there."

I feel as if I've had the wind knocked out of me. I should be relieved, I suppose. To have the apartment all to myself, the inconvenience of stepping over suitcases gone. But instead, I feel like I'm being abandoned.

"When are you leaving?"

"Day after tomorrow."

"When did you decide this?" I can't believe it's so sudden.

"Today, when I got the call about the project in London. It's a famous composer. I'd be insane not to take it." He lights a Silk Cut.

I have to be happy for him. I can't be selfish for me. He can't stay forever, no matter how much I want him to. "Well, we should do something special before you leave. Maybe I should try and see if I can get tickets to *Rent.*"

"Oh, that would be terrific, but I doubt you can."

"I'll call Ticket Master."

Hayden's going to work with a famous composer and I'm going to end up sitting in a parked cab on Eighth Avenue, waiting while my Banana Republic boyfriend buys crack from a teenage hustler. That is, assuming he's still alive. I hate that I love him.

The intercom on the wall next to the door lets out a lame squawk. Hayden and I both look at it; we've never heard it before. Nobody ever visits me and I always pick up, never order in for delivery. I go over and push the TALK button. "Yeah?"

"Auggie, it's me, Foster."

"Brilliant!" Hayden says, excitedly rubbing his hands together. Hayden has never seen Foster before. Suddenly there is the possibility of drama.

I buzz him up. A few seconds later, he knocks on the door. I let him in.

"I had to see you." And then he starts crying, grabbing ahold of me and sobbing against my neck. I look at Hayden who mouths, *Crack.* I mouth back, *No shit.*

"Foster, what's going on? C'mon, pull yourself together and tell me what's happened."

He sniffs, wipes his nose on the shoulder of his T-shirt and says, "Hi, you must be Hayden. I'm Foster. Nice to meet you. Sorry for barging in like this, but—"

"Yes, that's whom I assumed you were. Nice to meet you, too."

"I picked up again, Auggie. Big time. I couldn't stop myself. I'm out of control."

"Where have you been?"

"The U.N. Plaza."

"What? The U.N. Plaza? For two days?"

"The windows open so the smoke can get out. Anyway, I want to get better. I'm checking into rehab."

"Well, I'll leave you two lovebirds alone. I think I'll go peruse Barnes & Noble for something to read on the plane. Something inspiring like *Final Exit.*"

"Thanks, Hayden. See you later. I'll call Ticketmaster, see about *Rent.*"

"You guys are going to see *Rent*?" Foster asks. "I wanna go."

"You wouldn't like it. You can't smoke inside the theater," I tell him.

Hayden leaves and Foster takes my arm and pulls me over to the bed, where he sits.

"I've never seen where you live before. It's . . . small."

It occurs to me that no matter how rock-bottom Foster became, he would never be able to live in something as humble as my apartment. And my apartment is probably not too humble by ordinary standards. He's completely spoiled. "Yeah, I know. Forget about the apartment. Listen, you better get to rehab. You're a mess, a real train wreck."

"I know, Auggie. Please, will you forgive me? I can't help it. You know what that's like, remember? You used to be a mess."

"Yeah, I know," I admit, "I do remember what it's like to be out of control." Odd that I say this in the past tense.

Foster gives me a small, sweet smile. "I do love you, you know. Even though I know I'm no great prize, I am *your* no great prize."

"Why did I ever agree to group therapy?"

"No, Auggie. You got a lot out of it, you really did."

"Like you?" I ask nastily.

He rolls me over on top of him. "Yeah, like me."

After *Rent*, we walk over to Ninth Avenue and hail a cab to take us back downtown. "There's really no reason to ever go above Fourteenth Street," I say as we fly down Ninth, making all the lights. "Except for the brief excursion for live theater."

"Are the meat samosas filled with lamb or beef?" Hayden asks the waiter at the Indian restaurant.

"They are filled with *meat*," he replies proudly.

Hayden orders the vegetarian samosas.

"At least I can better understand your attraction to him now, after seeing him," Hayden says, breaking off a piece of papadum. "He's possibly the most attractive man I have ever seen in my life. He's quite literally breathtaking. I no longer blame you at all for your shallowness and lack of judgment."

I smirk. "Yeah . . . well." I take a sip of Diet Coke, the Ketel One martini of those in recovery. I'm so sick of Diet fucking Coke.

"It's almost like a male Liz Taylor thing."

"How do you mean?" I ask him.

"You know, if she weren't as beautiful as she is, people wouldn't admire her *struggle* with booze and pills. They'd just cross her off as a hopeless lush. We're a very visual society."

"I don't know. My obsession with Foster is kind of fading. It's like he's severed my give-a-shit nerve. I'm over him."

"Ha! You are so full of shit. He's done just the opposite; he's reconnected your give-a-shit nerve."

"No, it's not true. I don't deserve to be in love with such a mess."

"I'm not talking about what you deserve. I'm talking about what you feel."

"I hate it when you play therapist. Especially with *your* accent. It makes everything you say sound so BBC."

The first course arrives and we start talking about rehab. "Don't you think it's odd," Hayden says, "that you spend thirty intense days with these perfect strangers, you become this really tight little dysfunctional family? And you never hear from anybody again?"

I stab a piece of tikka chicken kabob onto my plate. "I do think about that sometimes. Like, I wonder if Dr. Valium is okay. Or Big Bobby, I wonder if he's cross-addicted to White Castle." In rehab we learned that it's easy to cross-addict from one thing to another. Like you give up crack and you pick up dope. Or you give up booze and pick up a crack addict.

"I'm sure Pregnant Paul is out there using again. I have no doubt about that," he assures me.

"And that girl, what was her name? The cutter?"

"Sarah," he says.

"That's right, Sarah. She's probably sitting at home right now with a serving fork stuck in her thigh and a syringe in her arm, having multiple orgasms."

"You've really only slept with Foster once?" Hayden asks as he spoons some maatar paneer gravy over his saffron rice.

"Twice now, actually."

"When was the twice?"

"Yesterday, after you went to Barnes & Noble. But I only count it as the first 'official' time."

"And why is that?"

"Because this time, I looked."

Back home, Hayden gathers his things together from around the apartment, stuffing them into his suitcases, double-checking under the sofa and in the bathroom for anything left behind.

Foster calls just after we turn off the lights to go to sleep. He calls just to let me know he's okay and not using. He doesn't want me to worry, he says. He's content tonight to just stay home, curled up on the sofa reading *Bastard Out of Carolina*. After the operator cuts in and asks him to deposit twenty-five cents for an additional three minutes, Foster doesn't call back. But I can see him: standing there on the corner of Eighth Avenue and Forty-Seventh Street, banging his head against the hung-up phone receiver, saying *shit, shit, shit.*

I help Hayden carry his suitcases downstairs to the black Lincoln he ordered from a car service to take him to the airport. "No cocktails on the plane," I warn.

Hayden gives me a hug. "Good luck to you. Please get to some meetings, they'll do you good."

"I know, I know. I will. I promise." Even as I say this, I know I won't. I'm so over AA.

"And good luck with Foster. Be careful."

Hayden has become my common sense. I don't want him to go. I'm afraid of what I might do, what might happen. Without him, who will keep me in check?

He climbs into the backseat, slides the window down and leans out. As the car pulls away he shouts, with feigned earnestness, "And remember, you *are somebody.*"

Hayden is gone. And suddenly I feel so completely alone. I stand on the sidewalk, surrounded by apartment buildings, cabs, cars, people packed into every available inch of this city. And yet I feel alone. It doesn't feel like we're each going our own separate ways. It feels like he is moving on and I am staying behind.

I begin to smell it in the hallway as I walk toward my office. It gets stronger. When I finally reach my office door, I realize I have reached ground zero for the smell. I bend down, swipe my hand across the gray wall-to-wall carpeting and then bring my finger to my nose and sniff. It's unmistakable: scotch.

I open my door. The smell hits me in the face like something physical. Fumes so powerful that if I were to light a match, the room would probably explode.

My office has been drinking, has relapsed without me.

Because I don't know what to do, I sit at my desk. And amazingly, the alcohol fumes are only more intense. I can only sit there like I am meat marinating.

A moment later, Elenor passes by my office saying a casual "Hi there" as she passes by. Then she reappears, standing in my doorway, nose upturned. A look of alarm passes across her face. She steps inside, sniffing. "Augusten," she says, "what's going on in here?" She looks around. I don't know what she is looking for. A party?

"I haven't been drinking, Elenor, if that's what you're wondering."

She eyes me suspiciously. My credibility is stretched to the breaking point due to the obvious olfactory situation at hand.

"It smells like a distillery in here."

"I noticed," I say.

She leans around and looks in my trash can, glances under my desk. "Any idea why your office smells like this?"

One word comes to mind. "Rick." I stare at her. "He poured a bottle of scotch in here. It's probably his idea of funny."

She stares back at me blankly. "I don't think Rick would do that," she says. Then she crosses her arms over her chest and gives me a little smile like I'm some child who is lying about the toothpaste all over the hairbrush. "So everything's going okay with you? You know, in terms of your . . . situation?"

I can't believe this. I want to grab her and shake her, scream, *I DIDN'T FUCKING DRINK! DON'T YOU REMEMBER THAT ASSHOLE WAS LOOKING THROUGH MY BACK-PACK? DON'T YOU UNDERSTAND HE HAS IT IN FOR ME??!!* Instead, I get up from behind my desk and grab my bag, slinging it over my shoulder. "I'm fine, Elenor. Thank you for asking. And I think you're wrong about Rick. I think this is exactly the kind of thing he would do."

"Where are you going?" she asks, turning.

I let out my air and look at her like, *You just don't get it.* "To a keg party, Elenor," I say.

Walking down the sidewalk, I fume. I shoulder my way through the throngs of workers, clutching their Starbucks cups, *Wall Street Journals*, briefcases. The sounds of traffic, which I normally don't even hear, are deafening, oppressive. I pass a building super hosing down the sidewalk and there's a rainbow in the mist. I step on the rainbow, soaking my shoes.

I can't call Foster, can't depend on him. And Pighead has enough to worry about without worrying about me. Hayden is probably sleeping off his jet lag. That's my sober network. It's a very short list. I walk quickly, imagine not stopping. Could I walk all the way to California?

If I had gotten a sponsor in AA like I was supposed to, I could call him. And he could tell me, "Let go and let God," and I could think, *Bullshit.*

I could go to a meeting now and just vent. I could.

On the corner I spot an Irish pub. It's open, even at ten-thirty in the morning. *Pathetic,* I think. *The kind of place you'd have to be a hard-core alcoholic to step foot in.*

I go inside.

That smell. Stale beer, cigarette smoke, wood, gin. There's no other smell like it. It's bar smell. And at once, I feel like I have come home.

It takes a moment for my eyes to adjust to dim light. I make my way to the bar and sit on one of the stools. I set my bag on the bar and my hands are shaking. I can't do this. I can't be here. It's not worth it.

"What'll it be?" the weathered old bartender asks in a gravelly voice, the skin around his eyes creased, his mustache yellowed from years of exhaling Marlboros.

And I am torn. I am split down the middle. Anxiety spreads through me, as if whatever had been containing it cracked, burst. My heart races in my chest. Just one shot. I could order just one shot. I need to take the edge off. The edge is too sharp. I'm cutting myself with this edge.

"A Diet Coke," I say after a long pause.

The bartender looks at me for just an instant longer. It's as if he has been able to read my mind, knows what's going on inside of me. And it occurs to me that he's probably seen this many times before: the demons wrestling.

When he sets my Diet Coke on the bar he says, "Enjoy."

I suck through the thin straw. I suck until only the ice is left.

THE MIRRORS OF LA

Greer and I are in LA shooting the commercial for Wirksam. Shutters was booked, so we're staying in bungalows near the Château Marmont. This is a surprise to everyone. The client is so cheap, I'm amazed they didn't make us go to an animal shelter. However, they have said they will not pay for any meals. And we are to use our personal calling cards if we use the phone. And they even tried—though I will say they did not press the issue—to double us up, two in a room.

After we check in, we meander by the oval pool. A couple of busty female extras are sunbathing on red striped towels and a man with a hairy back is in the water. So hairy that at first I think it's his front, but then realize it's his back. LA allows this?

"Isn't this the place where John Belushi overdosed?" Greer asks.

"No," I tell her. "But somebody else probably died here."

"Yeah, it must be pretty easy to OD in this town." She looks at me and I can read her mind. She is thinking, *I hope you remembered to bring your alcoholic books with you.*

She slides her sunglasses down from her head. "Well," she says, "I'm exhausted. I'm going to go take a nap. Where are we going tonight?"

"The Ivy," I say. "The Nazi gets in at five; we're supposed to meet out front at seven."

"I hate babysitting clients," she says. "They think that just because they put you up in a nice hotel they own you. I wish he would just order room service and leave us alone."

"I hope he doesn't wear shorts," I say.

"Yuck, I hadn't considered that," Greer says, crinkling up her nose.

"Oh well, see you later," I say and head off to my room. As I'm walking away I can hear Greer's thoughts as she passes by the sun-bathing extras: *You girls are going to get malignant melanoma and then nobody's going to cast you.*

The room is very nice. I go to the minibar out of habit and am depressed when I realize that its contents are off-limits. They have *No Smoking* rooms, they should have *No Temptation* rooms as well. I take a seven-dollar bottle of spring water from the door. I gulp it down. I have four hours to kill before dinner. In the past, this would have been just barely enough time to obtain a comfortable buzz and establish my relationship with the bartender. Now it seems like more than enough time to perhaps write a screenplay. Alcohol time is very different from sober time. Alcohol time is slippery whereas sober time is like cat hair. You just can't get rid of it.

I go back to the minibar. It is all-powerful. I say the words out loud, thinking it will castrate my desire. "I want a drink." Instead, it has the opposite effect. By admitting this, I've reinforced the craving, made it fiercer. I once read about a guy who lost his arms in a fire. The nurse took pity on him and gave him a hand job. I don't even get that.

I pace. The room has a wealth of mirrors, and I am compelled to stare into each of them as I pass by. It's impossible to go into the bathroom for even a washcloth without looking at my body from every angle, my pores magnified and illuminated. I stare at my stomach and pinch the thin, determined layer of fat that blocks my abs. I tell myself that it's the LA mirrors. I am more ripped in my New York mirror. This one makes me look skinny, yet with a thick middle. Then I have a terrifying thought: maybe LA mirrors are better, sharper, more accurate. Maybe this is why physical perfection is so common in LA, because people have the truth of their reflections. I have fooled myself into believing that I have a good body, but obviously that is only by Manhattan standards, by inaccurate Manhattan mirrors.

Actually, I think I was better looking when I was drunk, because then I only saw myself through one half-opened eye. And through my own cloud of internal fame. I only saw myself when I was holding a tumbler of scotch in front of the mirror, which to me reflected as an Academy Award, while I gave my acceptance speech. Sigourney Weaver was always standing next to me, looking tearfully proud.

LA is just awful. It's too sunny. And it makes me even more self-conscious and shallow than I already am. I suddenly wish I had some Valium or an appointment with a local doctor for dimple implants. Something to look forward to. If I can't drink, I need something. A goal. Preferably one involving dissolving stitches.

I've only been here for a few hours and I already feel like a mess. At my core, I am a vain and shallow person, and being in LA always brings this buried truth closer to the surface. I fear that my soul wants not tranquillity and wisdom, but long, blond hair extensions that hang loosely down over my eyebrows and a ripped, liposuctioned stomach. I want pec implants and a chemical peel. I want Gucci loafers. I want Rupert Everett to be in love with me, a Range Rover and a new, small cell phone in my pocket.

I want reservations. No, this is wrong. I want to be somebody who never needs reservations. I want my reservations to be unspoken, a given.

I want my nose to be the same shape, but smaller, more in proportion to my face. I want to earn the respect of these LA mirrors. I want to be able to be able to say, in that disinterested Valley way, What*ever*.

I go to the window and fog it up by hyperventilating. I realize that I actually fear returning to New York because now that Hayden has gone back to London, I am worried he has taken my mental health with him. That he accidentally packed it in his suitcase along with his dirty socks and the hard cheese he bought at Dean & Deluca.

I would like to be sitting in a whirlpool right now. But not drunk at four in the morning like the last time I was in a whirlpool. I don't even want to think about that time.

At dinner, Greer and I sit on either side of the Nazi, out of professional duty. He scowls at everybody who asks for the butter. He sees butter as a weakness. We try to make the dinner conversation light and enjoyable. But he will have no part of it. He pulls his preproduction booklet from his sinister black briefcase and starts talking about his "wardrobe concerns."

Greer stares at her watercress salad, absently drumming her fingernails against her water glass. Elenor refills her wineglass constantly. And Rick sneaks glances at the waiter's crotch and I catch him every time. It is astonishingly satisfying to look at him and think, *Closet case,* and know he can read my mind as he looks away, flushed. All Mormons are gay, I believe. Rick is merely a further example.

The account people smile while they chew, nodding at everything the Nazi says. I look at his arms and notice for the first time that they are furry. Pathetically, this makes me like him slightly. And miss Foster.

If I were straight, I am certain I would be one of those guys who goes to wet T-shirt contests and votes with great enthusiasm.

By the time dessert is offered, everybody at the table is drunk except for me and the Nazi. Even Greer has had two glasses of Chablis, which for her is drinking to blackout. I sit there and think how it isn't fair that I can't drink at all, even a little. I realize I have crammed an entire lifetime of moderate drinking into a decade of hard-core drinking and this is why. I blew my wad.

Fuck.

Walking back from dinner past the Santa Monica pier, I notice that a lot of the homeless guys out here are pretty hot. I start thinking that it's like there's this whole, untapped resource of guys I hadn't even thought of before. All these jobless, alcoholic Mel Gibsons. Like daisies sticking up through the sidewalk cracks.

The next morning, Greer and I are waiting for the light to change at the crosswalk on the corner of Pico and Ocean. We see a bus heading toward the intersection. It's empty except for the driver and a single passenger in the very back. HELP . . . CALL POLICE . . . is scrolling across the marquee above the windshield.

"Oh, shit!" Greer cries, reaching in her bag for her cell phone.

I watch as the bus runs the red light.

Greer cups her hand over her other ear and speaks into the phone. "Sharon? It's Greer. Listen, remind me to have the Wirksam outdoor ads resized to fit buses. I totally forgot to do it before we left. Talk to you later." She snaps the phone closed and tosses it back in her bag.

"Greer, what the hell were you doing? I thought you were calling nine-one-one. We need to call the cops about that bus."

"Oh," she says. She bites her lip.

The bus makes a sharp left out of sight.

Greer shrugs. "Well, it's too late now."

I turn to her, stare hard.

"Don't look at me like that! Jesus, I'm not the only person in LA with a cell phone. Somebody else will call."

"I can't believe you," I say. "That was really horrible."

We make it to the other side of the street. Greer stops and faces me. "Look, commercial shoots are stressful. My mind is focused on work. When I saw the bus, it reminded me of something, that's all."

"Didn't you see the sign in the front? Lit up in the front?"

"I can't take care of everybody," she says. "What do you expect me to do? Go swim out there off the coast of Florida and escort all those Cubans to the shore? Or maybe help the Mexicans dig tunnels under the border?"

"What?" I say.

"Augusten, I'm not an alcoholic like you. Getting all this free therapy and having all these personal transformations all the time. I'm just a regular person living a regular life. I can't be Florence *fucking* Nightingale."

"Don't worry," I tell her. "You're not in any danger."

After lunch, we're sitting by the pool and Greer looks up from her *Town and Country* magazine. "What do you think happened with that bus, anyway?"

I look over at her. "Whoever was in the back probably shot the driver, stole his wallet and took off."

Greer shakes her head. "You'd have to be crazy to take public transportation these days."

"How's your magazine?" I ask.

She smiles. "Scandinavian Airlines prints poems on the sides of the engines for the passengers in the window seats to read. I just think that's wonderful."

"Mmmmm," I say. "Wonderful."

She glares at me. "Well, it *is* wonderful. It's thoughtful. It shows they're thinking about people, about their passengers."

"They only do it for the press it generates," I say.

Greer lays the magazine across her legs. "You can be really cynical sometimes," she tells me. "For all your talk about recovery, you're a very angry, bitter person."

"Happy Hour's over. What do you expect?" I snap.

"There are other ways to be happy," she says, "besides drinking."

"Like?" I ask the expert of happiness.

"Like just sitting out here, taking some time for ourselves, enjoying the sun." She smiles a fake smile that she thinks looks real.

"While some poor bus driver bleeds to death on the side of the road because you didn't call the police."

"That's not fair!" she cries.

"No, it's not."

Greer picks up her magazine and begins thumbing through it again, snapping the pages.

I close my eyes and imagine how easy it would be to walk into the hotel bar and have a cosmopolitan. Nobody would even know.

A moment later, she says, "Oh, wow. A new pill that prevents male pattern baldness. One hundred percent effective, it says."

I bolt upright. "Where? What?"

She smirks and pretends to read. "Made from the blood plasma of slain bus drivers."

Horribly, I laugh.

So does Greer. "God, I really am an evil monster."

"No you're not," I tell her.

"How do you know?" she asks.

"Because if you were truly evil, the Nazi would like you more."

She considers this. "True."

"As long as the Nazi hates us," I say, "we can't be *all bad*."

"We mean well," she says.

"Mostly," I add.

"It's advertising," she says. "Advertising does it to us."

"I hate advertising," I say.

"I know. We should be bus drivers."

Later that afternoon, we are called to the set to approve the final wardrobe. Because we hate the commercial we are about to shoot, both Greer and I see this as an enormous task, something better left to God, or if God is preoccupied, then a coin toss among the stylists.

"I really couldn't care less," Greer says to me in the minivan.

"Dress them all in black. Put everybody in green armbands to tie into the bottle," I say.

At this point, we're not shooting our second or even third campaign choice. We're shooting something that Elenor and Rick basically forced on us. Something that features dancers and the flag of Germany, along with a couple of puppies.

"It's all just one big *so what*," Greer says bitterly.

Once we're on the set, I locate the M&M and potato chip table. It's next to the director's chairs where the agency is supposed to sit. Greer and I toss our stuff on one of the chairs and each grab of handful of corn chips.

"Ho hum," Greer says. "Isn't advertising exciting and glamorous?"

"It's better than manual labor," I point out. "The least amount of work for the maximum amount of money."

"I guess," she says, crunching a chip. "If you don't mind handing over your dignity."

"I don't have any dignity," I tell her. "I never have. That's why I'm in it." I eat some M&Ms. "Besides, I was drunk for so many years, I didn't really even realize I was *in* advertising."

"I was painfully aware of it," she says, glaring at me.

After we nod our heads at the costumes, speak to the director for five minutes and choose a glass for the product shot, it's time to go back to the hotel. Only two hours of actual work, yet it's drained us completely.

"I'm just going to sink into the whirlpool," Greer says, her head against the window of the minivan.

"I'm gonna order a salad and watch TV and then crash," I say, hardly able to keep my eyes open.

Although it's only six P.M., we seem to have contracted some sort of brain-numbing disease. The threat of tomorrow has made us drowsy.

"Normal people in America don't realize how stressful commercial productions are. They just think advertising must be really fun. They don't realize it's hell," Greer says, absently twisting her diamond tennis bracelet.

Belinda is unconscious on the daybed in her trailer. Belinda is the model we hired to wear the silver swimsuit and dance on top of a giant beer cap. Unfortunately, Belinda suffers from an eating disorder and after bingeing on forty or fifty Mint Milanos, she collapsed near the toilet in the dressing room.

"Just our luck," Greer says, plucking lint off her sleeve. "The first day of the shoot and already there's a problem with the talent."

We're guarding the snack table. Elenor and Rick are sitting with the Nazi, distracting him with a spreadsheet program on Elenor's computer.

"This is great. Just what we need. More down time," I say, stuffing a handful of party mix into my mouth.

Greer paces like an anxious ferret. "Never work with children, puppies or bulimics," she says.

The director walks over. "This sucks." He folds his muscular, tattooed arms across his chest. "She threw up all over her hair, so we have to re-do her."

"Oh, that's just grand," Greer says. "Thank you Anna Wintour for ruining the female body image."

I say, "Did she wake up yet?"

"Yeah, she's awake now. But she says she's really dizzy. She's afraid to get back on the bottle cap. Afraid she'll fall off."

Greer narrows her eyes. "Bribe her with a slice of cheesecake and some Ex-Lax."

Watching the playback monitor, it's immediately clear that this will be one of the worst commercials Greer and I have ever shot. The Nazi is not ranting or grinding his teeth, so we know he is happy. And this means the commercial is an abortion of the worst kind.

Greer sits with her legs crossed, foot tapping at the air.

Elenor is hunched over her computer.

Rick wonders out loud whether or not one particularly handsome assistant producer "is a fruit." Truly, he can't take his eyes off him.

And I am trying to see if I can remember how a martini tastes. It's like trying to picture a dead relative in my mind, trying to see their face, their smile.

All the while, Belinda writhes on the bottle cap, looking gaunt and vaguely unsteady.

"Don't worry, we can add some color to her skin in postproduction," somebody comments.

On the plane home, I decide to do my expense report. Greer is writing an angry letter to the company that makes her alphahydroxy face cream because she says it burned her skin. I ask her for a pen.

"How do you spell 'catastrophic'?" she asks.

I spell it for her and unfold my bill from the hotel. I lower the tray table and spread the bill out, along with an expense report form from work.

"Is 'crucify' with an 's' or a 'c'?"

"Jesus, Greer. What kind of letter are you writing?"

She snorts at me. "You have to word these things strongly if you want to get anywhere."

"What do you want from them?" I ask.

"A year's supply."

"It's crucify with a 'c.' Now leave me alone." I start adding my hotel room, tax and meals for each day. Then I see the minibar charge. The total is sixteen hundred dollars. "How is this possible?"

"What?" Greer says, turning to me.

"What the fuck?"

"Augusten, what is it? What's the matter with you?"

"My minibar charges. Look." I hand her the bill.

"These aren't your charges?" she says, looking over the bill.

"Of course not. No. I only took bottled fucking water."

She stops chewing her gum. "You *did* read the little notice on the minibar, didn't you?"

"What little notice?" I say.

Greer, ever the A student, recites the notice from memory: "For your convenience, you will be automatically billed for each item removed from your minibar."

"But all I drank was the water!"

"Okay. But did you take things out and then put them back?"

"They bill you for *that?*" I say, horrified.

"Of course. All the good European hotels do it now."

We weren't in *fucking* Europe. I say nothing.

"What did you do? Take all the liquor bottles out every day and then put them back?" She laughs like this is not something within the realm of actual possibility.

Unfortunately, it is. Because that's exactly what I did. I fondled all the bottles, constantly. Sixteen hundred dollars' worth of fondling. That's like hiring a prostitute every night for a week. And not even having a drink to break the ice.

Back in my apartment, I phone the hotel and explain the unfortunate situation.

"I'm sorry," they tell me.

"And . . . ?" I say.

"And that's why we put the notice on the minibar door," the customer service representative tells me with great smugness. Smugness that seems to say, *Richard Gere wouldn't bitch about this.*

That's it. I lose. Once an alcoholic, always an alcoholic. For the rest of my life, there will be a bar tab.

"He's German, he's supposed to be punctual," Greer says, annoyed, checking her Cartier Panther watch. "I could have *used* this extra time to sleep!"

I'm sitting in conference room 34A with Greer, Barnes, Tod and a few other people who make up the "Beer Team" at the agency back in New York. We need to show the Nazi the commercial we shot and get his approval so the spot can be shipped to the networks and, regrettably, aired.

The Nazi is half an hour late.

Half of the pastries that the catering department brought into the room for the meeting have been eaten, croissants with their corners spitefully pinched off, the jam centers of donuts scooped out by fingers.

Barnes, the account guy, looks at his watch, spits a breath out of his mouth. "Guys, if he's not here in fifteen minutes, why don't you go back to your offices and I'll call you when he gets here. This is so rude."

Greer leans over, whispers in my ear. "How much do you *loathe* advertising?"

"I despise it," I whisper back.

The conference room phone rings and Barnes answers it. He places the receiver to his ear. "Conference room 34A," he says. He widens his eyes, looks at us and nods.

"Get your armbands on, the client's here," I say under my breath.

Barnes hangs up. "I'm just going to go stand by the elevators for him," he says as he leaves the room.

"I am not in the mood for him today," I say to whoever's listening.

A few moments later, Barnes returns with the black-eyed, frowning client. The client's nasty black leather briefcase is attached to his fist. Everybody rises from their seats, a courtesy. I am tempted to hail him with an outstretched arm.

The Nazi walks directly to the table with the bagels, cream cheese, pastries, coffee and lox.

"Wouldn't it be hilarious if he took some lox?" Greer whispers.

"Shut *up*," I say back with an evil grin.

Nazi pours a cup of coffee, flips a couple of the pastries over with his fingers and makes a disgusted face as he walks to the conference room table and sits. *Fwap! Fwap!* The fasteners of his mysterious black briefcase spring open. He retracts a pad of graph paper, then reaches into his jacket pocket for a mechanical pencil. He checks his watch. "Ve need to make zis brief, as I have anozer engagement across town viss ze pee-ahh people."

P.R. As in *public relations*. This man has a way of making every sentence sound like a steel cable being stretched to the point of breakage.

Greer kicks me under the table, turns her head and gives me the eye.

Barnes starts the meeting. "Well, we're here today to show you the cut. Let me just say that we're all very excited about this commercial. We think it came out great. And the goal is for you to sign off on it today, so we can get it to the networks in time to make our air date." He claps his hands together as punctuation.

The Nazi is taking notes, of what I can't imagine. His scowl-ing face is bolted to the pad of graph paper, fingers gripping his mechanical pencil so tight his knuckles are white. "Ya, go on, I'm lizzening," he says, not looking up.

"So . . . then . . . I'll turn the meeting over to Greer and Augusten, our creatives. Guys?" And he makes this presentation motion with his hand, like he's a game show hostess displaying a twenty-seven-inch flat-screen television.

The Nazi doesn't look up, but continues to write.

Greer rolls her eyes.

Barnes looks at her and motions for her to go ahead by giving her the international hand symbol for "hurry up"—rolling his hands around each other in midair—while mouthing the words, *Let's go.*

Greer simply places one hand on the table before her, then places the other neatly on top. When Greer wants to, she can be hypnotically sexy and captivating. And she wants to. "Hans?"

The Nazi looks up immediately.

Greer smiles her Meg Ryan smile. "Hi, I hope I'm not bugging you. You look so busy there taking notes." She gives a subtle, prac-ticed laugh. Though he'd have no way of knowing it's practiced.

I could be imagining it, but I believe he blushes. Or perhaps it's merely capillaries bursting in his forehead, as a result of his anger at being interrupted. The equivalent of a smile crosses his lips and he dramatically slams his mechanical pencil down onto the pad of graph paper, folds his arms on the table and says, "*Guten morgen*, Greer. I'm sorry if I vas rude. Please, go ahead."

"Great. I just wanted to move things along because I know you have somewhere important to be." She's still doing Meg Ryan. She does a *great* Meg Ryan. I know Greer, and I know that inside, she is thinking, *I would like to chop you up into small, manage-able pieces and grill you on a hibachi, then feed you to my shar-pei.* But all that comes out is *Welcome to moviefone!*

Greer and I rise together. We are performing the *Ballet of Two*

Who Pretend to Actually Give a Shit; a private performance for our client. Greer steps aside and motions for me to go to the video player. She does this because Greer couldn't so much as find the power switch if her life depended on it.

I slide the tape into the machine. It makes a *whirrrrr* sound, then a *ker-chunk,* then a buzz. After you hear the buzz, you can push PLAY. But I wait.

The tape in place, I now face my client to give my little pre-viewing speech. "Now, Hans, as you know, this is a rough cut. The picture hasn't been color-corrected yet, the titles aren't perfect, so what you're seeing is a very *rough* cut."

Greer, ever the flawless professional, is already standing across the room beside the lighting control panel. "Ready?" she chirps.

"Greer," I reply.

And with her seventy-five-dollar manicure, she depresses the LIGHTING ALL button. Smoothly, the lights above us fade from bright to medium through dim, past faint all the way to darkness.

I push PLAY. The machine makes a deep, throat-clearing sound. The monitor displays some video crackling, then immediately the familiar countdown: 5–4–3–2–1. A beat of blackness. Then our horrible, cheesy commercial.

Shots of beer bottles being pulled from icy coolers.

Male models, female models hugging each other.

Puppies scrambling in the grass.

A kite soaring up into the sky.

A man leaping into a water fountain, despite his dress shoes and suit pants.

A woman on a bicycle, arms and legs outstretched.

A bride in her wedding gown juggling lemons.

Over all of this, a song: uplifting and motivational. Product name mentioned within the first six seconds and repeated eight times. A catchy tune, designed to be permanently tattooed on the brain. A tumor that causes one to purchase. At the end, the singers sing the slogan: *Germany in harmony . . . with America.* Then the beer bottle appears with the slogan printed beneath it on the screen.

After the commercial plays through once, I push REWIND and say, "I'll play it again for you." I must have said this a thousand times in my career.

As the tape is rewinding, the room in darkness, Greer says, "Maybe I should check to see if he's pushed the right button, sometimes he scares me." She must have said this a thousand times.

After it rewinds, I push PLAY.

Just at the scene where the redheaded model opens her hands, setting the firefly free, the door to the conference room opens, a wedge of light spills into the room. My secretary closes the door again, heads toward me. I move to her. She cups her hand around my ear and whispers.

I walk over to Greer. "Come here," I direct, as I pull her arm. I open the door and lead her outside.

"What?" she asks, whirling around toward me.

"It's Pighead," I say.

"Oh my God, what?"

"He's in the hospital. He was taken there by ambulance." Something's rising in me. Dread, panic, confusion, I don't know. Something's either rising or falling, I can't be sure.

"You should go now," she says.

"But I can't, the meet—"

"I'm not kidding, Augusten. Just leave. I'll take care of things."

I chomp on my thumbnail. "Shit, Greer. I've been so fucking consumed with this nut from my group therapy that I've totally ignored him. That and this stupid job. I didn't even call him once during the shoot. And now he's in the hospital." I want a drink. Rubbing alcohol, even. That is my default, wanting a drink. And no amount of rehab, no AA meeting will ever be able to switch that default to, say, orange juice. I want a fucking drink. I don't want to go to the hospital to see Pighead. I want to go to a bar.

"Go," she says.

I seem to be frozen in place. I know I need to go. Now. But I can't. My feet are getting along really well with this particular square of carpet.

"Augusten," Greer begins, "you can't run from this. Whatever *this* is. It might be nothing. It might be something. But whatever it is, you have to face it."

"Now who sounds like a self-help book?" I say, stalling.

She doesn't smile. She walks to the elevator bank and stabs the button. I join her. "Call me if you need anything. Do what you need to do."

"Thanks, Greer," I say.

The elevator arrives and I step inside. I go down.

RUNNING UNDERWATER

Pighead?" I say softly as I open the door to his room.

"Fuckhead, is that you?" he wimpers, his voice cracking.

I walk into the room. Pighead is lying on a bed, feet elevated. The smell of bleach has soaked the air and something else, sickeningly sweet. Distinctively hospital. I walk to his bed and sit. I lean over to give him a hug.

"Watch the lines," he says.

I pull away. It's true, he looks like the back of my computer, connected everywhere to everything. "Sorry, did I hurt you?"

"No, it's just easy to get tangled up." He sounds very tired. He looks awful.

"How are you feeling?" I ask, as if I need an answer. I'm stiff, almost formal.

"Oh, I'm just great," he answers. "Never felt better."

Last time I saw him, he looked like him. Now he looks like somebody who is very sick. His face is so thin. It's *that* look. The AIDS look. *As Seen on TV.*

"Seriously," he begins, "I'm not doing so well."

I clear my throat. Blink hard. "Um, what's going on exactly?"

He sighs and looks across the room at nothing. "Well, Sport, I don't know exactly. And neither do they." He waves his hand in the general direction of the doctors, outside the room.

"I don't understand."

"I don't either. Nobody does. My blood work is normal. T-cells are fine. But there are things that should be a lot higher given everything else."

"What should be higher?"

"All the things you don't pay attention to." He doesn't say this with anger. Just a little sadness. I realize what a difference it would have made to him if I had paid even a little more attention.

"When are you coming home?"

He rolls his eyes. "I don't know. They tell me in a couple of days, so we'll see."

"They're not telling you anything?"

"They're concerned about the hiccups because they don't know what's causing them. They just don't stop."

"Aren't they doing anything?" I ask. This makes no sense. None.

"Well, there's a new class of drugs called integrase inhibitors. So my doctor, Barbara, says, 'Let's get him the drug.' But once again, it's not available yet and the current trials are only open to patients who are naive to all other drugs."

"Naive?" I ask.

"People who've never taken anything." Pighead has taken everything. "If I'm lucky, she said by October we should start to see compassionate-use availability. But that's a long time away."

"It's not all that long," I tell him. "Not at all."

"Well, the amazing thing about these drugs is that they're trying to develop them to be a once-daily pill. Imagine, just one pill."

I picture his kitchen counter, littered with prescription medications. Which I had always found so odd because he'd never been sick or looked unhealthy. If anything, he was tired sometimes, or miserable with side effects from the medicine. But overall, he's been fine. Besides, nobody gets really sick from AIDS anymore. They certainly don't die from it.

"I told Barbara, 'I want to get *off* of the heavy-duty antibiotics I'm taking to allegedly prevent MAC. To give my body a break for a while.' " He looks around for something.

"You want some water?"

He nods his head.

I take the urine-yellow plastic water pitcher on his nightstand and pour some water into the paper cup, hand it to him. "Why are your hands shaking?" I ask, trying to control the shaking in my own voice.

"Yet another new and fun thing." Water splashes out of the cup, soaking the front of his hospital gown.

"Why did you have an ambulance take you here? Why didn't you just call me at work and have me take you in a cab?"

Something in his eyes frightens me. "Because the hiccups wouldn't stop long enough for me to talk. I was losing the ability to breathe."

Jesus. "They're not so bad now," I say.

"Morphine calms them down for some reason."

It dawns on me that the two people I most obsess over are seriously involved with narcotics. I put my head on his chest, listen to his heart. It's beating so fast that I'm afraid just listening it to it will make mine beat along with it and I'll have a heart attack. His heart sounds like a bird's, not a man's. He falls asleep instantly and for some reason, this makes me profoundly sad.

• • •

Will I ever stop smoking? Do I need more paper towels? I sprayed the TV screen with Windex, but maybe I should go back and clean in between the ventilation crevices in the rear. And this is all that's on my mind, all I can think about even though Pighead is in a hospital room being very sick.

My thoughts seem thick, ketchup stuck in the bottle. Like trying to feel someone's face while wearing goosedown mittens. I've played all my sad music; nothing works. Nothing makes me realize, understand that it is *Pighead* in that bed.

His hand shook as he held the tiny paper meds cup. It trembled under the weight of less than an ounce of tap water. He winced in pain as he swallowed and collapsed back on the bed, exhausted as if he'd just done bench presses.

I'm out of soap in the bathroom. And there was no mail today. Strange. There's always something. Coupons at least.

The last thing he gave me before I left his hospital room last night: a yellow sticky note on which he'd scrawled PLEASE REMEMBER I LOVE YOU.

I should go back now and lie in bed next to him and hold him in my arms. This is what I ought to do. Lean back on his articulating steel hospital bed with the thin, scratchy sheets, rest his head on my chest, wrap both arms around his new, tiny frame and hold him. But what if he died there in my arms? If the embrace was so comforting that it took the edge off his fight? I did not want to see Pighead sigh deeply and relax into death.

So, I look at a shirt that I wore once, just to run to the store, and threw carelessly across the back of a chair. I will fold it. Put it back. A numb coward with folded shirts.

I almost sob. Like an almost sneeze that, at the last moment, swallows itself. I almost sob and then I'm blank. I light a peach-scented candle to mask the cigarette smoke, to sweeten the room.

I called. Just now. He's so tired that he couldn't talk for a full minute, even to me. I told him I could come up. But he's running a fever of a hundred and four and has chills and can barely breathe and is due for medication in an hour and he's just so tired. It seemed okay that I'm not there with him. He's busy concentrating on the business of breathing.

He said, "I want them to find out what this is and I want them to treat it, no matter how horrible the treatment, and I just want to move on." They say it could be a parasite or lymphoma or any other number of things his AIDS-wracked immune system can't contend with.

Who knows? Nobody. I feel as if something essential is rushing out of me and there is nothing I can do to stop it. I cannot find the valve. I'm bleeding out, deflating. There is the sensation of speed. Spiraling. Of falling.

Foster is lying on my sofa, shirt off, eating Ben & Jerry's Rocky Road ice cream from the carton and reading the Narcotics Anonymous Blue Book. "This is really fascinating, profound stuff," he says with his mouth full. "It's so true. I can see it all so clearly now—shit, this stuff is so cold it hurts." He opens his mouth to warm the ice cream, then he sets the pint on the floor beside the couch. Every once in a while, he laughs out loud or says, "So true, so true." He could almost pass for a normal boyfriend, if only the cover of his book was something like *Investment Strategies You Can Live With*.

Foster is staying with me for five days, until he moves into his new apartment. He decided that part of the reason he's feeling so crazy is because he's still living in the same apartment he shared with the crazy Brit. When he asked to stay here, I thought it was the only good, friendly thing to do. I also thought it would be a good minitest of us together. A relationship terrarium. And I needed him, that's the truth. I needed somebody to be with me. Somebody to stop the spinning.

I go over to the couch. "Shove over," I say. He sets the book down next to the ice cream on the floor and opens his arms. "C'mere," he says warmly. I wrap my arms around the mess and close my eyes. Foster is my source of comfort. A frightening fact.

"I'm really worried," I say.

"I know," he whispers. "Just close your eyes and take a nap, right here next to me."

Shit, I wish I could count on you, I think.

"I know," Foster whispers.

At my last therapy session, I tell Wendy about Pighead being in the hospital, Foster being in my apartment and me being a mess.

"Are you going to meetings?" she asks.

"No," I tell her flatly.

"Well, they might help," she says. "I really wish you'd go."

I nod as if I plan to. But the truth is I hate AA meetings and have no intention of going back, ever.

As always, the subject returns to Foster. "Even if he does go to rehab or start taking his sobriety really seriously, I'm always going to be living on the edge, waiting for his relapse. I just don't see how it's possible. It's bad enough having to make sure *I* don't relapse, but then having to worry about him."

I ask her if there are any precedents. "As a general principle, should recovering alcoholics be with other recovering alcoholics? Or should we find teetotalers?"

She, of course, says there are no hard and fast rules. And this annoys me because I want her to tell me what to do. I explain that, "Another alcoholic is the only person who could ever really, truly understand me, the way my mind works, my Void. But I'm afraid to be with one, because I feel like if they relapse, I lose them."

She nods.

"I think I love him, but I also think that you can love people who aren't good for you."

Wendy crosses her legs. "One of the qualities I have seen in my experience as a therapist, one of the 'traits' if you will, is that people I associate with long-term sobriety all have a sense of perspective in common. As if they can step back from their life, step back from the play, and watch the performance and make judgment calls. You seem to me to have this quality."

This feels like the closest I will ever come to a stamp of approval. I almost wish she'd write this down on her letterhead so I could carry it with me, as evidence of emotional health and stability. I could then pull it out on the third date, when a future potential boyfriend's questions and doubts arise.

"How do you feel about this being our last session?" she asks. I am wary and feel this could be a trick question. I must be careful how I answer, because I do not want her to revoke my mental health.

"Well, it's a process. You know." *Process* is an excellent word. I continue, more confident. "I mean, I won't ever reach a place where I can say, 'Okay, I'm together now.' But I do feel like my immediate crisis is over, I'm sober. And now it's just a matter of using the tools I got in rehab and in therapy to stay sober and continue to grow." As I say this I am impressed with my own ability to think on my feet; a skill absolutely honed in advertising. Of course, I have no idea if any of what I've said is true. But it certainly sounds good.

"You really don't talk about Pighead very much. Yet I get the feeling that there's more to the story." She looks at me as if I have some sort of reply.

"Hmmmm," I say. "Maybe so."

Her eyes widen ever so slightly. Just enough so that I can see that *she* can see a crack in my glossy, sober exterior.

• • •

After therapy, I go to the gym. As I do bench presses, I think about Pighead unable to even manage a small paper cup. And Foster, unable to manage his life.

Later at home, I play the soundtrack from *Falling* and drink lemon seltzer water while I sit at my computer and write radio commercials for my German beer client. Half an hour later, the buzzer sounds. I jump.

"Who is it?" I say into the box on the wall.

"I'm a friend of Foster's," says the voice. The voice with a British accent.

I buzz him in and stand by the door until I hear the knock. I open up and there, standing before me, is one of the most mortifying sights. A needle-thin man with dark circles under his desperate eyes. His clothes look—and smell—like they haven't been washed in weeks. He could be a member of an eighties punk band who just woke up from an overdose.

"Where is he?" he asks urgently.

"Who are you?"

"I'm Kyle, goddamn it. Who the hell are *you* is what I'd like to know?"

I don't want to get into a fight with somebody who might have a fistful of syringes in his back pocket. "I'm just a friend of Foster's. How did you know he was staying here?"

"What do you mean, how did I know? How the hell do you think I know? He's my boyfriend. I know where he is." He edges closer. Letting him in is not an option.

"Well, Foster's not here now. I'll tell him you stopped by. Okay?" I begin to close the door.

His hand flies up and blocks it. "Where the hell is he?" the maniac wants to know.

"Look, asshole. I don't know where the fuck he is. Get lost." I lower my voice and narrow my eyes. I channel Jeffrey Dahmer. "I mean it. Leave now." I give him a look that I hope makes him

understand I am not a rational, sane person. That I might actually
enjoy making soup stock out of his cranium.

"Fuck you," he spits. He turns and walks down the stairs. I
stand there until I hear the door below open and close. I stand a
moment longer listening for breathing. Convinced he's gone, I go
back inside my apartment.

By eleven o'clock, there's no sign of Foster. I go to bed at two;
still no Foster.

I dream that he walks in the door and I feel relieved. Only to
wake up and realize I was dreaming. I have the same dream
throughout the night, a terrible loop.

At work the next day, I feel edgy and worried and frustrated and
angry and sad and confused and relieved and every other emotion
on that damn rehab feeling chart. Sometimes, a few feelings collect and have a sort of party in my head. Then it seems they all
leave and I have no feelings at all. I remember in rehab someone
saying that nine months was a turning point. A lot of people go
back out and use at the nine-month point. It's like the seven-year
itch. I think this must be because we have nine months programmed into us from our time in the womb. After nine months
we are ready to make a dramatic change. Be born, or go get
drunk.

Our Wirksam commercial is being tested in focus groups.
Greer really stresses about this. She is worried the commercial
will not test well, that people will not like it. I, on the other hand,
could not care less. Advertising feels like this piece of dog shit I
can't seem to scrape off my shoe.

I sneeze.

Greer sees me eyeing my sleeve. "Do you want a Kleenex
brand facial tissue?" she asks.

"Huh? A what?"

She reaches into her desk drawer and retrieves a small packet of tissues. "A Kleenex brand facial tissue. Do you need one?"

"Greer? What's wrong with you? Why are you calling them that? They're Kleenexes."

She sets the tissues on the desk. "Augusten, you of all people should know better. Kleenex is a registered trademark of Kimberly-Clark. They're not 'Kleenexes,' they're tissues. Kleenex *brand* tissues."

"You're completely mad," I tell her.

"No. You're just being a selfish alcoholic. Kleenex is their brand. They have a right to protect it. And I, for one, respect that. I respect other people. You can't just go around changing things into what you want them to be. Just because you want to call tissues *Kleenexes* doesn't make it fair or right." She's very angry.

"Um. You're taking this whole *Kleenex* thing way too seriously. What is this really about?"

"It's about the entire world revolving around you, Augusten. Because you know what? It doesn't. We all have to make compromises and get along." She picks the tissues up and throws them in my lap. "And be civilized, okay? Don't use the sleeve of your sweatshirt to wipe your goddamn nose." She stands to walk out of the room.

"It's not a sweatshirt, Greer. It's a Gap High Performance Fleece Athletic Crew Top."

At a little after noon, I phone Pighead at the hospital. I'm alarmed when his mother answers. Why can't he answer the phone himself? "How is he?" I ask.

"He not so good," she says in her thick Greek accent. "He have very high fever. No food, nothing. Can't eat. Last night, very bad. He ask about you. You come?"

"I'm on my way."

• • •

When I walk into Pighead's room, I'm confronted with his mother and two of Pighead's friends, whom I know only by name, from Pighead telling me deeply personal and embarrassing things about them. I nod to the friends. "Hey," I say to his mother. She turns to me. Her eyes contain confusion, panic and ancient Greek spells. I walk to the bed.

Pighead's eyes are wide open, too wide. "Hey, Pighead," I say.

He looks at me. He extends his shaking hand. I take it. "Augusten," he moans, "please don't hit me."

His mother looks at me quickly, sharply. "He's only teasing," I say. And I can see a tiny smile on his face, but it's so small it's almost like what's left after a normal smile. He closes his eyes, which for some reason makes me feel better.

I ask him if he's feeling okay and he shakes his head from side to side. "No."

And suddenly he's asleep, which does not make me feel better. Because falling asleep that fast is more accurately termed "losing consciousness." "What's going on with him?" I ask his mother. "He wasn't this bad the other day."

"He'll be fine," she says, walking to the nightstand and removing a used tissue, a paper cup and a peeled but uneaten banana, which has begun to turn brown. I note that she is wearing latex gloves. The diamond ring on her wedding finger pokes up through the rubber, stretching it.

I walk back over to Pighead, and suddenly his eyes are open again. He motions me to lean closer. He wants to whisper something.

"You," he asks. And then he slowly raises his hand up and points to me. Faintly, he smiles. His hand falls back on the bed and he is asleep.

I whisper back. "You."

• • •

Foster comes home a little after eight P.M. He looks ragged, horrible. He slinks in the door, sad and defeated. He glances at me only once. Then wordlessly, he collects his few things and puts them in his knapsack. Then he sits on the sofa, head down, and says, "I'm sorry, Auggie."

"Your friend stopped by last night," I tell him.

"I know," Foster says.

I shoot him a glance. "You know? How could you know?"

He looks up at me. "Augusten," he begins, "I want you to know that I truly love you. I love you so very much. But I can't . . ." He stops. "I can't . . . I'm not good for you and I know it."

"What are you saying?" I ask him.

"I bought a brownstone in Brooklyn," he tells me.

I cannot believe what I am hearing. "What? You what? When?"

He exhales in utter defeat. "A couple of weeks ago. I bought a brownstone." Then, as if it can't possibly get more disgusting, "Kyle's going to be staying with me. For a while."

"Wait a minute, Foster," I say. "Are you telling me that you are moving back in with that psycho Brit?"

"It's just for a while. He's doing really bad, Auggie."

And suddenly, I can see it all very clearly. The insanity. The parallel universe of it. How it mimics normal life enough to fool you while you're in it. But when you step back, wow. I realize that this is one of those three-hundred-empty-bottles-of-Dewar's-in-my-apartment-that-I-can't-see things. Yet instead of rage, I feel sorry for him. He's caught in the same place I was caught. It dawns on me that to be with him would be like living with my old self again.

I go and sit next to him. I want to think of something profound to say, but nothing comes to me. I put my arm around him and tell him I love him. I say I wish there was something I could do. "But there's not, I know. Not really."

On the way out he says, "I'll give you the new phone number as soon as we have a phone." He stammers, "Um, I mean, as soon as *I* have a phone."

So they're going to be a *We*. "Foster, why Brooklyn?"

He pauses in the doorway. Turns. "I wanted to be as far away from Eighth Avenue as I could get."

Rae appears in my head, as she often does, carrying a quote with her. *You can't move away from your addiction, it will follow you wherever you go.*

He sets his bag down and we hug. He feels so fucking good. But then, so does scotch.

THE BUTTERFLY EFFECT

I've been at Pighead's apartment since six A.M. I've changed his diaper three times, given him four injections and watched while he vomited peach Yoplait onto the Philippe Starck hall runner. I can't help but think that having a hangover while placing the soiled diaper into the red plastic biohazard bag would not be the end of the world. In fact, a hangover might improve my outlook. I took a week off from work, so at least I don't have to deal with that shit. Just this shit.

Pighead is operating in slow, drooling motion. Within the space of a month he has been transformed into a skeleton without bladder control. The only reason he's home instead of still at the hospital is because they ran out of tests to perform. Life is a question mark now.

"Do you still feel thick in the head?" I ask him while he sits on the couch watching the TV, which, incidentally, is off.

He nods slowly. A strand of saliva, as thick as yarn, sways from his lower lip. I use a tissue to pinch it off.

The visiting nurse that comes every day taught me how to give Pighead his intramuscular injections. This might be part of the reason Pighead always looks at me as if I am about to harm him. We ordered the tiniest needles possible for the tiniest amount of pain. I even injected myself with water to see how much it hurt. I was surprised that I could barely feel the prick. So I think it's the medicine itself, not the needle, that burns. I don't dare inject myself with his medicine. The stuff is deadly.

His mother has moved into his apartment. She spends the day muttering prayers in Greek and simmering lamb bones on the stove. Originally, the diaper changing was her department. I figured, she did it before, she can do it again. But she was unable to do it without sobbing, so I took over the task. Clearly, nothing is going according to plan.

"Do you remember last fall when we took a drive to Massachusetts to see the leaves?" I ask Pighead.

He turns to face me. I'm sitting next to him on the couch and the effort of turning his head seems large. He nods. He raises his arm and places it on my shoulder. He speaks very slowly. "I would give every penny I have for just one more day like that," he says. His arm falls from my shoulder and lands on the sofa. I think that arm is too bruised; we need to move the IV to the other arm.

Last year at this time, Pighead looked like a soccer player. Handsome, stocky, healthy. One would easily have hated him for his fine genetics. Now, his cheekbones look like two luggage handles protruding from either side of his head. His legs are the diameter of Evian bottles. And the mind that was formerly valued at seven figures on Wall Street probably could not add ten plus two.

Meanwhile, I have discovered a latent talent for nursing. I find comfort in thumping air bubbles out of the IV line before inserting it. I like opening the little sterile alcohol pads before swabbing his arm and the cap of the medication bottle. I feel whole while I count and organize a week's worth of his pills and place them into the pale yellow Monday-through-Friday plastic pill box with snapping lids over each day. Sometimes he will smile at me and I know that this is the old Pighead smiling. I smile back and then take his temperature. It is a play and we are in our roles. I am performing from a script.

I wonder if I were a normal person, instead of an alcoholic with a highly evolved sense of denial, whether or not I would be more of a mess right now. Instead of thinking, *My best friend might be dying*, I am thinking, *I need to take that retrovirus inhibitor tablet and split it in half*. I feel alarmingly stable.

Hayden calls from London to tell me that he relapsed in a pub near Piccadilly Circus. Well, well, well. Deepak Chopra finally made a bacon cheeseburger out of the holy cow of India.

"How tacky," I tell him. "You relapsed in a tourist area."

Shamed, he admits, "It was a poor choice."

"What? Relapsing or where you relapsed?" I ask.

"Both," he says. Then, "You don't sound nearly as surprised as I expected you to be. I feel rather let down."

"Nothing surprises me now," I tell him. I am stoic. I am Joan of Arc, with liver damage and an unused penis.

"Are you going to meetings?" he asks when I tell him about Foster moving back in with the Brit and Pighead being in a free fall.

"Ha," I snort. My life has become a series of choices based on triage. "I don't have the time. Besides, you're not one to talk about AA. You went every day and look what happened to you." Hayden is now proof to me that AA is crap.

"I wouldn't have relapsed in New York," he says. "I had a sober network there. Here, well, I don't have anything."

"Bullshit," I say. "You chose to relapse. You didn't have to." I hate it when alcoholics relapse and then act like somebody cut the brake lines on their cars.

"I suppose it was building up. I suppose it was inevitable."

I wonder if it's building up in me? I wonder if I would be able to tell? I wonder if the fact that I must wonder is my answer. "I'm not frightened about Pighead," I tell him.

He's quiet for a moment and I swear I can hear the Atlantic Ocean churning over the phone lines, even though I realize they aren't lines but satellite signals. So maybe it's interstellar dust motes banging around. "I don't know if that's a good thing or not," he says finally.

"I don't feel anything, actually," I point out.

"Hmmmmm," he says.

I know exactly what he means. Then remembering something, I ask Hayden, "Where do whales go when they die?"

"They beach themselves," he says immediately.

"Oh," I say.

"You really ought to go to a meeting, Augusten. I'm telling you this as somebody who has recently imbibed and who is now counting days once again and steeping in his own misery."

I want to ask him if it was just a little bit fun, a little bit worth it. "It was really awful, huh?"

"You see?" Hayden explodes into the phone. "You're asking *buying* questions. You want to know if it was really awful as opposed to semiawful. I swear, Augusten, I'm worried. Go to a meeting. Don't drink."

Hayden is annoying me. I had no intention of drinking. He's the one who got smashed in the Times Square of London. He's the one who threw his sobriety against the wall and now has to go clean up the mess.

All I have to do is change a few diapers.

• • •

Greer is not pleased when I tell her, over the phone, that I am taking a leave of absence. But because of the reason, she is forced to bite her tongue. Probably literally. Probably it is bleeding. "Well, that's a very good thing you're doing," she says, like I have volunteered to serve turkey to homeless people in the Bowery.

"I'm a little late," I say with some disgust at myself.

"Late for what?"

"Late for showing him that I actually give a shit. Late for everything."

"It's never too late," Greer chimes. I picture her wearing a horribly expensive sweater made by a seven-year-old Cambodian orphan with head lice. "I'm sure you're helping."

"How's the Nazi?" I ask, changing the subject to something neutral.

"He was furious that the music house wanted forty grand. He wanted us to 'Jew them down.'"

"He didn't say that."

"Oh yes, he did. His exact words."

I wonder how much of my soul remains after spending so many years as an advertising copywriter. Will I end up in Hell along with the Hamburger Helper Helping Hand, Joe Camel and Wendy, the Snapple Lady?

"Call me," Greer says.

I know she doesn't mean to call her and chat. Or call her for updates on work. She means call her when it all goes down.

For three days in a row, Pighead has had no hiccups. He stopped drooling and seems more mentally alert. Enough to call me "asshole Fuckhead" when I accidentally spill Ocean Spray CranApple juice on the arm of his pristine white sofa with the down cushions. It's not a large stain, but it will be permanent, a fact Pighead has the mental capacity to remind me of more than once.

Even Virgil has crawled out from under the bed. For weeks, he has been afraid of Pighead. Probably because Pighead no longer smells like Pighead but like something made by Pfizer.

His mother rolls pastry dough with a toilet paper dowel in the kitchen and I sit at the dining room table reading *Esquire:* "101 Things Every Guy's Gotta Do Before His Number's Up." Number 73 is: paint a woman's toenails. I add my own number 102 to the list: clean diarrhea off your ex-boyfriend's legs. "Your eyes look better," I tell Pighead. "Brighter," I add.

"I feel a little better," he says.

Virgil sleeps in a wedge of sunlight in front of the fireplace. He cannot be roused, even with the squeaky carrot. Dog denial.

If it weren't for the seven boxes of medical supplies stacked next to the front door, the biohazard bags, the disposable diapers, the rubber gloves, the IV pole with the Plum XL3M Series Pump, the fact that most of the furniture has been moved to the sides of the room to make space, and the visiting nurse who is quietly connecting two lengths of clear plastic tubing in the corner, this might pass for an ordinary day.

On my way home, I surprise myself by stopping into a liquor store on Seventh Avenue and Twelfth. I surprise myself even further by buying a pint of Black Label. On the way out, I think how strange it is that liquor stores never redecorate. They never get cool-ized. But then, they don't need to be hip. They are like urinals—people will go there no matter what.

THE DEEP END

At home, I sit at my desk and open the bottle. I bring my nose to the opening and inhale. The smell is sharp, powerful. For a moment, I think, *How could anyone drink this stuff? This could power a lawn mower.* But then I'm pouring it into a plastic cup and bringing the plastic cup to my lips, like a lawn mower with hands. I talk to myself. "I can't relapse, this is just classic. I know better. I should go *immediately* to an AA meeting. This is a code blue."

It burns going down.

My head is filled with fumes. I am more than mildly uncomfortable. But then I feel the warmth of it. As if Liquid Foster has come from behind and wrapped his arms around me. I honestly feel a sense of home. I feel safe.

I finish the pint and want more. I feel only slightly bad that I have done this. And I'm not sure that all of me believes I actually have. But then another part of me feels like it's no big deal. Because there are certain facts that I need to begin grasping. Fact number one is that my best friend is not doing so well. Fact number two is that I didn't see it coming because I was too busy doing absolutely nothing of any importance. Fact number three is that I don't want to be sober anymore. I do not want front-row-center seats for the crucifixion. I would like to conveniently sidestep what is happening in my life at the moment.

The Boiler Room is packed when I get there a little after eleven. Packed with gay guys from the East Village wearing stiff G-Star denims and knit skullcaps. I am wearing frayed khakis that I bought years ago at the Gap, an *Avid* T-shirt I got free from an editing house and white sneakers that are closer to gray. I am the opposite of *kewl* and look completely out of place here. So naturally, a guy comes up to me immediately.

"Hey," he says, gripping his Rolling Rock.

I nod, half-smile. "How's it going?"

"It's all right, man. My name's Keith," he says, offering up his hand.

"Augusten," I say, shaking it. "You been here long?"

"Nah. Just got here ten, maybe fifteen minutes ago." He takes a sip of beer.

Keith is shorter than I am, about five-eight to my six-two. He has dark hair, dark eyes and good features. But best of all, he's talking to me. "So what are you up to tonight?" he asks me.

"Getting shitfaced," I tell him.

He grins. It's the grin of someone who understands the concept of shitfaced. It's the grin of someone who might want to join in on the fun. "Let's drink," I tell him and walk smoothly to the bar, like an expert pool player who is about to begin the national championships.

He follows.

And I realize this is exactly what I came here for. I came here for someone to follow me. I came here to be Alpha wolf.

We drink. He feels up my ass, I feel up his. We drink some more.

An odd thing happens. Instead of getting sloppy drunk, I get focused drunk. Far from wanting to lose myself in the lyrics to the theme song from *The Brady Bunch*, I have the clarity of mind to know that the reason I am drunk and in a dark bar with a strange guy is because I am desperate to control something. I want this man to drink when I tell him to. Laugh when I crack a joke. Blush slightly when I look at him *just so*. And leave when I say it's time.

"Let's get out of here," I say.

"Sure," he says. If he were a dog, his tail would be wagging, ears flopping in opposite directions. "Where to?"

"Your place. I don't want to be in my apartment."

He seems happy enough with this suggestion. We head for the door. He pauses. "Um," he says, looking at me with tentative hope, "should we get some blow?"

"Excellent idea." I slap him on the back and his smile broadens. I reach into my front pocket and withdraw a wad of twenties and fifties. "Here," I say, jamming some of the bills into his hand. "Go get some."

I stand by the door looking at the other guys who are themselves looking for other guys. The whole thing suddenly strikes me as beyond sad. All of this exposed loneliness. These raw nerves firing into the dark. I imagine the guy leaning against the pool table hooking up with the guy poking at the jukebox. They're both good-looking and aloof. Maybe later, they'll speak to each other. Then fuck. Then—and this is the part that interests me— fall asleep together. Naked, snoring men. Strangers with their arms around each other or their backs pressed together. The thought revolts and fascinates me. It reminds me of two puppies that just met, curling up together and sleeping, then drinking out of the same water bowl.

Keith returns looking very proud of himself. "Ready?" he asks in a way that can only be described as genuinely friendly. I look at him for a moment and realize I am a complete goner.

"Sure, let's head out of here," I say, in my best normal voice. I don't tell him about the pool table man or the jukebox man or the sleeping puppies. He is not for epiphanies. He is for surfaces. Or maybe that's me. I suspect it is.

Luckily, Keith lives only blocks away. His apartment is a fifth-floor walk-up. I manage the stairs and am uncomfortably sober by the time I reach the top. I am hoping he has alcohol in the apartment. And then I remember the blow. Once inside, Keith tosses his wallet and keys on the kitchen counter and removes miniature paper envelopes from his pocket. He produces a razor blade from the junk drawer in the kitchen and goes about the task of cutting lines. He works wordlessly, like an old-world craftsman. His face is pure scrimshaw. I, on the other hand, would simply drag out the corner of my Amex card, poke it into the dust and start snorting.

"Wanna go?" he asks, producing exactly half of a plastic straw from thin air.

I take the straw. "Sure," I say as I lean over the counter and, like a practiced anteater, begin inhaling line after line.

"Whoa, man. Take it easy on that shit."

I turn my head sideways and look at him with the straw still at my nostril. "Don't worry," I tell him. "I'm fine." I inhale another two lines and pass the straw to him. I pinch my nostrils together and sniff whatever dust remains.

Keith displays admirable moderation, snorting only two lines. "That's enough for me for a while," he says.

"Take off your shirt," I tell him as I stretch my own T-shirt over my head.

"Holy shit," he says when he sees my chest. "You have an incredible body." He reaches his hand out to touch my stomach. I feel no pleasure in his compliment or his touch, only impatience. This is the only feeling. I feel like the paper on which my mood chart is printed.

"Here, I'll do it," I say as I tug his shirt up, snagging it on his head. He pulls his head out and tosses the shirt onto a chair. His chest is very handsome—strong and solid. But this isn't what interests me. What interests me is seeing what I can get him to do. The coke has made me incredibly horny and also borderline suicidal. I'm split 50/50. Do I want a blowjob or do I want to jump out the window?

"Does this feel good?" he asks later in bed, my cock in his hands, slick from his mouth.

No, it feels awful, I don't tell him. But want to. This is not what I expected, he was the wrong guy. His touch is too personal. Affectionate. It could split me open.

I gently pull him up, rest his head on my chest. I stroke it as kindly as I can possibly stroke a stranger's head. "I have to go," I say. "Sorry."

"Hey, Augusten, what's the matter? You seem like you're upset about something. Like maybe you wanna talk. I really like you, you know. It's not just about sex or anything. I mean, there's something about you that, well, I don't know," he trails off. "Something I guess I'm really attracted to. And I don't mean the physical stuff."

He's a really nice guy. If only I weren't me.

Greer calls me to tell me that our commercial didn't do well in focus groups and that we need to do a re-edit.

"I can't care about this now," I tell her. I am deeply hungover.

She's silent for a moment. "Well, it's our commercial. I mean, I know you've taken a leave from work, but . . . Well, you are the writer."

"Greer, I have a lot of shit happening," I say. "You are just going to have to deal with this yourself. Hire a fucking freelancer."

"Why me?" she explodes. "Why must I always clean up after you?"

My head is pounding and my nose is dry. "Greer, just calm the fuck down. I'm not getting paid to deal with this crap. Get it? *Leave of absence* means I'm not there."

"Well, what about me?" she cries. "I need some support here."

"Advertising is not the most important thing in the world, Greer."

"No, of course not," she spits. "You are."

I glance over at the empty bottle. I would need to be very drunk to speak with her now. A gram would help, too.

"Look, I gotta—"

"I'm sorry," she says. "I didn't mean that. I just mean that I need help, too."

"I can't be your support system," I say. "I have too much going on in my life. There's not enough of me left over."

"I had a dream about you last night," she begins. "I dreamt that I was working late at the office and all of a sudden, there was a tornado. And the windows started to blow in and there was glass everywhere. And in the dream, I knew you were the tornado."

"Sorry about your dream."

"I bet you are," she says and hangs up.

An hour and a half later, she calls back. There is apology in her voice. "I just thought you'd like to know what happened to Rick," she says.

Rick is now the farthest thing from my mind, but whatever happened to him, I can only hope it was something that involved a stun gun. "What?" I say, weary, half interested, half not giving a fuck.

"He was promoted," she says.

"That's wonderful," I say, ready to hang up.

"To *Direct*," she adds.

A thin smile comes to me. Rick is now in Direct Marketing, the lowest of the low. His life will be about getting people to open their envelopes and send back the SASE. If ad people are bottom-feeders, Rick is now a catfish with no dorsal fin and an extra eye.

I drink to Rick.

"He coded. It took five people just to get his heart going again. He hasn't regained consciousness." These are the first words I hear this morning, not counting "Grande? or venti?" from the Starbucks guy. Pighead's brother is standing next to me in ICU. We are both standing in the doorway to Pighead's room. Pighead himself is attached to many busy machines.

"I don't get it," I say. My fingers burn from the hot coffee in my hand.

"He started complaining last night. Saying his chest hurt. He was cold and sweaty. My mother freaked, called nine-one-one. I got here at about three."

At three, I was still doing lines. This reminds me that I brought one of the packets with me. "I gotta run to the bathroom. Be back in a sec," I say, turning and walking down the hall. Inside the bathroom, I open the little envelope and set it on the stainless steel ledge above the sink. I open my wallet and pull out a credit card. I go to work on the coke. I do maybe a quarter of it. I fold the envelope back up and stick it in my pocket. Then I decide, fuck it. And I take the envelope out again and do another quarter. I take a leak and my piss smells like scotch. Then I go back outside. Jerry is still staring at his older brother. I walk past him and go to Pighead's bedside.

"Pighead," I say. "You in there?" I poke his arm with my index finger. He doesn't respond.

"Wake up," I say very quietly. It's an effort to speak softly because the coke is pushing me. I'm hitting my brakes constantly, skidding inside.

Nothing. Less than nothing. The ventilator is incredibly offensive, breathing for him like this. Giving him these expansive, healthy breaths. For the first time today, I notice that I'm wearing jeans and a tight white T-shirt. The veins along my arms stand out like highways on a map and I feel ashamed. It feels obscene to look this healthy.

On the way home, I tell myself he's dying, that I have to accept this fact. Then I tell myself, no he's not, I don't have to accept anything. I can feel the small pouch of coke in my pocket. It's like this tiny powder hard-on that wants attention. But the thing is, I don't really love coke. So I stop at a liquor store on University Place and pick up a bottle of Dewar's.

Pighead's mother calls me three times, leaving long messages on my machine. Messages that say things like "When are you coming?" and "Still no change." I listen to her speak into the machine, unable to answer her calls. "Maybe he would wake up if you come," she says.

No, I want to tell her, *he wouldn't.*

I notice that I have polished off nearly half of the Dewar's. I glance over at the picture of Pighead in the car from our trip to Massachusetts all those years ago. And a picture of me in that fucking motel pool. I look at it and think, *The deep end.*

And then something else hits me. Something so blindly obvious that it's no wonder I have been unable to see it. The problem is that it's been eight years since that trip to Massachusetts, six-and-a-half since he learned he was positive, six-and-a-half since I decided to *get over him in that way.* And I didn't. I didn't get over him. I never got over him. My feelings simply went into remission. They were pushed out of the way by the olive in the bottom of my martini glass.

No wonder I don't feel anything. I'm about to lose everything.

It's after visiting hours when I arrive at St. Vincent's. The receptionist at the front desk lets me up despite the fact that I probably smell like the floor of a bar. She lets me up after checking her computer. "Go ahead," she says, handing me a pass. I want to turn her computer monitor around and read what it says. Why is she letting a drunk up to his room near midnight? Does it say, "Lost cause, admit all"?

ICU is dark, though pulsing with the electronics of life support. I get the feeling that nobody here is sleeping. They're just unconscious. I walk softly, trying not to let my sneakers squeak against the tile.

"Pighead?" I say softly. "I'm here," I tell him. I look to see if his eyes are moving beneath his eyelids, to see if he's dreaming.

His right eye opens. The eye closest to me.

"Pighead?" I say. "It's me. It's okay. If you can hear me, squeeze my hand."

He doesn't squeeze my hand. *But still.* There's something in his eye. Something of him. I need to tell him. Now.

Except I can't say anything. I can't say anything that will make him think something's wrong. "Pighead, you know how much I . . ." and then I say, "It's okay."

A tear wells in his eye. It wells and then spills down his cheek. And despite being pumped with booze and coke, I can read that one eye as clearly as a billboard for cigarettes. Only instead of saying *Alive with Pleasure* it says, *I Have to Go Now.*

"You're going to be okay, Pighead. They're going to fix you. You need to fight this off. Fight as hard as you can." *Plop, plop, plop*, my own tears hit his sheet.

His eye says, "I can smell the liquor on your breath, Fuckhead. What the hell are you gonna do without me?"

"Pighead?" I whimper.

His eye says, "I have to go now. Don't follow me. Be good. Stay dry."

I need him to get up and start making hot dogs. I need him to yell at me for something. I need him to absolve me of every bad thing I have ever done to him or anyone else. I need him to know I won't run away or be shallow anymore.

His eye closes. A nurse enters the room. "Your friend had a very fitful evening. I think it's best if you let him rest. He needs to rest."

"How is he?" I ask her.

She looks at me like, *What, are you kidding?* "I'm sorry," she says, touching my arm as she leads me out of the room.

Well, there's my answer.

"He can get better, you know. I've seen him do it before. I mean, he was fine only a month or so ago." I think, *It has been only a month, hasn't it? Or has this been going on longer? Have I lost track of time?*

"You can come back tomorrow," she says. Then she adds, "You should probably sleep some yourself."

At home, I drink the rest of the bottle and finish up what little coke is left. I play the last message Pighead left on my answering machine. He left it before any of this shit happened. I saved it because it was so unusual. It said, "It's eleven-thirty, you must still be at work or over at Foster's. Anyway, Augusten, I just wanted to let you know that I love you."

At the time, I thought, *Huh? What's this shit all about? Why is he so Hallmarky all of a sudden?*

Now I know.

I wake up to the nagging ring of my phone. The machine picks up. I hear a hang-up, then the phone rings again. I drag myself out of bed feeling flammable from the alcohol fumes that are wafting off my skin. On the counter next to the microwave is the empty bottle of Dewar's, along with a dozen empty bottles of hard cider. Funny, I don't recall buying hard cider last night.

"Hello?" I answer. This seems to me more acceptable than "What the fuck!?" Which is my first thought.

"Augusten, Jim."

"Oh, hey. What in the world are you—"

"Pighead died. I just got the call."

In an effort to wake from the dream, I speak out loud. "What are you talking about?"

"I'm so sorry, Augusten. He was pronounced dead forty minutes ago. Heart failure."

"Wait."

"We're handling the arrangements. I recognized his name. We're always the first to know. I'm sorry."

"He's dead?"

"Yeah, he's dead. I'm so sorry, kiddo. Want me to come over?"

Why didn't his family call me? Why didn't his brother call me? Why did he die? And why is the undertaker telling me this? "I have to go," I tell him and hang up. I walk into the bathroom and look in the mirror. "He's dead," I tell my reflection. "Do you understand? Pighead is dead. You will never see him again. How does this make you feel?"

My reflection says nothing.

The wake is at four. I arrive at one. It's impossible for me to see people right now, anyone. Especially his family. It seems hardly possible that I am even capable of walking, having consumed nothing but alcohol for the past thirty hours. Which may explain the frown I get from the woman who answers the door of the funeral home. "No, Jim is not in at the moment. But you may view the body if you like." *View the body.* As if he's a Fabergé egg.

I walk into the viewing room. Harps gently play "Somewhere Over the Rainbow" through discreet speakers in the ceiling. Banquet chairs with padded red vinyl seats face the front of the room. There are flowers everywhere, an extravagance of blossoms. The aroma is Grandmother's Powder Room on steroids. He, I feel certain, would approve of the casket. It's a solid walnut Batesville with an ivory crepe lining. Jim suggested it personally. This is the first time I have ever seen, firsthand, how exquisite the undertaker's taste truly is in these matters.

I peer into the coffin.

So still. No heaving chest. No shaking. No sweating. No face winced in pain. No hiccups. No diarrhea. And a tuxedo.

"Hey, Pighead? Are you there? Pighead?"

I guess not.

I look at his face a while longer. I want to touch it but am afraid. I think, *Now I can remove your number from speed dial on my phone. I can forget your birthday. I don't have to put rubber gloves on and inject you with medication. I don't have to worry about getting stuck with a needle. Or fill your humidifier. Or change the lightbulb in the kitchen. Or answer the front door. I don't have to wonder how long you'll live. I don't have to tell you I can't see you today. I don't have to ever put more ice in your glass or pick up hot dog buns on the way to your apartment.*

In my head, I go over all these new benefits.

Days pass. They come and they go and I drink. This is all that happens. I suppose the mail arrives but I don't check. Greer leaves a message to see how Pighead is doing. She deliberately does not mention anything about work, so I know this is probably the real reason she called. I send her an e-mail saying just, *He's dead.* On my list of priorities in life, Greer is at the bottom along with vac-uum cleaner bags and my career.

Jim calls drunk and leaves a weepy message. Something about how he did the best he could. How he prepared "the body" him-self, as a favor. How Astrid left him because she thinks he's a drunk. "Ain't that a pisser," were his exact, slurry words.

And I can't stop thinking about Pighead. I wish I could talk to him and he'd talk back. Use some sort of spirit-world sign lan-guage. Make the lights flicker, or if that's too hard, he could cause a draft in my apartment. Or maybe it's easier to come back in a dream. Maybe he could visit me there. The only problem with that is that I'd always think it was just a dream. So maybe he needs to learn how to turn street lamps off when I walk beneath them. If that's too tricky, maybe he could just make them blink.

I keep talking to him but I don't hear anything. Maybe it's too soon. Maybe there's a holding area or something. *A process.* Like going through customs with a dog. How it has to stay in quarantine for a few weeks before you can take it home. Maybe it's like that. Or maybe you just die and that's it. Maybe there *is* nothing else. Maybe your body heat simply evaporates and adds another billionth of a degree of heat to the world.

The phone rings. I take a hurried swallow of scotch and answer it. It's Foster. Why am I not surprised? "Well, well, well," I say.

"Hey, Auggie."

"Hey, Fosty," I mimic, hatefully. "Where's your little Brit tonight?"

I hear the flick of a lighter, a sharp inhale. "He's gone. Been gone for three, four days," Foster says as he holds his breath.

"And you?" I ask.

He exhales into the phone, which I guess is my answer. "I'm fucked up. How's life?"

This makes me laugh. It's the first time I've laughed in days. It's bitter, like the first twenty seconds of water coming out of an old faucet. "What's your address?"

It takes me about fifty minutes to reach Foster's apartment by cab. I tip the driver three bucks and walk to the front door of the brownstone. He answers wearing a tank top, sweatpants and a blue bandana on his head. I walk through the door without saying anything.

"Want the grand tour?" he asks with zero enthusiasm.

I'm standing in the foyer. In front of me is a staircase that winds up to a second floor. To my right is one large room and to my left is another. There is no furiture. Various articles of clothing are strewn about; underwear, jeans, a sock and—inexplicably—

a football helmet. I follow Foster through the living room and into the kitchen. Although it would be considered a "gourmet, true cook's kitchen" by a perky real-estate agent, it's just another empty room. The Wolf stove, the Sub-Zero refrigerator with the glass doors, the slate countertops all ignored. "Nice kitchen. Bet you make some really lovely dinners here," I say.

"Oh yeah," he says, "I'm always cooking up a fucking storm."

"Why'd you even bother?" I ask him.

"Gotta live somewhere," is his answer.

I look at the copper backsplash and get the cliché lump in my throat. "Pighead died, Foster. And I'm drinking again." I go over and wrap my arms around him and tuck my face against his neck.

"Shhhhhh, baby." He strokes the back of my head with his fingers. "Let's smoke."

I ease away from him as he opens one of the drawers in the kitchen. He removes a glass pipe and a small plastic bag, along with a yellow Bic lighter. "C'mon, let's go get comfortable." He leaves the drawer open.

We sit cross-legged on the futon in his bedroom. He hands the pipe to me. I place it to my lips and our eyes meet. "Ready?" he asks.

I nod my head.

He lights the white rocks at the end of the pipe and I draw. A dreamy, warm smoke fills my lungs and goes immediately to a place inside of me that I have been unable to reach my entire life. The taste is both chemical and slightly sweet. I hold it in my lungs until I feel vaguely faint and then let it out.

This is perfect.

Nothing can compare to this.

It is instant and it is profound. This is what has been missing from me my entire life.

Foster smiles so warmly at me that I lean over and hug him as hard as I possibly can. He kisses my face over and over. Then he lights the pipe for himself.

Back and forth we trade it. He lights it for me, I light it for him.

Later, while Foster is lying on his back with his shirt off, I bring my face close to his stomach and study the ripples. They fascinate me. How did he get them? Where did they come from? God, the body is so breathtakingly amazing.

As if we are thinking one continuous thought, Foster begins doing crunches. I watch the muscles in his stomach bloom red with heat and blood. He does crunches and he doesn't stop. Sweat begins to form on his forehead. His face becomes liquid. I take the pipe and light it myself, watching. Sweat drips from his nose. His face is contorted with pain. He goes on and on and on.

When I can't watch anymore, I walk over to the window. It's floor-to-ceiling and I bring my hand to the glass. Although I can see the ripple, I can't touch it. The glass feels smooth, solid and cool. Yet I know glass is a liquid, always in motion.

Once I accidentally cut my wrist on a broken glass in the sink. How can a person slice their wrist with liquid? It's incomprehensibly brilliant and clever, glass.

It's dark outside and I can see Foster in the reflection. He's lying still now, breathing heavily.

"Augusten," he says.

I turn. "Yeah?"

"This is me. Now you've seen me."

I walk over to him. Sit beside him. "I could live here," I tell him. I take the pipe from his fingers. "I mean *here*," I say, holding it in front of his face. "I could live right *here*."

"Come curl up with me," he says, patting the space on the futon beside him.

I do. I climb beside him and lie on my side, hands between my legs. It seems like only a few minutes pass before Foster is sound asleep. But I can't sleep. So I go to the window and sit on the floor. I lean my head against the molding and stare at the street. Sometimes a car drives by, but mostly it's calm.

Time passes. A harrowing amount of it.

DRY

Months later—perhaps ten?—I walk down St. Mark's Place and I am insanely drunk. It is after midnight but the street is jammed with people and the vendors are selling Yankees caps, temporary tattoos, bootleg videos. Halfway down the block I see two beefy black guys sitting on the tall stairs that lead to a converted brownstone. As I pass by, one of them says, "Rock?"

I stop. "You have any crack?" I ask.

They rise and come down the stairs. "You a cop?" one of them asks.

I laugh. "I am so not a cop," I say.

They do not laugh. They ask again. "Yo, man. You're not a cop, are you?"

I say, "No. I am not a cop."

It's difficult to stand without swaying. Normally when I am this drunk I am sitting at my computer. I am not accustomed to standing.

"I need crack," I say.

A small plastic bag is produced; it contains two white rocks. "Fifty," one of the men says.

I remove my wallet from my back pocket and open it. I have a quarter-inch of twenties and remove three of them. "Here," I say. I have cashed in my 401k and feel incredibly rich, with over sixteen thousand dollars in the bank.

"Ain't got change, man," says one.

"Hurry this shit up," says the other.

"Whatever. Fuck it," I say, motioning for them to keep the change. I have always been a generous tipper. I used to work at a Ground Round restaurant in Northampton, Massachusetts, and I got very bad tips. So I know. So I tip.

"How do I do this?" I ask. Foster did it last time and I didn't pay attention. But I don't know what to do with them on my own.

"Oh, man. We ain't got time for this."

They walk away, fast. Almost a run, but not quite. But I don't know why they are afraid. Nothing will happen to them. Or me. I feel we are all protected. The alcohol in my system gives me a powerful sense of immunity.

I slide the bag containing the crack cocaine into my front pocket and turn around, walking back in the direction I came. Except now I feel more powerful, having the crack in my pocket. But I don't know how to smoke it on my own, so I feel like I have just bought the most amazing Corvette and I can't drive a stick. It is a feeling of supreme power together with utter dependence.

I need somebody who knows what to do.

I walk north on Third Avenue and then make a right on Eleventh and walk toward Second. Often there are prostitutes on the corner of Eleventh and Second and prostitutes know how to smoke.

I feel charmed when I see one, sitting on the sidewalk, her

back against the side wall of the sushi place on the corner. "Of course there's one here," I say to myself. My confidence is total.

I stop when I reach her. "What's up?" I ask. I am smiling, trying to look friendly and not horny.

"What you want?" she asks, flat. She sounds exhausted, empty. Like a clerk in a Wal-Mart who does not want to help, who wants to go home, but must be there for a few more hours.

I produce the plastic bag. "How do I do this?" I ask.

She stands, smiling. "Whatchu got there?" she says, suddenly very sweet.

"I just got it," I say. "But I don't know how to smoke it on my own. I need somebody to show me."

"That looks fine," she says. And when she says "fine" she makes the word glow.

Because I am so drunk, time becomes elastic. I don't know how long we are standing there before the black car pulls up to the curb. There are three young black men in the car and somehow, I find myself sitting in the car, on the backseat. The hooker is on my left. An older man I hadn't seen before is on my right. The bag with the rocks is up front with somebody else.

I see the lights of the boats on the water as we cross over a bridge.

The car is so dusty inside that I think, *They've never cleaned it.* This fact makes me feel safe, as though I can go unnoticed.

I fall asleep.

The sun spilled into the room. The windows were open and the breeze was caught in the madras bedspread hung at the window. It billowed into the room and reminded me of stained glass, the way it glowed. I remember there were plants everywhere, their leaves green and shiny. Somebody watered them and dusted their leaves. Maybe it was Serena.

When I woke up, the car had stopped in front of a building and we all climbed out. We went into a building. The men talked, the hooker spoke out loud, a list of things she wanted. Tissues, some beer, a comb.

One of the men stopped on the steps and turned around. He said he'd be back in a while. He was going to go to the store.

The rest of us went into an apartment. We sat. I sat on the sofa. The hooker busied herself, opening drawers, locating a lighter, a pipe.

One man sat at the small table below the window, another sat next to me on the sofa.

I was the subject of some amusement and interest. "What the hell you doin'?" somebody said.

"I am crazy," I said. "And bored."

"Man, you don't know what the fuck you doing."

But I did not feel threatened, in the least.

These people knew each other well and they began to talk around me, resume a conversation they had begun maybe days before. They were catching up. "No, man. I gotta go to work today. I can't party all night. I got to be at the train."

Later, they were talking about somebody else who worked in a garage. Somebody who repaired cars.

The hooker told me her name. I do not remember asking. I do not remember her telling me her name. I only know that some-how, she became Serena.

The man who had gone to the store returned. Had I given him twenty dollars? I remembered, then, that I had given him money. He carried a bag of groceries. SOS pads. Essentials.

He started talking about his uncle.

Somebody lit the pipe and the smell made me drool. It was passed to me second, after the person who lit it. After the man who sat at the table lit it, took the first deep drag. Serena took it from his fingers and gave it to me. Which struck me as very kind and unselfish.

I inhaled. And tried to keep the chemical smoke in my lungs for as long as I could, like I was swimming underwater.

The pipe was passed around the room and what surprised me was that nothing happened. The men, now three of them, continued talking about their daily lives. Uncle somebody who was fixing up his house in Queens. Some guy who worked in a garage. Somebody else who had to go to work soon. We could have been having coffee.

I faded into the sofa. Perhaps I slept.

In the morning, I was alone with Serena.

I watched her tuck the sheet in between the box spring and mattress, smoothing it with her hand. She fluffed the pillows, dented them with the spine of her hand, just so. Sometimes, she would turn to me and smile. She offered me coffee, boiled in a pot on the stove.

The ceiling fan turned slowly, not because it was on, but because the breeze pushed its blades. A pigeon landed on the windowsill and then took off.

The apartment had no door. I rose from the couch to find the bathroom in the hallway. None of the apartments in the building had doors, only empty hinges. I walked down the hallway, past people's homes, their lives open. Pancakes sizzled in cast-iron skillets, the sound of a knife chopping against a cutting board, the low mumble from a TV. Children in white cotton underpants, thick black hair woven into cornrows, tied with ribbons.

The bathroom was clean. This surprised me as much as anything that morning. How many people used this one bathroom? At least the whole floor. And how many apartments were there on this floor? Five, maybe seven. And not a single door among them. I pissed into the bowl and my urine turned the blue water green.

"You leaving?" Serena asked when I walked back into the apartment. She had lit a candle and already I could smell the apple scent.

"Yup. I gotta go," I said. I was no longer drunk. I was suddenly extremely sober.

"You don't belong doing what you're doing," she told me. There was no blame in her voice. Just kind observation.

"I have to change," I told her. Out of my clothes? Out of my life?

"Everybody can change," she said. I believed her. But why didn't she believe herself?

"You?" I asked.

"I'm doin' what I can do."

I wanted to hug her, and so I did. Then I gave her a hundred dollars in twenties because I had a hundred dollars in twenties, and then I left.

Outside, I looked up at the building. So many windows smashed. Angry sprays of white paint looping over the brownstone steps. Crushed cigarette butts, broken beer bottles, a condom.

Empty glass vials lined the path to the front steps, a few of them crushed almost back into sand. The geraniums of a crack house.

I walked down the sidewalk, the only white man for half a mile. Certainly the only gay white male advertising copywriter wearing a Rolex for half a mile. I walked and I thought, *That apartment without a door or electricity is nicer than my apartment. It is more lived in. It is lived in, not rotted in.*

I took the subway home, but could not bring myself to look at anybody. I knew I must have smelled insane, like chemicals and alcohol and something perhaps unfamiliar, yet sinister. I looked, instead, at people's feet. I saw their stockings and their black banker shoes, I could smell their shampoo and their hair gel.

I thought, *This is it. I am rock-bottom, on the subway. I have to stop. I cannot end up like that.*

When I finally entered my apartment, it was two in the afternoon. My apartment, once again, a debris field. Even the ceiling above my chair was yellow from nicotine. It was worse now than when I came home from rehab. And then it occurred to me: I have relapsed for a longer period of time now than I was sober before.

I was drunk by four.

I wake up slowly, gradually leaving a dream where I've fallen asleep in the woods, out back behind the house I grew up in. I'm cold and damp. The dream leaves, the sheets are soaking wet; the feather bed drenched. I climb out of the bed, disgusted. Two nights in a row I've peed in the bed. Last month, I am smoking crack in the South Bronx and this month, I am urinating in my own bed. This is not progress.

I make my way to the refrigerator, stepping over all the clothes, empty Chinese food containers and unopened mail that covers the floor. There is a vague path from the bed to the refrigerator, then from the refrigerator to my table. Mounds of papers, containers, empty cigarette packets have been pushed out of the way to make this path, or flattened. I take out a bottle of Evian and gulp, then I catch my breath and gulp some more. I drink water in the morning and the middle of the night.

The machine is blinking.

"*What do you want??*" I say out loud as I stab the PLAY button with my finger.

The polite voice of an older, unfamiliar man begins speaking. "Hello, um, this call is for a Mr. Augusten Burroughs. . . ."

I go to the computer, poke a key to wake it up.

". . . Mr. Burroughs, my name is Mercer Richter, and I'm calling from . . ."

I hunt around the empty Marlboro Lights boxes on my desk, looking for a cigarette.

". . . Robison Jewelers on Spring Street. The piece of jewelry . . ."

I see a cigarette on the floor, unsmoked, and bend over to pick it up.

". . . that somebody named 'Pighead' had made for you . . ."

I freeze. My heart rate quickens. I throw the cigarette back onto the floor, leap out of my chair, go to the machine.

"What, what, what about Pighead, who is this?" I'm poking at the machine, raw panic, where's the STOP button? *"Stop!"* I yell over the voice as it continues to drone on. I finally hit the right button and the machine is silenced.

"Okay, okay," I say. Calm down, easy. I carefully look for the REWIND button, make absolutely certain that it is not the DELETE button. I push it. The AT&T digital answering machine rewinds instantly.

I gently push PLAY once again, lean my elbows on the counter, my head just under the kitchen cabinet, as close to the machine as I can get.

"Hello, um, this call is for a Mr. Augusten Burroughs. Mr. Burroughs, my name is Mercer Richter, and I'm calling from Robison Jewelers on Spring Street. The piece of jewelry that somebody named 'Pighead' had made for you, it's finally ready to be picked up. Now, I tried the first number that Mr. Stathakis gave me but it's apparently been disconnected, and this is the only other number I have, so I hope I've got the right person. Feel free to call me at 555–8389. Bye, bye."

When I take my elbows off the counter, my hands are shaking so violently that I just stare at them, fascinated.

What was that man talking about? What is happening?

I go to the phone and lift the receiver, then realize I didn't write down his name or number. I'll have to play the message again, except I can't. It's just too confusing.

I'll go to Robison Jewelers on Spring Street. I know just where it is.

Robison Jewelers is a small, exclusive jewelry store with a poured concrete floor, Knoll chairs and tiny pinprick halogen lights.

A petite, attractive young woman with a pageboy is at the counter. I approach.

"Hi, a man called me about some piece of jewelry or something that I'm supposed to pick up . . . I didn't get his name."

"That would be Mr. Richter. One moment and I'll see if he's available." She quickly spins away, her bouncy little pageboy swinging.

There's a tall guy in a dark suit standing by the door; he must be a security guard. I'm surprised I didn't notice him when I first came in, but then I'm not surprised.

A silver-haired man appears behind the counter, holding a black box. We introduce ourselves and I shake hands. "I understand you have something for me."

He chuckles softly, curiously. "Actually I do, I have it right here. Oh, but I'm sorry to ask, could I just see some form of identification?"

I reach in my back pocket, pull out my wallet, hold my driver's license toward his face. He looks at it, then at me, then back at it. "That's fine, thank you.

"Yes, so um, Mr. Stathakis came into my store, oh, must have been months ago," he says, smiling kindly. Then concerned, "By the way, how is Mr. Stathakis, he wasn't feeling well at all when he was in here. As a matter of fact, he could barely—"

"He's dead," I say flatly.

"Oh. Oh my goodness, Oh my. I'm terribly, terribly sorry to hear that. I had no idea. Oh, I'm terribly sorry."

"Sir, I'm not feeling well myself today, I have to actually be someplace fairly shortly, so if . . ." I trail off.

"Of course. So like I said, he came in a few months ago, and he had this very specific piece of jewelry that he wanted made . . . for you, Mr. Burroughs." He laughs softly again. "Like I said, he was very specific. And, it's a mighty unusual piece, I must say. But our craftsmen did a beautiful job, if you'd like to see." He opens the box.

I lean forward. Whatever it is, it's wrapped in velvet. "Here we go, let me just remove this pouch and . . . there you have it. There's an inscription on the back, certainly the *most unique* inscription we've ever done."

At first, I can't tell what it is except that it's large and gold. I reach my hand toward the object in the box, but before I touch it, I see clearly exactly what it is.

It's a gold pig's head. A Pighead.

It comes out of me at once, propelled by a force all its own, a noise I've never made before.

A gigantic laugh straddling a guttural sob. The older man flinches, startled. "I'm sorry, I'm sorry." I'm trying to speak, but it comes out messy and wet. I slide my glasses off my face, drag my sleeve across my eyes. A laugh comes through, then a choke.

"Can I, may I please . . ." And I take the Pighead out of the box. The back of it is flat, engraved. I have to swipe my eyes again to get the blur out so I can read what it says.

In the tiniest italic print, it says:

I'M WATCHING YOU. NOW STOP DRINKING.

I remove the golden Pighead, palm it and start to leave. "Mr. Burroughs," the man says. "The box?"

I say, "I don't need it." And I don't. I absolutely do not need anything else.

I walk outside. And there is no word for this. I walk and I walk and I walk and I walk and I walk. Something is building in me, and I know what it is, so I chant, "Let it out, let it out, let it out," as I walk, not caring if I seem insane. Not looking at the other people on the sidewalk who must be staring at me as I talk to myself.

And then I am weeping. I am bawling. I am not holding any of it back. I am not thinking of ducking into a doorway and covering my face or swallowing it whole so that it goes deep inside my chest again. I am walking and everything is draining out of me.

And like a moron, like a wasted disaster of a man, I open my hand and see that my palm is still filled with this obscene mound of gold, this message from the dead. And I bring it to my lips and I kiss it and I say, "I fucking love you."

Except I am not saying this. I am screaming it at the very highest altitude of my lungs.

I feel as though helium has been injected into the spaces between my cells. I feel lighter and also slightly intoxicated.

It is only when I get home, the Pighead glowing warm and gold in my pocket, that I sink.

I am excited that Pighead has communicated with me from the dead. I want to summon the actual, live Pighead and tell him this. "It's a miracle," I want to tell him. "A message."

And as I step into my apartment and twist the deadbolt, it hits me. He's dead.

And suddenly, I feel tricked. As though someone has played a horrible joke on me. Given him to me, then taken him back. My elation—a message from Pighead! I can go over to his apartment again and ignore him!— seemed to imply that I'd found a sort of portal.

Like when I sleep. I look forward to going to sleep because I hope, or sort of wish, that I will dream about him and that it will be so real, I will have no choice but to accept that I slipped through some kind of wormhole, over to the "other side" and that the Pighead I met in my dream is the real Pighead.

The gold Pighead had opened a door. It was a message, and it's rude not to return a message.

This is followed by the crushing of fact. He ordered the Pighead before he died. It was a message from the living. From the dying, actually. But still. There is no door.

My apartment, perfect squalor, closes in around me once again. The empty cartons, some with leftover, uneaten food dried and molding in the corners, comfort me. My mess, my disgusting nest. Bottles, everywhere. The mattress, soaked with urine, left to dry, only to be pissed on again. Flies skid across the surface of the sheet, itself unwashed for months—perhaps sucking salt or other minerals from the fibers.

On the stove, in the center between the burners where I always keep my "current" bottle, is my current bottle. It is half empty and, like a baby, this makes me long for more. I will need to go to the liquor store on Second Avenue and get two more bottles. Two is the most I can manage to force myself to buy at once. More than two, and I feel ashamed, chronic, like a wino.

I remove the gold Pighead from my pocket and place it carefully in the cabinet above the sink. This is where I keep important things—birth certificate, passport, the sterling silver cup my grandmother gave my mother the day after I was born. I place it in the cupboard next to the cup and I close the door. Inside the cupboard is the only clean space in the apartment. It is protected from dust, debris. The air is rare and clean, the door blocking most of the stale cigarette smoke and a rotting life.

I walk to the liquor store, get my bottles and return home. I drink. Why couldn't I let Pighead's gold Pighead be what he meant it to be: a message? He knew he'd be dead when I got it. It was his way of finding me.

Yet, I drink. And I feel sick with myself that I do.

I sit at the computer and get lost, drinking, smoking, going deeper and deeper into the screen. I am rereading Pighead's old e-mails. There are dozens of them and I read them all. Drunk now, I am looking for something I missed.

"I miss you," he writes. "And yet, what can I say? It seems that you will always think I am asking so much—too much from you. When all I want is your company. Just a movie, just some time. But you're always busy, advertising or drinking or, I don't know, Augusten. I'm just so tired."

In bed, I turn off the light and the dark pulses around me. My eyes adjust, the thick black dissolving, giving way to shapes in the room—my bookcase, a mound of magazines, some years old. And then I see the spider. It moves quickly from one corner of the room, along the seam where the ceiling meets the wall. I think it has something to do with my eyes adjusting to the dark. But I watch as it pauses, and then changes direction. It's big, and its apricot seed–sized body is supported by long legs. It waits. Does it see me? Carefully, I reach over and turn on the light. I do this without moving my eyes from it; I do not want to lose the spider. I will turn on the light and see if it scampers away and if it doesn't, I will get a magazine and squash it.

The light is on and the spider is not there.

And this is absolutely impossible, because my eyes did not leave the spot for one instant, my finger turning on the lamp switch beside the bed by feel. But the spider is gone.

It defies reason. I go to sleep.

The next evening, I drink again. I finish the first liter of Dewar's and then go to the cabinet to hold the gold Pighead.

I feel its weight in the cup of my hand. Gold is heavy. For the first time I think, *This must have cost him a fortune.*

It scares me to have the Pighead exposed to the air in my apartment. The air feels filthy, as though it will contaminate this treasure the way I feel contaminated myself. I place it back in the cabinet and sit at my computer.

I type chatty e-mails to friends in San Francisco and I am okay. I finish both bottles.

I go to bed and I see the spider when I turn off the light. To-night, there are many spiders. The ceiling is filled with them.

I turn on the light and there are none.

I understand now that I am hallucinating. In rehab I learned that chronic, late-stage alcoholics hallucinate. Seeing spiders is, in fact, not uncommon.

I go to sleep feeling impressed with the powers of the mind.

The next morning, I am sick. I feel like I have the flu. My lungs hurt. I have a fever. I cannot move.

I have been in bed for ten hours. It is, in fact, not morning but afternoon. I put a pillow over my eyes, tucking it around the bridge of my nose so I can breathe. I sleep.

When I wake up, I feel worse. My body aches, as though damaged.

I understand that I will not drink today. I will not smoke, either. I am too sick to drink or smoke, my interest in both replaced by the knowledge that I am not afraid of death. I feel like shit. If I died, it would be okay. The cliché *When you have your health, you have everything* is very true. When you do not have your health, nothing else matters at all.

I sleep for another ten hours. When I wake I am shaking all over. I hold my hand out in front of me and it vibrates.

I feel worse.

My heart is racing. This, in fact, is what woke me up. My heart beating so wildly in my chest that it woke me from my dream, like someone pounding on the front door.

I sit up in bed, pillows stuffed behind me. What the fuck?

That night, I am worse still. My whole body is shaking and hives are making swift progress across my entire body. They have covered my legs in red welts. They are spreading to my arms and my chest. They are ringing my neck, just above my clavicle. My mouth tastes metallic. Every sound—a horn outside, a distant shriek from somebody on the street, startles me. I lie down, thinking I must sleep this off. But as soon as I begin to drift off, I have the sensation of falling, and startle awake.

The hives are fusing. They are not splotches now. They are like ropes, wrapped all around me. I am afraid.

In the middle of the night I understand that I am in alcohol withdrawl and that it is serious and that I need to be in a hospital. But I cannot walk across my apartment, even to pee. I must pee in bed, sober, not asleep. I must pee in bed because I am too sick to walk. When I stand, I become massively dizzy and begin to black out. My legs itch and I have caused them to bleed. My throat feels like it has narrowed. Like I have hives inside my throat now. They feel like hands around my neck.

It takes me three hours to prepare, but by morning I am dressed and I am walking down the two flights of stairs. I walk into the Korean market that is just downstairs and never closes. I go to the beer case and I buy hard cider. I am in agony as I wait for my change, having handed him a twenty. Finally, I cannot wait while he answers the phone. "It's okay," I say, and leave without a bag.

Upstairs, I uncap a bottle and I drink from it as though it is water. And the effect is nearly immediate, but it is not enough. I drink three more in succession. My hands stop shaking and I feel calmer. The hard cider is medicine, now. Like in rehab, this is what they do with the really, really bad cases. They feed them small volumes of alcohol to lessen the physical withdrawal. They call it tapering.

I stash the remaining bottles in the refrigerator and get back into my filthy bed. I turn on my right side, not my heart side, and I try to sleep. But again, as soon as I begin to drift to sleep, I have the feeling that I am falling from a great height and I am startled awake.

I am going to die. If I fall asleep, my heart will stop and I will die. I need to be in a hospital now. I have alcohol poisoning.

Oh my God, what have I done to myself? I am too afraid to move.

Forty-eight hours later, I am better. The hives have reduced, though my legs are covered in welts, some split and bleeding. But I can tell they have lessened. My hands are not shaking. I drank the remaining bottles of hard cider and today have had no alcohol. I have had cranberry juice.

I feel as though I will not die.

And also, I feel as though I came very close to death.

This is not a joke, I tell myself. *I poisoned myself with alcohol. I almost killed my fucking self.* I look around my apartment, standing in the center of it, the filth, everywhere, in piles, on surfaces, dead fruit flies, living fruit flies. Who would have found me? And when?

I sit at my computer and there is still some Dewar's in the cup next to me. The cup sits on top of the two-year-old box my computer came in. This is my table. Its top is concave, ready to implode. I drink from a Santa mug, a holiday mug I bought at the pharmacy downstairs for two dollars because I was sick of drinking from plastic cups and decided I deserved a real cup.

A film of dead fruit flies cover the surface of the liquid.

I will never take another drink for the rest of my life.

I am in no position to say this. It is the One Thing an alcoholic should never say. It is the one thing an alcoholic cannot be certain of. It is unrealistic, part of denial.

I will never drink again.

And I will clean this apartment and reinvent myself and change every single thing until I am unrecognizable. I will new and improve myself, like an ad.

I will start now.

I take my mug to the kitchen sink and I pour the liquid into the drain. But what do I do with the mug? There is no trash can here. It's all a trash can.

I am so tired.

I set the mug on the counter. I need to sleep. I wonder if I can.

I get back into bed and this time, I fold a T-shirt into a strip and tie it around my head to block out the light.

I go to sleep.

And I do not die.

ONE YEAR LATER

Anyone here counting days?"

Jim raises his hand, reluctantly. "My name is Jim and I'm an alcoholic. Today is day ninety."

Everyone claps and Jim's sponsor winks at him. I nudge him with my elbow and grin.

After the meeting, Jim and I walk along West Fourth. "Fuck. I really want a drink. I mean, I'm not gonna drink, but I really want one. Does the *want* ever go away?" he asks.

"Well, I'm no expert. But no. Probably not."

"*Great*," he says, shoving his hands in his pockets.

"That's the bad news," I tell him. "You can never replace it. The good news is you do learn to live without it. You miss it. You want it. You hang out with a bunch of other crazy people who feel the same way and you live with it. And eventually, you start to sound like a cloying self-help book, like me."

We pass by a secondhand bookstore and stop to look at the antique globe in the window. "It seems so easy for you," he says. "It's like you just don't drink, period."

I recall the months after Pighead died where I entered my coma. What else to call it? Drinking from the moment I woke up until I passed out. Going to bars and trying to find a penis and then not having any idea what to do with it. Smoking crack with Foster. And then meeting Serena.

And then the pig head. *From Pighead.*

And then the plain, almost monastic process of waking up, taking a shower, going to an AA meeting and then doing this again and again, day after day until an amount of time had passed and it became not a struggle, but a routine. "You've got to be kidding me," I tell him. "It is so not easy for me. It was easy the first time. And look what happened. This time I have to really stay on top of it so it doesn't sneak up on me. But you're right in one way," I say. "I just don't drink." And it doesn't hurt that Foster has moved to Florida to open a bar. One less temptation in my geographical area.

"What about tomorrow?" he asks.

I spot Thailand on the globe, then Kuala Lumpur. "I don't know anything about tomorrow," I tell him. "The only thing I know about tomorrow is that I'm meeting Greer for this freelance thing we're doing. Assuming a runaway bus doesn't have other plans in store for me." At first I was worried that I might have too much time on my hands as a freelancer. But it turned out to be the best thing. I don't have to be in an office every day with assholes like Rick. And the day rate for freelancers is outrageous. I can afford really excellent underwear to sit around all day in.

"It's good that you and Greer are getting along again," he says.

"Yeah, I didn't think it would stay bad forever." Greer and I didn't speak for almost ten months. Then she quit work and started taking anger workshops at the New School. She also took up painting. All her paintings are black. "It's better now. We both speak *recovery*."

Jim goes into the tobacco store on the corner of Christopher and Seventh for some cigarettes. He comes out with a pack of American Spirits and growls, "It's just so fucking uncomfortable." A match flares at his fingertips.

I nod. "I know, I get like that. I get where I feel like I'm gonna drink anyway, eventually. So I might as well do it now. It's awful. Sometimes I feel like I have hives in my brain that I can't scratch."

"What do you do?" Jim asks, very hungry for the answer, as this has probably described perfectly the way he feels at this moment.

"You're supposed to go to a meeting. I mean, as much as you hate them or if they feel stupid or you just don't want to go. The thing is, if you go to a meeting, you won't drink that day. It's like a minibrainwash. It kind of fixes you for a little while." But then I say, "Of course if I'm really wallowing in self-pity, then I'll tell myself, 'Pighead would give anything to feel this uncomfortable right now.'" So there's always the auto–guilt trip method.

We make a right on Bank. As we walk below a street lamp, a curious thing happens: it flickers and then illuminates. A wiring problem seems to have developed over the past year within the New York City street-lamp system. Many times I've noticed a street lamp coming on in the mid-afternoon, just as I pass by.

"Hi, Pighead," I whisper.

"What'd you say?"

"Nothing." I smile, but it's small, and only to myself.